MEMORIES MILESTONES AND MEMOIRS

Selections from a Writing Workshop

Edited by Emily Rosen, M.A.

THREE EM PRESS
MMM

authorHOUSE™

1663 LIBERTY DRIVE, SUITE 200
BLOOMINGTON, INDIANA 47403
(800) 839-8640
WWW.AUTHORHOUSE.COM

First published by AuthorHouse 11/10/05

ISBN: 1-4208-8257-0 (sc)

Printed in the United States of America
Bloomington, Indiana

This book is printed on acid-free paper.

DEDICATION

I dedicate this book to my sister, Rhoda Tillett, whose all too short life was full of stories – told and untold. She is the title character in a book as yet unwritten. She had, among her other traits, an eye and a soul for art in all its forms and was responsible for bringing so much of it to the island of St. Thomas in the Virgin Islands, where her legacy lives on.

Also, I dedicate this book, to Dr. Irwin Rosen, my husband of 50+ years who was supremely sanguine about sacrificing me to my computer for what must have seemed like an endless measure of time. Without his indifferent yet co-operative willingness to support my solitude throughout the editing period, this book would not exist. He is probably reading this now for the first time and so I say, "Thank You, darling, for leaving me alone."

P.S. I was always available for dinner and whatever !

TABLE OF CONTENTS

FOREWORD

Retiring to Florida – so sayeth the pundits – is tantamount to waiting to die. This didn't scare me one bit, since I planned to be so busy that I wouldn't notice that I was on a holding pattern. In fact, I may actually have died already, and this is possibly the heaven they talk about.

With combined training and background in journalism, education and mental health it seemed like a no-brainer for me to stir those ingredients into a stew and come up with a writing workshop to encourage people to dig into their family and personal histories. Thus was born, *MEMORIES, MILESTONES AND MEMOIRS,* my first class a giveaway at the then recently built community center of the *Boca Raton News.*

For a city with a reputation as a locale for homogeneous gated communities, I was thrilled and amazed at the disparity of "people types" who came to that first class – and to the subsequent ones – eager to dig and tell. Freebees, however, are not forever and with some difficulties, I finally alighted on a more reliably permanent venue for my classes at the *Boca Raton Community Center.*

People came to my classes for a variety of reasons all stemming from their desire to record parts of their lives. My sense of how to establish trust in a group, provided an undercurrent of safety and camaraderie. Combined with the pedagogical goal of improving writing skills, I felt it important to encourage students to expand their reading choices in recognition of and in search for good writing. Group cohesion and a reach for improved craftsmanship, produced the right atmosphere for eager writers to examine different aspects of their lives as well as their writing skills.

I came from the mantra, "Everybody Has A Story." Every examined life can become an interesting read. And many seemingly quotidian incidents and events, as well the "ordinary" people in our lives who become extraordinary in retrospect -- if written about with a mixed soupcon of humor and openness to feelings, can and have become classics of literature.

My classes attracted beginning writers, seasoned professionals, competent "wannabees" and some aspiring to best-seller-dom. As they revealed their work, it was easy to classify them: people who just wanted to write their stories and whose writing style reflects that simple goal, people whose prose is adequate enough to depict interesting events in their lives, people whose writing is competent and skilled enough to tap into their emotions as they learned how to develop character, place and voice, excellent and talented writers whose words paint pictures, whose work is well focused and who, if willing to work at it, will eventually be recognized.

And here's what I loved the most. There was no hierarchy of writing skills in terms of the kinds of feedback and attentiveness each class member received. I never had the feeling that people were sitting in their seats interested only in their own work. We had a level playing field of respect for each work, and recognition that everyone, even the most talented can learn from the work of others. The writing process also involves awareness of the importance of listening skills – listening to others and especially, listening to oneself.

In the workshops I've been teaching since 1999, I try to spark the artistry and creativity that lie in the depths of our souls. Sometimes I did that with prompts and suggested assignments, At other times, the give and take of focused discussions ignited bursts of memory. Recognizing students' growth, giving encouragement and personal attention to the editing process and acceptance of limitations in abilities, all kept the process fresh and fruitful.

People need to feel that they are being heard, and that their stories have resonance. My students did listen to themselves and in this volume you will be reading some of the personal stories that had them wandering far from Florida's flat landscape and splashing shores.

ACKNOWLEDGEMENT

Some wonderful people held my hand through this experience. But one in particular is responsible for shoring me up every time I began to falter, every time it became too formidable, every time I lost sight of my reason for doing this. She was also my launch inspiration, getting initial material into the computer for me, pointing out some simple rules of organization. Thank you, **Lucia Leao** for also being my soul mate.

And to **Nancy Miller**, **Luciana Duce Dugan** and **Steve Kates**. Your sideline cheers kept me moving, albeit slowly, but at least to the finish line.

WRITERS ON WRITING

Writing Hurts

Luciana Duce

For me, the process of writing hurts. The words never sound the same on paper as in my head.

The sentences get stuck like rubber soles on chewing gum. I push and pull and try to pry them loose. The language that carries the perfume of expensive writing escapes me. How to link the feelings with the phrases?

When they're in my head, I see words like neon flashing on and off but spilling out on the paper they lose their luster...no glow...opaque like a bad watercolor painting. My hand moves across the paper with ease but the sentences lag behind.

So why do I continue week after week to try to write? What kind of sadistic muse is behind this awkward adventure? Who lures me to the page day after day with no sign of fulfillment?

When I am writing I feel my existence. The motion of my fingers forming letters delights me.

The content becomes secondary as the movement contains the energy, the feeling of life in the fingers, then in the hands. AHA, there it is. Writing for me is an act of giving life to my thoughts, to my emotions, to my fantasies, to my imagination, to my "self".

It is Life-giving and like all birthing, pain lives side by side with the new life. So I surrender to the process and trust I will be in love with the fruit of my womb no matter how misshapen she appears.

Why I Write

Dorothy Dworkin

I write because I can.

I write because once, a long time ago, a favorite teacher said, "Dorothy, you are a writer. Never forget it."

I write because he believed in me and therefore, I believed in myself.

I write because I am willing to share my feelings and by doing so, I hope I can help others to get in touch with theirs.

I write because I have something I want to say and perhaps someone else will want to hear my words.

I write because I want my family to know who I am and value the life I've led.

I write because it gives my pleasure to touch another person's heart and have them recognize themselves in some of my words.

I write to record my experiences and by writing remember them.

I write to reduce pain and re-live pleasure.

I write because I want to leave a record that says, "I was here and it mattered."

I write because I spend most of my time with other people and writing lets me be alone with just myself.

I write because of the satisfaction I get from putting pen to paper and creating coherent thoughts and ideas.

I write because I can imagine a world beyond my present reality.

I write because once, a long time ago, a teacher believed I was a writer and I never forgot his words. Now, I believe it too

I write because I know I can.

Why I Write

Joan Krukewitt

I write because I can. I feel a competency in writing. I can take words and convey ideas with them. (I strive for simplicity.)

I write because I like to read and appreciate succinct language. I write to clarify my thinking, to form an opinion. (There are so many others around.) I write to have something of my own. I write to create, to release, to make concrete, to pin down. I write to seize ideas that are always hovering. I write to capture the infinite. I write because I sometimes connect with something bigger than myself and sometimes I write "better than I know." It's like reading someone else's work.

I write to communicate on a deeper level. Letters can be read, reread and read between the lines. They put meat on the bones of communication.

I write to remember. I write because so many have told me to write. (Can they all be wrong?) I write to show respect to my Maker. If He has given me a talent, obviously, He'd like me to use it.

Having said all this. I have to force myself to write. I take writing classes to get back to writing. I'm writing this piece so that I can turn in an assignment. I'm not sure why I do this.

Why I write

Z. McGrath

Many times I wonder why I want to write especially when I sit frozen in front of my word program and the little professor is waiting patiently with hands behind his back blinking his eyes. Every clever idea that flowed like liquid gold at two A.M. lay on the page as lifeless squiggles of lead. Each attempt at writing is quickly backspaced. Maybe I should simply kill the stupid professor.

I write because I'm filled with the magic of words in the same way a musician might be taken with the magic of notes. I love using words to tease out a fragmented thought. I'm amazed that when the same words are arranged differently how meaning can be altered.. I'm struck with the potential power words have -- to uplift or plunge into despair, creating feelings as diverse as love, hate, joy, sadness, anger and passion. I'm awed at how words were first used by man replacing the economic straightforward body language of thrusting arms, shrugs, nods, pointing and all facets of facial expression along with the occasional grunt. Even now, so long after our ancestors uttered the first sounds, no matter what words I choose to give someone, my ancient body language speaks even more clearly. But gratefully the written word can befog any such evidence.

I love that words build a bridge between you and me. I love the elegant sophistication of some words. I love the clear simplicity of other words. I love using words to tell a story. I love writing words that reveal who I am. I love using words as a cloak to conceal me. I love to record what I see, what I know, what I feel. I am grateful that have overcome my fear of a blank page. I feel satisfaction when I see a completed page and I think mostly, I write to say, "I am"

Why I Write

Zachary Plesser

I often find myself musing about why I write. There are moments when I think I have the answer. There is not just one reason that drives me to pen and paper.

Here are my best guesses:

I write because writing provides me with an emotional catharsis, a way to relieve my brain of a lifetime of accumulated thoughts and feelings. Without writing, there would be no release for me from all the remembered experiences and emotions.

Enter my ego. Writing is speaking on a page. I like hearing the sound of my own voice. I like reading my writing to others. It makes me feel big, even superior, if you will.

Writing allows me to express myself with a crystalline clarity. Speaking, in person, on any subject, is always affected by emotions emanating from an audience. True feelings or beliefs, are always muddied by the emotions that accompany spoken words. Only when I write, can I convey the pure essence of my feelings.

The act of creation and writing is just such an act, It fills me with satisfaction. I feel at peace with myself after surveying a personal accomplishment and for me, writing is such an accomplishment.

In short, writing just plain makes me feel good

Why I Write

Sonia Ravech

Why do I write? I can express myself more comfortably with the written word than the spoken one. Feelings and emotions flow onto the written page: whereas, in conversation, I often struggle to clearly convey my ideas. When I write, I feel free. I can reveal my most personal thoughts without fear of being judged. Writing is permanent. I can record a memory in my journal and store it away. Years later, if I chose to reread the journal, the memory is there waiting for me to retrieve it. Writing can be edited. If it doesn't come out right the first time, it can be rewritten and rewritten again. Once words are spoken it is much more difficult to retract them.

Why do I write? I do so to leave a legacy for my children, grandchildren and future generations. Through my writing, I hope to help them understand the woman that I am, the deeds that I've done, the successes I've achieved, the failures I've overcome. I write to keep the memory of my life alive for them

I write to share with others the joy I find in music, in nature, in travel, in theatre, in friendship and family. There is so much beauty in my world. Through my writing; I hope to let others view that world.

I write to dissipate my anger. With my pen I can release my frustrations, using the most vitriolic language. I read and reread my words, until the tension subsides. Then I tear up the pages and toss them in the trash along with any leftover feelings.

Writing is creative. It's challenging. It's personal. It's therapy. It's fun. It allows me the freedom of expression to be myself without reservation or pretense. This is why I write.

Storytellers

Susan Violante

At first, I didn't think I would enjoy the writing class but I registered for it anyway. I don't even know why. I had so many disappointments with the other classes I had taken. I expected to come into class and find the usual group of people who wanted to learn how to write.

Instead, I found storytellers. Storytellers don't think about writing as something that needs to be taught. They write not because they are in search of fame and money, not because they want to live the writer's lifestyle. Storytellers write because they have no choice. They are like sponges spending every day absorbing life, until words start dripping out.

To my surprise I found myself surrounded by people like me. I don't know what excuse the others found to register for this class or the excuse the instructor found to teach. But I know why we are all here. We need to listen to each other's words flow.

Don't get me wrong. Writing is also a craft and we all can use some direction on how to put the words together, but that is not why we gathered.

We are here because we needed help to get the words out so that we could make space for new experiences coming in.

Oh the joy, when I realized I was not only being helped getting the words out, but found myself absorbing so much life from these story tellers.

THE STORIES

Claire Rifkin Aronowitz

I've wanted to be a writer ever since I was in Junior High School when I received an "A" in a composition about how my father had been smuggled out of Russia. The success of my first creative writing effort encouraged me to continue. Many of the stories and poems I wrote during high school were published in the school magazine. Unfortunately, difficulties at home prevented me from carrying out my plan to enroll in a journalism program at Syracuse University.

Through the years, I honed my writing skills by taking writing courses at The New School and participating in many writing workshops. When my children were in college and I was in my early forties, I went to The Fashion Institute of Technology, majoring in Advertising and Communications. The curriculum included copy writing, journalism and public relations. I graduated with High Honors as an Associate in Applied Science.

Writing was an important part of my duties on several jobs during my working life. I wrote press releases for a Public Relations firm, craft directions for McCall's Needlework magazine, and educational material for a division of McGraw-Hill.

I have been working on my Memoir, which is a collection of short stories, essays, exposition and poems, for over thirty years. For the past four years, with the help and encouragement of Emily Rosen's Memories, Milestones and Memoirs Writing Workshop, my Memoir is almost ready to be published.

Our Wedding Night - 1945

By Claire Rifkin Aronowitz

It was 4:A.M. when the cab driver dropped us off in front of the Barbizon-Plaza Hotel. We were wearing our custom-made matching suits, and I had pinned the large white orchid from my wedding bouquet to the lapel of my suit jacket.

The lobby was deserted, except for two clerks behind the check-in counter and a bellhop sprawled on one of the couches. I was embarrassed and self-conscious as I stood in the middle of the room surrounded by our luggage, while my husband, Marty, went up to the counter to register.

I'm sure they can tell we're newlyweds, I thought. I imagined they were thinking about what we would be doing up in that room. We followed the smirking bellhop. He opened the door to the room and placed our luggage inside and stood there grinning.

"Have fun," he said as he pocketed the dollar Marty had given him.

It had been a long exhausting evening. We ate, drank and danced our way through our loud, lively wedding celebration. And tired as I was, this was our wedding night, and I felt it was our duty to consummate our union. This was 1945.

I rummaged through my suitcase and pulled out a new white satin, lace trimmed nightgown.

" I'll only be a few minutes," I promised as I went into the bathroom. I took a shower, ran a comb through my hair, dabbed a few drops of *Evening in Paris* behind my ears and between my breasts, took a deep breath and went back into the bedroom.

Marty seemed to have fallen asleep in the easy chair.

"Wake up honey. No sleeping yet," I said as I kissed him.

"I'm not sleeping Just closed my eyes for a minute," he answered as he struggled to stand up.

"Okay, okay, then hurry up," I said pushing him into the bathroom.

We were novices, lacking the expertise as to exactly how to get the job done. I had looked through a "How To…." handbook which I had safely tucked away in my suitcase for further reference. I thought I was prepared, but facing reality was an entirely different matter. We knew about using a contraceptive, so Marty had taken care of that detail. I had prepared the items I would need, which included douching apparatus.

We turned the lights down low, tuned into soft seductive music and began. Unfortunately, inexperience and anxiety may have caused the prophylactic to break. I pushed him away and leapt out of bed.

"The douche! The douche! I must douche," I shouted. "The book says if something like this happens, you must douche immediately."

We rushed into the bathroom where I had put the douche bag, the special powder and a measuring cup

"I'll read the instructions and you mix the solution," I said.

He worked frantically, measuring, mixing and pouring like a mad chemist, then left me to figure out how to use the contraption so I wouldn't become a victim of an untimely pregnancy.

When I came out of the bathroom, Marty was sound asleep. I fell into bed next to him and slipped into oblivion.

Over breakfast the next morning we laughed at our clumsy, inept efforts.

"I'm sure we'll do much better once we're up in the mountains at the hotel," he assured me.

And we did!

MMM

Michael's Friend - 1971

By Claire Rifkin Aronowitz

In stead of saying "hello" or giving me a hug and a kiss, which my son Michael always did when he came home, he burst into the apartment with a young woman at his side and announced, "Ma, this is my friend Laura. Laura this is my mother, Claire."

I was a bit confused. I didn't expect him to come home with company.

"Oh. Hello, nice to meet you," I stammered.

"Sit down Lore. I'll be right back," he said as he picked up his duffle bag and went down the hall to his room.

She sat primly in the club chair with her sandaled bare feet firmly planted on the floor and her hands on her knees. Her long curly hair framed her pretty face.

"Where do you live?" I asked.

Obviously, Michael had given her a ride home from school. I expected her to mention someplace in the area or one of the towns on Long Island.

"Ohio. Shaker Heights in Cleveland," she answered.

"Ohh?? Well…I guess you're not going home this weekend. Right?"

"Didn't Michael tell you about me?" she asked.

"Noo…he didn't. I guess he forgot. But it's okay. Michael's friends are always welcome," I assured her trying not to sound as annoyed as I felt.

Why would he bring a friend with him this week-end, I wondered, since the reason for his visit was to attend my niece's wedding on Sunday?

"You'll have to call Aunt Ceil and tell her you'd like to bring a guest to the wedding. I'm sure she won't mind," I said.

"Sure I'll call, but we can only stay for hors d'oeuvres and the ceremony. It's a long ride and we don't want to get back to school too late," he explained.

"Oh, Michael, no. Why can't you stay and leave Monday morning? You can miss one day."

"No Ma, we can't. We'll be at the wedding for the ceremony. It's the most important part, isn't it?"

While my husband was surprised to find that his son brought home a guest, he didn't seem to mind. At dinner Michael was more animated than he'd been on previous visits, as he told us about what was going on at school. Laura was quiet, but graciously answered my husband's questions about herself and her family. I played my usual role as nurturing Jewish Mother asking, "Can I get you some more brisket? Have more gravy.."

Although there were twin beds in Michael's room, there was no doubt in my mind that Laura would sleep in Michael's room and he would be on the Castro Convertible in the living room. When I told Michael about these arrangements, he just nodded, but said nothing. While they were watching television, Marty and I opened the couch and made up the bed.

"Sleep well. See you in the morning," I said as we left them and went to our room.

The next morning I tip-toed out of my room, not wanting to wake my son and his guest. The door to his room was closed. Good. Laura must still be asleep, I thought. I peeked into the living room, but Michael was not in the bed, nor did it look as though anyone had slept in it. Well, I thought, I tried to do the right thing. Let *her* mother worry.

In the kitchen I found a note taped to the refrigerator door.

"Hi. We got up early. I'm taking Lore to the City to see the sights, then to Chinatown for dinner. Be home tonite. Love, Mike."

Unable to contain my disappointment, I woke Marty to tell him about his son's inexcusable behavior.

"Calm down, honey," he said as he crawled out of bed. "It's no big deal. They're young and spirited, and she seems like a nice person."

Later that morning, as I was putting the finishing touches on the dress I'd made to wear to the wedding, I wondered what Laura would wear. She didn't seem to have any luggage other than the knapsack. I went into Michael's room and carefully flipped through the clothes in the closet. There was nothing belonging to Laura. I looked through the dresser draws - nothing. My anxiety level was escalating.

I flew out of the room to share my concern with Marty.

"Michael must have told her about the wedding. I can't imagine that she would think jeans and a T-Shirt are okay. I'll die of embarrassment."

"No of course she won't wear jeans," Marty tried to allay my fears. "Maybe she didn't have anything suitable up at school. I'll bet they went shopping."

"Maybe," I said. "Let's hope so."

When Marty and I went to bed, they had not yet returned. I tossed and turned unable to find a comfortable spot, filled with the same anxiety and fear that I had experienced when my children were in high school and went out for the evening. I finally heard the key turn in the lock and fell asleep hoping that Laura had a suitable outfit for the wedding.

At breakfast they could not stop talking about their day in Manhattan.

"What an amazing place," Laura said. "The view from the Empire State Building was incredible, and I definitely must get back to the Museum of Art. We walked for miles and I loved being in Central Park"

"It was great!" Michael added.

Not a word about shopping, but I didn't think it would be a good idea to ask. And, much as I was tempted, I didn't say anything about their sleeping arrangements.

Soon it was time to get ready for the wedding.

"What if she wears jeans?" I said.

"Stop it!" Marty shouted. "There's nothing you can do about it. Hurry up. Let's go."

From the living room we heard, "We're all ready and waiting."

My fears evaporated when I saw Laura. She was a vision in a striking floral print halter-top gown.

"You look beautiful," I told her. "Did you buy the dress yesterday?"

"No," she answered. "I bought it in Buffalo."

"But where was it?" I asked.

"Oh it's a cotton-knit, so it doesn't wrinkle. It was rolled up in my knapsack.

I was especially proud to introduce Laura to the family that day and have continued to be proud of her for more than thirty years.

MMM

Facing Up To Time

By Claire Rifkin Aronowitz

"Hello, I'm Dr, Herbert. Please have a seat," he said. "How can I help you?"

He was short and slight. His smiling blue eyes looked directly at me from behind horn-rimmed glasses. There was a new unused quality about him that made him look very young.

My heart hammered as the words tumbled out of my mouth, "I've been thinking that perhaps I might want to have a face lift, but I'm not sure. I'd like your opinion"

He ran his slim manicured fingers along the side of my face.

"You have wonderful skin. We won't have a problem," he said handing me a mirror. "I'll just pull up the skin in front of your ears," and he continued to describe in graphic detail what he would do to achieve the desired result.

"You won't look sixteen again," he laughed. But I can promise that you'll have a fresher, brighter, more youthful appearance."

I wondered if during the procedure, the years would roll off one by one. Sixty, fifty-nine, fifty-eight, fifty-seven. Will the doctor know when to stop, or will I have to tell him what age face I want to retrieve?

"Well what do you think?" Dr Herbert asked.

"It sounds wonderful, but I'll have to discuss it with my family."

"By all means," he said. "If you decide to have it done, call my secretary to make the necessary arrangements. Any questions?"

"Well yes. A couple of things," I was hesitant. "Uh, uh, How much will it cost?"

"I never discuss fees," he seemed embarrassed. "Miss Anderson at reception desk will give you that information."

"There is something else. It's probably silly, but no matter how much I diet, I can't get rid of this," I said patting my stomach.

"I can't help you there. I only do above the neck. You'll have to see my associate Dr. Kenneth. Ask Miss Anderson if Dr. Kenneth has a few minutes to see you today. If not you'll have to make an appointment."

Miss Anderson gave me a copy of the fee schedule and a brochure. When I asked about seeing Dr. Kenneth, she said if I was willing to wait, he would see me.

"Sure, I can wait," I told her.

Miss Anderson was tall and slender. Her long blonde hair swung from side to side as she walked, her short white uniform clung to her well-defined curves. I felt like the "Hulk" as I trailed after her.

We stopped in front of a small alcove. "Have a seat," she said pointing to a chair between two seated young women.

"Dr. Kenneth will be with you shortly. Meanwhile look through the photo album on the table. You'll get an idea of how talented the two doctors are."

One woman looked up from her magazine and nodded. I returned a forced self-conscious smile. She looked so small and slight that at first I though she was a child. The second woman was an attractive dark-skinned brunette. She acknowledged my presence by fluttering her long black lashes and smiling broadly.

I leaned back and closed my eyes. I remember how upset I had been when I first noticed that my sharp angular jaw line was beginning to sag, that my once youthful swan-like neck was becoming prune dry, and my sensuous lips were being surrounded by small telltale wrinkles. My efforts to camouflage the damage, by the prudent use of make-up and silk carves was only moderately successful.

Advertisements for magic-formula skin products and cosmetics making extravagant claims to "minimize wrinkles" and give a more youthful appearance began to jump out at me. I was seduced into trying a couple, but saw no improvement. There was a rumor that Preparation H was the new underground remedy to shrink wrinkles, but I couldn't get myself to try that one.

I noticed articles about celebrities having breast reduction or augmentation, facelift, fanny lift, or tummy tuck. Television talk shows featured plastic surgeons extolling the benefits and joys of "having a little something done."

Several of my friends were having cosmetic surgery. They really needed improvement, I told myself. But not me. And I had been lavish with my compliments.

"You look wonderful. So attractive. So much younger."

I found myself spending a great deal of time looking at my face, pulling up the skin around my eyes and mouth. I had to admit I did look better when the wrinkles and laugh lines were smoothed away.

One morning I caught a glimpse of my underwear clad body in my full-length mirror. Red and blue spider veins ran crazily up and down my legs like a medical drawing of the circulatory system. The skin rippled down my inner thighs ending in a lump above my knees. My stomach protruded like a pregnant woman in her fifth month, and my full breasts bulged up over my bra. It was then that I realized that even if I were to have my face smoothed out, the rest of my body wouldn't match. There seemed to be so many cosmetic surgery commercials offering state-of-the-art procedures utilizing computers, board certified surgeons, and an overnight stay in their on-premises clinic.

An attractive spokeswoman on one of these commercials seemed to be speaking directly to me in a soft persuasive voice. She explained how simple, how safe, and how inexpensive their methods were. She made is sound as though it were my birthright to push back time. Repeated over and over, I heard the enticing offer of "Free Consultation. Free Consultation."

I opened my eyes. The two young women were still in their seats.

"They certainly make you wait, don't they?" I said breaking the uneasy silence.

"They do, but it's worth it. Dr. Kenneth is the best," the brunette answered.

She was so attractive; I couldn't imagine what her problem had been.

"What did you have done?" I asked.

"Well, I lost over 100 pounds and there was so much loose skin under my breasts that I couldn't wear a bikini," she explained. "Dr. Kenneth tightened it all up. I'm here for my final check-up."

"I turned to the younger woman," What about you?

"My nose was too long and too wide. It was just awful. Dr. Herbert gave me this wonderful new one," she answered holding her face out toward me.

"Now I'm here to see Dr. Kenneth about having my breasts made larger," she said looking down at her bosoms, which barely made a ripple in her sweater.

"I have enough for two. You can have some of mine," I said, and we both laughed.

"What are you having done?" Brunette asked.

"Oh, I'm only here for a consultation. I don't know if I'll have anything done," I answered.

"Well good luck whatever you decide" the younger woman smiled and went back to her magazine.

The brunette was the first to be called into the doctor's office. Her visit lasted only a few minutes. After the second woman went in, I picked up the photo album. Page after page was filled with "before" and "after" photos of faces, noses, buttocks, and bellies of every size and shape. Wrinkled faces looked glumly out at me from "before" photos, while in the "after" they were smoothed out, all smiles.

An enlarged "before" photo showed the naked torso of a woman with ungainly rolls of fat in folds around her middle. In the "after," several rows of black stitching ran around her body like railroad tracks.

Ugh, how disgusting, I thought. What am I doing here? I must be crazy. Who needs this?

I quickly gathered up my belongings and hurried back to the reception area.

"I've changed my mind. I'm sorry," I apologized to an annoyed Miss Anderson.

Before she could say anything, I ran out the door into the bright sunshine, took a deep breath and walked briskly down the street. I stopped when I saw my reflection in a store window. I stood up straight, pulled in my stomach and smiled approval.

"You look terrific old girl," I told myself.

Janis Ashley

I was born in 1951 in Astoria Queens and we moved to Brooklyn. Shortly after, I attended Brooklyn College for s short time but dropped out after two years as many of my compadres were at the time, "turning on, tuning in and dropping out".

I moved to California for a few years and then dropped back into a University in Mexico for a few years before returning east. I have made South Florida home for the past 30 years as I wanted to be a resident when my folks retired there

MMM

Momalach

By Janis Ashley

It was Spring 2004, when on a routine visit to Mom's, I saw a stack of unpaid bills on the dining room table. She said her hands hurt while making out the checks and she jumped at my offer to take on the monthly task. Thus began the odyssey of becoming my mother's keeper.

Now, as part of the thrice-weekly routine, she entices me with offers of ketchup – she had a coupon- or toothpaste, or tissues. "You always were the 'snotty one," she said, reaching for a laugh.

Seated in her easy chair with bills, checkbook, and return address stickers, I began my new job. At first she insisted on signing the checks herself, but since my name was also on them and I assured her that my signature would be acceptable, she allowed me that privilege.

I make sure that we talk daily and soon noticed that Mom was losing words for everyday items and events. My sister Rhona and I laugh about what Mommy "came up with" this time, and at Rona's urging, I began to write things down lest I forget. Once, after thanking her for the great genes, Ma replied that she never gave me dungarees.

One time I called and she didn't answer, and the machine did not pick up. I raced over to find she was not home and found her at the clubhouse pool telling jokes. She had no idea her machine was not working After chastising her for frightening me -- what if she "had fallen and could not get up" -- I fondly became her parole officer with whom she had to check before making commitments. The other day she called me her "county commissioner".

On yet another visit she was wearing her COP hat, Citizens on Patrol, seniors driving the neighborhoods who alert the police if they notice anything unusual.. "But Jani," she told me, "We are not allowed to use the siren or go shopping." Still, she was so proud to be useful.

Her imagination is incredible. She tried calling me at the office once, but "the girl in the phone", said I was on another call. Apparently, "voice mail" is an entity living in my phone. The other day she told me she had taken a little nap. When she woke up it was 7:00 o'clock, so she dressed, had breakfast, and waited for it to get light. When it didn't, she realized it was "pajama time" instead.

Some things are hard for her to understand. After a power surge on her phone line, her message "went away". I told her how to rerecord and she did so successfully, but never hit "stop" so callers were unable to leave a message. I played it back for her to show her that unless the other person got a beep, they could not leave a message.

Four years ago I changed offices and noticed an elderly gentleman who made daily visits to the dog groomer next door usually carrying a bag of produce. I thought of my mom, a widow of twenty years, and the gears began to turn. He was a widower according to his niece, the dog groomer, so I asked him if he'd like to meet a "nice girl".

He demurred, but I could tell his interest was piqued, I assured him there was no pressure and I slipped him her phone number. To avoid surprises, I told Mom that "Al" might be calling. A few weeks later, he did call and they met. They have been an item ever since, and I truly believe she has added much laughter and quality to the autumn of his life. They base their dates on shopping for veggies at the dollar store and later feasting on their purchases. During the first year of their relationship, Al turned 80 and his family threw a party in New Jersey. Of course Hazel went with him and the last scene of the "This Is Your Life" video was Mom and Al kissing with the caption, "He saved the best for last."

There are times when Mom embarrasses or irritates me, yet when others meet her, they always tell my how lucky I am to have such a sweet and adorable mom. One particularly irritating moment was the morning she called to ask what my plans were for the day. I had none.

"Oh," she said, "I thought you were going to Miami to see your friends."

"Not today," I replied.

"You'll never guess where I am, Jani", she said.

"Where?" I demanded.

"In the hospital, and they are going to release me soon. I didn't want to bother you if you were busy."

"Of course I'll come right away but why are you there?"

She had had chest pains the night before and called the paramedics, who picked her up. "I'm fine, and they are sending me home," she replied.

When I arrived, health care workers surrounded Mom and she was telling them jokes. They were actually sorry to see her go, wishing they had more patients with her attitude.

Each morning she wakes up early and goes to Albertson's. Although she might seem like just another ordinary, bothersome old woman, when I go with her, I see deli girls giving her samples to taste, the cashiers always offer big smiles, and the manager once said, "Oh, this is your mother. We know she sleeps here but we can't figure out where."

On the phone the other day, she told me that Al's family was due here from Jersey, but they hadn't arrived yet. When I asked if they were flying or driving, she replied, "How can they drive down? How would they pick up their rental car?"

When they first started dating, I remember thinking he was a great catch since he drove at night. Now it scares me to think of either one on the road day or night. They went to look at an assisted living facility the other day, but just drove around the complex looking because they could not find the office. Once they went to a large mall and lost the car but Mom had the presence of mind to have security drive them around the parking area.

We have begun the dialogue of what to do when and if Al needs to go into an assisted living facility. In my mind it is a matter of not driving anymore and not really cooking, even though he cooks every Sunday for Mom and his niece. For the "catch" that used to drive at night, he's dwindling into someone who should not drive at all, but they are not willing to admit their frailty and the resulting loss of independence. Who could blame them?

One day they had plans to meet at noon. She drove to his house and let herself in as he drove to hers, and waited. Eventually, they found each other..

Hazel's birthday was approaching last November, and one day while going through "important" papers in a box under her bed, I found her birth certificate. I was surprised to discover that she was born in 1924, not 1926 as I had been led to believe. She lied about her age when she eloped and wanted Daddy to think she was 17.

She had discontinued her home health care premium because of the high cost, and healthcare at 80 was totally unaffordable. Thus began a process of self-education regarding her options, but my immediate concern was her upcoming 80th party.

"No presents", she had said. I ignored her request and watched with great pleasure as she excitedly opened each gift. My special gift was a life-sized poster of her new trim figure which now hangs in her hallway.

Mom lost sixty pounds and is so very proud of how adorable she looks. She has a wardrobe of slim, trim clothing and accessories too. Al has built racks for her new wardrobe, and I never find her in a housedress

New wardrobe, new figure, new teeth. Her teeth had been slipping, and I was only able to persuade her to get new ones, by telling her that her petite figure needed petite teeth. She was sold, and now she is able to chew. This is a good thing, because she loves to cook for friends, and bake for everyone. I guess seniors have an affinity for banana cake and brownies.

They also have an affinity for dirty jokes, though my dad used to say she always blew the punch line. Once, when she was young, she wrote herself a note on a napkin after hearing a good joke from a comedian. The note was "cop joke". She couldn't wait to share it with her mother-in-law. She pulled out her napkin and began with the opening line. "I bet you can all guess my name. I'm long and hard and stand at attention when I get excited." After waiting expectantly for an answer, she announced, I'm a cop!" Actually, the answer was Dick, and needless to say, she began taking better notes.

These days, she never goes to the pool without her "crib sheet", and she is called HaHa, for Hazel Ashley. I'd like to see her do stand-up, but no one has to prompt her to tell jokes. In her next career, I'm sure she'll bring down the house, though I have taken to printing cute jokes off the Internet so she always has material, and maybe she will clean up her act a bit.

She keeps her cash in the freezer in a tangerine can under a plastic bag of frozen schmaltz, which gives a whole new meaning to cold cash. But let's face it. I don't think any crook would get past the bag of frozen chicken fat.

Sidney Awerbuck

Sidney Awerbuck was born in Kiev, Russia (now Ukraine) in 1921. No date, no birth certificate, When he was three, his parents left Russia for America, but at the time, there was a hold on immigration to the United States, and so his family went to Canada as farm labors, in Kitchener Ontario. After a short time they moved to Windsor across the river from Detroit where his mother had three older sisters, and where Sidney grew up and attended high school. .

He joined the RCAF in 1941 at the beginning of WW2 and remained for four and a half years, stationed in the western prairie provinces where he was involved in construction.

After the war he started a small Plumbing and Heating Company which is still in existence and eventually, he ventured into home building and mobile home manufacturing.

In 1964 he married Cele, an American, and moved to Detroit where he purchased a small Fire Protection Company (sprinklers) that was in trouble. Within 10 years the company was operating in four states with 200 employees and eventually it became a public corporation.

In 1980 Sid decided to "cut back and smell the roses," and moved to Boca Raton where he eventually became a permanent resident.

The Awerbucks have four children, nine grandchildren and three great grandchildren.

An enthusiastic scribe and recorder of life stories, Sid looks back on his life and in succinct summation, says "Not bad for a Russian immigrant

My Father: A Lesson in Morality

By Sidney Awerbuck

My father, my partner, my friend, taught me honesty and good judgment. At the age of sixty my father found retirement difficult. Having worked since he was fourteen, he found that inactivity was dull and uninteresting.

My life, in contrast at that time, was full of activity because I had a growing construction and real estate business. Bringing him into the business as a partner would restore his independence and feeling of self worth. He was a quiet and undemonstrative man.

Although our relationship was good, we were not close. So this partnership was a double blessing for him and for me.

I arranged a separate office for him and a weekly salary. He refused the office but accepted the salary. His reason for refusing a private office was that he insisted on hanging out with me while sitting quietly and listening to my telephone conversations and my experienced manner in making deals.

One day we had to appear at a closing for a property that we were purchasing. The seller insisted on cash rather than checks, and so I drove to the bank a few blocks away and withdrew the necessary money. When I returned to my office to pick up my father, I recounted the cash and to my surprise there was a thousand dollars more than I had signed for.

My father instantly said, "Take it back." But I stood up with the thousand dollars clutched in my hand and shouted, "No way, Pa. The bank has plenty of money and how will they know that we have it? It's their mistake." And with great determination, I thought I had uttered my final word on the subject, "We keep the money."

My father leaned over my desk and put his hand gently on my shoulder and said simply, "If you don't take the money back to the bank, our partnership is over"

With perspiration running down my face, I quietly sat down to think. I should have known better than to test his honesty and character.

We closed our deal at the lawyer's office and then I drove to the bank. It was after four o'clock and they were closed for the day. I tapped on the window and the manager opened the door and let me in. I greeted him with a big hello and waved an envelope in his face and said, "This is for you".

He fired back at me with, "I hope there is a thousand dollars in that envelope."

Sitting in the adjacent office was a young teller, in tears. It was her first day back to work from a two week honeymoon.

There was no excuse for my impetuous behavior. A warm and loving relationship with my father, my partner, my friend, developed after that experience. This lesson in good moral judgment has lasted my lifetime.

A Walk on the Bridge

By Sidney Awerbuck

In 1930, I was a ten year old newsboy for the now defunct Detroit Times Newspaper Corporation. It was a great company which provided their carriers with many incentives and prizes for selling the most newspapers in a one or two week period.

I was among the twenty five winners lucky to be the first to walk from Windsor, our home town in Canada, across the new Ambassador Bridge, spanning the Detroit River and connecting Canada to the United States. After the walk, we were to see a

Detroit Tiger baseball game. At the time, the game interested me considerably more than the bridge, which was an anticipated bore. But to be at Navin Field and see Tommy Bridges pitch,

Charley Gehringer at second base and of course my hero Hank Greenberg covering first base, for this I would walk to Chicago in my bare feet on broken glass.

When we arrived at the foot of the bridge on the Canadian side as we left Windsor, we were given both, a Canadian and an American flag to wave as we were crossing this amazing structure, which was over seven thousand feet long and forty seven feet wide, the longest bridge in the world. The girders, the cables, the steel beams and heavier cables were awesome to me. And the idea of such a structure having the power to connect two countries kept playing around in my imagination. But mostly, in my ten year old mind, I wondered, "Will this bridge be strong enough to hold all this weight? Hurry, hurry, don't miss the bus to the ballpark"

It was a beautiful sunny time for a ballgame. We were all given tickets for hot dogs and cokes and expected to enjoy the wonderful day at the park, but the game was slow and unexciting and when the loud speaker announced "Ball four," my reaction was, "Who cares!" I had lost interest in the game and could not take my mind off the bridge.

Instead of seeing ballplayers running the bases I saw steel girders pointing into the blue sky. I saw boats moving around below fighting the currents of the Detroit River. I wanted to go back to the bridge and look at it again and make sure that it was still there.

After seventy years and one thousand miles of distance, I recently went back to see my bridge. It was still standing there in its magnificent glory. It has not aged as much as I have. There were some changes that were obvious. The automobile crossing fare had increased from seventy five cents to four dollars. There were more than a dozen coats of paint applied since my first walk. But the most significant change, the one that brought me back to the reality of today's world, were the military armed guards with their AK47's checking all approaching vehicles.

As unsettling as it was to see those weapons, it gave me a great sense of relief to see that my bridge was well protected from any harm. But I still longed for the innocence of my first walk from one country to the other.

MMM

An Angel in Little Italy

By Sidney Awerbuck

There was a loud knock on my office door, a sound of authority.

"Come in," I responded, "The door is open". In walked Father Di Santi, the parish priest from St. Angelas church.

" I am sorry father but. I gave my donation to the Shaar Hashomayim."

The priest came towards me with a huge smile on his wise and friendly face as he stretched out his hand to wave away the thought of charity.

"Meester Seed I come to you for big favour."

"What can I do for you Father?" I felt somewhat chagrined at my misreading of his visit.

"My very good friend from my village in Italy is sending her son to Canada and I need a job for him. I know you are a friend with the Italian people, so I ask you please favor with a job."

"Ok,Ok. No problem Father. Bring him in to-morrow and Roger will take care of him."

"No Meester Seed I can't do, He is now on the boat and he comes in one week."

"Again no problem, Father.Bring him in when he comes off the boat."

The following week, the kind old priest brought in a 6 foot tall Adonis immigrant, wearing a suit jacket with extra wide lapels that had seen better days.

"What's your name?" I asked. He looked at me with frightened eyes as if I were the major whip cracker and he said two words. "No shpeek." Those words were the beginning of a 25 year friendship starting with the new words that I taught him

"My name is Joe Dinalo. Not Gussepi, but Joe."

Father Di Santi became a constant visitor to my office, bringing with him new Italian immigrants who needed employment in a new world where they found it difficult to be accepted. This was very similar to the situation that my parents had to cope with when they arrived in this country as immigrants, and it made me feel as though I were making a payment of some kind.

Over the years I was invited to many weddings, baptisms and church functions in "Little Italy."

It was a cold wintry day with tons of snow covering all the streets and sidewalks when the kind old priest came knocking on my door again. "Bonjourno Meester Seed."

"Bonjourno, Father.What brings you out in this nasty weather?"

"Meester Seed I have present for you and I have someting in my mind for a very long time I must talk with you." He reached under his arm and unpacked a large shoe box containing a home made lasagna.

"Thanks father. It looks – and smells – delicious, but it was not necessary for you to shlep all the way from your parish to give me this nice gift. So, what is it that you want to talk about?"

At that moment I felt I was the priest and he had come to me for confession.

"Meester Seed, you have done for me and the Italian people many favors and I look upon you like you are an ANGEL so I come to you for your acceptance of this honor."

"Wow, Father, Thank you for your generosity," I responded, a bit stunned, recognizing the huge honor and church ceremony that this entailed. "But, truly, I am not ready yet to be an Angel, I still have many more good deeds to perform before I can accept that honor."

Father DiSanti left my office pleased with our personal meeting but somewhat disappointed at my refusal of his offer. Within a few months, my good friend and holy Father passed away.

Many of the people he had guided to my company became prominent citizens in the community with businesses of their own. As I look back and review the last 30 years of my involvement in large and small corporations, I regret not accepting the honor that the old priest extended to me.

It was the weight of the wings that bothered me.

Geraldine Barry

Geri Barry, a San Francisco, California native, is a retired GE Healthcare Sales and Marketing Executive. This experience, combined with her background in Radiology and a Masters Degree in International Studies, provided a unique set of skills with which to embark on a global career, and also provides abundant material for the stories of her life. Ms. Barry resides in Boca Raton, Florida and is a volunteer with the American Cancer Society and Boca Helping Hand

MMM

Barry With An "A"

By Geraldine Barry

I was almost named Genevieve, after my mother, Genevieve Margaret Mary. But for the simple fact of her not wanting to live her life as "Big Gen", the almost-named "Little Gen", became Geraldine Barry, Barry with an A, not Berry, with an E.

Geraldine was a mouthful for the kindergarten set, thus, at a very young age, I became Geri, to all who knew me. I soon learned the advantage of being Geri Barry. Children loved to sing-song the name and "big people" rarely forgot it. In the official activities of my young life, my birth certificate name, Geraldine, had to be used. That, too, was not so bad, as Flip Wilson's character "Geraldine" elicited a bundle of laughs, and friends loved to address me in that same tone, Gerr all deeen !

It was in my adult years that I took my name more seriously. On a routine Friday night Xray Tech on-call assignment, I stole a few minutes to grab dinner in the busy UCSF Hospital coffee shop. Seated across the counter from me were two chatty women conversing loudly about the husband's illness and the other's search for her daughter's wedding dress. During a lapse in their conversation, a high pitched nasal tone came blasting across the Hospital page system, repeatedly pronouncing "Geri Berry" as if it were the fruit of the week, or pie of the day. The women began to laugh, and, as I slinked over to the phone and whispered my

33

name so they wouldn't know it was me responding to the operator, I heard one say to the other, "Can you imagine someone naming a child 'Geri Berry'?

The defining moment in my lifelong name game came years later, and a more seasoned Geri was spending time in Japan, talking, training, and selling the Medical Community on the new technological wonder, the CT Scanner. Although I have been told I should never play poker, I did a masterful job of masking my shock and stifling my laughter, every time I heard my Japanese associates introduce me as "Jelly Belly." And when mail arrived at my office in the U.S. addressed to Ms. Jelly Belly, that was it!

Seeing is believing. No more childish Geri Berry, Mary Fairy, Harry Carey jokes. No more blind date showing up saying his real name was Louie Dewey. The business cards were immediately changed, and, for the next 20 years, Geri was Geraldine.

And now, in a less formal, less structured phase of my life, I am Geri again; lighter, freer, call-me-what-you-willer. Name sensitivity is in the past. A few years ago, I knew I'd made a successful transition back to Geri, when I mailed my Hallmark Christmas cards depicting an ever smiling Santa Claus and his reindeer, a colorful card, with the inside script that read, "A Jolly Holly from Jelly Belly".

✳✳✳

Profile of a Short Encounter

By Geraldine Barry

I would not describe myself as romantic. A better label is sentimental. Included amongst my personal possessions and owning a treasured spot in my wallet, are bits and pieces, I call the sweet-stuff of my life; the In Memoriam card handed out at my Mother's funeral, the office memo referring to a last phone call "L.J. 2pm 2/14/98", a verse entitled *Success*, and two very significant short sentences on a worn scrap of paper. For me, not only were they words of encouragement, they were the final consult, each time I had to make a difficult life decision. I read these words for the first time in 1957, and countless times thereafter, at every fork in the road.

"Stories of past courage can teach, they can offer hope, they can provide inspiration, but they cannot supply courage itself. For this, each man must look into his own soul". *

I know that it was pure Karma that allowed me to share a few brief indelible moments with the author of these words. I was a college student and a guest at the Carmel Valley Mission Inn for the wedding of my friends, Diane, the beautiful Kim Novak look -a-like, and handsome, John Lyons.

We partied hearty throughout the weekend, treating ourselves to choice champagne, fresh Monterey crab, and the sound of the sea from the deck of the Roper family home along the Bay. On Sunday afternoon, tired and partied out, we casually drove the trails through Pebble Beach, a fresh, green, sunlit respite. Along our route, we spotted two lone golfers, at a stand still, likely contemplating the best approach to birdie the next hole. Two of us thought one golfer looked familiar, and, because we were in a betting mood, we decided to approach and find out for ourselves.

We were so surprised when they actually stopped their game, we momentarily had difficulty saying our names or identifying our different schools. One girl, at a loss for words, asked about the gentleman's wife and if she was a good cook. To which, he shook his head and only smiled.

We did pull it together when we were asked what it was like growing up in San Francisco. As I stood there, I thought I should tell him of the importance of his words. I could have recited them. but I didn't, and lost a glorious opportunity. The golfers seemed to enjoy talking with us, in spite of how little we had to say. We concluded, that better than most, they understood the aspirations of young people in 1960's America.

An unlikely group we were, temporarily hanging out in Pebble Beach; Geri, Bob, Bev, Bill, Paul, and John. That's Paul Fay Jr., Under Secretary of the U.S. Navy 1961 –1963, and John F. Kennedy, President of The United States 1960 – 1963.

We drove off in the sunset. Paul and John continued their game. We never knew what (and if) Jackie cooked for dinner. We knew we had shared a special moment.

On the back seat of the car from which we had hurriedly departed to approach the golfers, there was perched a camera, ready to use. Loaded and ready to use. Karma only goes so far.In our haste, we had left it in the car.

* <u>Profiles In Courage</u> – Senator John F. Kennedy 1956

Rene Blanco

Rene Blanco, famous author of short fiction stories and fiction books is also a therapist, and accomplished screen writer. Originally a New Yorker, René was raised in New England, studied at UCLA and Pitzer College in California for fiction and screenwriting, and lives in Florida. His TV and film accomplishments include a script for NBC's Top Rated drama *Third Watch* as well as the global thriller, _Noah's Descendants._ Fast fiction favorite *Pleasure on the Run* displays his special talents as a creative writer. Written for travelers as a fast read but appealing to all audiences, *Pleasure* is the perfect Flight Book™—with incredible power throughout, lasts a few hours, and takes you everywhere in the world of human experience. Excerpts from the next two Rene Blanco books, shock and thrill novel *Action Adventure* and the second Flightbook™ of stories, *Tender Concrete,* can be enjoyed at the author's website, reneblanco.com, along with much more

MMM

Grade School Sex and the Teacher of Desire

By Rene Blanco

I can't avoid looking back at my earliest grade school experiences and the teacher I'll never forget. What she taught me was not merely my ABCs. and to this day I still don't know if she taught me the right things. What I do know, is that she had a tremendous influence sexually and emotionally.

In 1960 and 1961, I attended a parochial school run by nuns. Miss Murphy, who was not a nun, taught first and second grade. She was much younger than my mother and the older kids talked about how sexy she was, but I could only think that with her round happy face, blue eyes and black hair, she wasn't ugly.

First grade was memorable only for John F. Kennedy's election, and the Mother Superior, who returned the graded homework. She sat behind a huge desk mounted on a high dais and each day she called out names and students would march up to get their graded homework. But when she called my name, she would whip my paper in the air or threw it on the ground for me to pick up. Maybe she didn't do it every time but it felt like she did.

My parents didn't like Kennedy but the Mother Superior did. Once on the playground, I found out the Mother Superior was giving out candy bars to kids if they said "John Fitzgerald Kennedy for President." When I told my mother, she pinned a Nixon button on me and sent me to school. The button came off when I saw the Mother Superior's angry face, and I'm still not sure if my special treatment was political.

But second grade was different. I felt a strange connection to Miss Murphy almost from the first day of school. Her black hair was silky, her face was bright, and under her blouse she wore thin lacey straps which wrapped around her chest. She usually dressed in dark colors with knee-length skirts and seamed stockings. Her shoes were simple leather flats but she had shapely legs, and when she looked at me she always smiled. I noticed, too, that she often twirled her feet and re-crossed her legs. From my assigned seat I could see her skirt slipping up sometimes, and I could see her under-thighs. She didn't bother to pull her skirt down until it began to creep too far up her legs, and I was very disappointed when she finally adjusted it. At the time I didn't know why looking at Miss Murphy's legs made me feel good and special, but it surely did.

As the year went on I did well in my studies but sometimes I wound up being punished, which meant that I had to stand in the front corner of the room, slightly to the side and behind Miss Murphy who sat at her desk. During these brief punishments, I listened to students take turns reading and I observed how she would listen and teach.

She half-faced in my direction while she taught, like she didn't want to leave me out completely, and she twirled those feet and re-crossed those legs and rubbed her shins along each other. Or, with her hands she would smooth her stockings, Occasionally, she would pull out a desk drawer to rest one foot on it with the other on the floor. Hidden from the rest of the class behind her desk, I began to see more and more shadowy space between Miss Murphy's legs, like she didn't care about me seeing inside. Her stockings stopped above her knees and there showed her creamy white legs.

She threw glances at me now and then, but she did not seem to discourage my looking at her since she made no effort to stop me. Perhaps she glanced at me to make sure I was being attentive to the lesson. Once, my dickie got so stiff, it stood straight up. At the time, I did not understand the connection and I had to stay facing into the corner for a long time until it went down. She didn't send me back to my seat, so she must have been aware of what had happened. That was the last time she imposed that "punishment" on me.

At the end of the school year, the first mini-skirt fashions came out and Miss Murphy wore a short skirt one time, but in the afternoon, I saw the Mother Superior talking to her and she changed back to wearing her usual outfits again.

The climax of my feelings happened during the final Graduation Pageant held for the parents. Our class, led by Miss Murphy sang songs with choruses of "Row, Row, Row Your Boat", but no costumes were used until the final rehearsal practice. When I saw Miss Murphy in her little sailor costume my feelings shot through the roof. Her costume was a tight one-piece red, white and blue bathing suit, high heel shoes and stockings which ran all the way up her legs and looked like fish netting.

She was pretty for sure—I knew that! When she walked and stood and sat beside me, it thrilled me but also made me feel confused and sad at the same time. Maybe this was the last time I'd see her, I thought. And when we sang our songs for the audience, I sang my heart out as we merrily rowed in our boat next to each other. Her face shone with beautiful light and her legs opened and pumped in perfect rhythm to the music with me. I had another stiff dickie and was scared and excited, too, realizing it was all because of my feelings for her. That night there weren't enough choruses of "Row Your Boat" for me!

My intuition was right about Miss Murphy. During the summer I went on an errand for my mother, and walked near the school which sat on top of a hill. From quite a distance I saw the Mother Superior and several nuns seated at an outdoor table with Miss Murphy. By now I could spot her perfect round face a mile away, She rose from the table with the nuns and everybody was smiling. She shook all their hands and seemed to be thanking them. They did likewise, but I had the feeling they were doing it to part ways forever. The sadness of the pageant hit me again, but my confusion disappeared. Whatever they were doing was done. I continued on my errand while thinking over and over about chasing Miss Murphy to say Hello, or Good-bye.

A month later I learned she had moved away and the school had been sold to a developer. But I wasn't sad anymore, because those thrilling feelings which she had caused in me, were still inside and I looked forward to having them again and again and again.

MMM

Higher and Higher

By Rene Blanco

I hated my life until I began smoking pot. It t was a constant drone of boring meaningless activities that I endured, like freezing weather. But I didn't get high the first time I tried it which was during the moon landing in 1969, when I said to myself, What's The Big Deal About Grass?

Woodstock was the following month and while a few kids with progressive parents got to go to the festival, I didn't even think of asking my up-tight conservative parents for permission. I did run across grass now and then, when a couple of black kids were smoking in the back of a bus and no one did anything. Another time, I smelled it in a store staircase.

I knew which kids at school I could ask about pot but I never made a point of looking for it.. There was so much news and conflict about drugs, about the Black Panthers, Abbie Hoffman and Jerry Rubin, and of course Vietnam that I just wanted to go underground and get away from it all. So, I studied hard, lots of science and math, and managed to get accepted early where my father was a teacher at MIT.

On New Year's Eve of that year my parents were out to a huge party while I stayed home. I felt like such a loser because I had few friends and nowhere to go, but I did have a joint of grass that was supposed to be great stuff. A couple weeks earlier I was taking out garbage at the fast food place where I worked and caught an older man with a long gray beard handing something over to one of my schoolmates. A joint dropped out on the pavement. Then they saw me, and froze. Their frosty breath pumped out fast.

"Don't tell anyone," my classmate said. He was not one of the "cool" kids at school I could ask about pot. He was a bookworm in fact. He had an A-rating from Harvard, meaning he was automatically accepted if he applied.

"No, I won't say anything," I replied. "Never thought you'd do that stuff, though."

"Why? It's great," he told me. "You never tried it?"

"I did," I answered. "It sucked."

"No," said the man. "This is the real deal, Acapulco Gold. I can also lay a little Honduran grass on you."

The man wore ripped hippie jeans, crooked patches and wildly messed up hair crowned with a halo of flowers.

When I thought about how weird he looked I saw myself reflected in a window, dragging those bulging garbage bags dressed in blood and ice cream-soiled clothes with a dark tired expression. I felt so unhappy with my life, like I was just sleepwalking through the years even though people said I had everything, a loving family, a good career and future waiting for me. The older guy had a happy twinkle in his eyes, though, not like he was doped up.

"Tell you what. Here." He handed me a rolled cigarette.

I considered his offer for a few seconds. The trash stink began to bother me and it was tooth-gnashing cold. I hurled the bags into the dumpster and stared at my classmate again. "You really think it's good?" I asked him.

My classmate shook his head emphatically like saying, Absolutely! "Of course it's good," he replied. "Remember the project we did on algorithms, what a pain it was? This makes even algorithms fun."

He was enthusiastic and also a smart student like myself. If it made algorithms fun then maybe it was OK. I took the joint and put it away for a special occasion.

So, six months after first trying pot and not getting high, I retrieved the joint I was given and fingered it until a few grains fell out that shined like gold dust. Unlike the first grass I smoked this had a sweet, almost perfume-like aroma, which changed to a thick pungent smoke upon lighting. The smell was reminiscent of incense. After a few small puffs I began coughing violently. Then, parts of the joint began exploding in my hands, shocking the hell out of me. It was a series of sharp pops blasting smoke out the sides and top of the cigarette as the marijuana seeds burst from the heat. Cinders flung up everywhere. This was nothing like the first cigarette I smoked. I expected big things from this experience. But, once again nothing happened.

What a rip-off this is, I thought. and totally lost respect for my school friend. He was a fool, throwing money away on nothing, on a myth. This pot thing was pure hype.

But as I was contemplating the misinformation about drugs along with everything else on the news, and without warning, I threw up my dinner. From one moment to the next, I felt a mass regurgitation shoot up my throat and out of my mouth in a spray that resembled a whale's blowhole.

"Screw this shit!" I yelled out loud and pressed my sleeves across my lips to hold back more discharge. In a muzzled voice I stomped around screaming, "I'm never freakin' doing that shit again, man!"

As I hustled for a rag and began mopping the area of projectile vomit on Mom's Persian rug, I realized that I was smiling to myself, and dabbing up the mess in slow circular motions. No, I didn't feel too bad about Mom's new rug, or scared that she would know. So I got sick, she would understand, but I didn't care anyway. In fact I was curious to see what reaction she would have, that dumb confused look on her face showing all the disappointment she felt in my behavior. I hated that look of, "You Should Feel So Guilty and So Ashamed for Disappointing Me." This would zing her tidy life. Then, she'd just change to that sympathetic but suspicious edge in her voice. "But...but, child, what were you doing?" I laughed out loud at the pathetic upset in her imagined voice.

At that moment I felt a soaring euphoria carrying me away from all the boredom and meaninglessness of my day in and day out existence. I entered a very thoughtful and deep meditative state, a dreamy feeling that descended on me like the soft touch of pleasure rubbing me all over. But I was alert at the same time, keenly aware of everything around, of each traffic noise outside the house, wind rustling the trees and rattling the windows, the low rumble of the heating furnace pumping heat through the pipes and the Three Stooges marathon on the TV at low volume. The sounds, the familiar surroundings, small details of the furniture that I touched, even the feelings of just sitting there taking it in with the heightened awareness of myself inside this bag of skin, everything about me and my life seemed brand new.

The kitchen clock ticked off second after second while I listened closely to it. Each split second contained a new amazing sensation or thought. My perception of all the old was changed in what I soon realized was a just few minutes of time. Objects seemed to glow with a fascinating aura. My perspective of me was altered as I saw my existence from a completely different angle, a much better one, I thought.

For the first time ever I knew that I was alive, actually feeling my heart sending warm blood through me and having something to compare to my normal state of interminable boredom. I always believed there was a good reason for living and for having feelings, and perhaps it was this—at least for me. It gave me a reason to be excited about waking up, other than that I should be doing whatever I was supposed to be doing according to Mom and Dad. Now, for myself, and my own satisfaction I had an alternative point of view.

But how long this would last, I had no idea. What if I never came down from the drug? I got worried and began feeling sick again. They said in the news that some people never came down. A sudden shot of fear coursed through me. What if I'd gone too far over the edge already? I got up fast, looked around at the walls, the doors, the windows with a frantic series of doom and gloom, thoughts running across my mind.

How was I going to get down from here? Not that I wanted to just yet. But, I didn't have any idea what was happening to me, and I seemed to be getting higher and higher, the volume on the Stooges marathon seemed louder and the Three Blind Mice theme song came on, anchoring my mind to something from my childhood. Their comedy took on a radically different meaning than it had as a child. At that time I thought it was stupid but now they began revealing their genius for satire. I laughed for an hour, revisiting the episodes where poverty and prejudice force them to take jobs selling the snake oil product, Brighto! And the one where they impersonate doctors to escape false accusations, and make each emergency worse as the hospital loudspeaker blares out, "Calling Dr. Howard, Dr Fein, Doctor Howard!" Then the episode where Moe plays Hitler, Curly plays Goëbbels, Larry Fein is Tojo and they maim each other over control of the plastic world.

I was having so much fun. Maybe it wasn't so bad if I never came down. But I also felt sorry because it was supposed to be bad; I was told it was wrong. And therefore I must be bad. I always feared I was bad and now I had proof because I enjoyed these wonderful sensations of happiness. But, was it really wrong, or were those people who said it was bad, wrong? Some people needed medicine to get through the day—mood stabilizers they were called—and doctors gave them out. Why was this any different? I thought, maybe I'll be one of those lucky ones who never come down.

George Britton

George Britton was born in the Bronx, New York in October 1924. and attended the prestigious N.Y.C .public Stuyvesant High School.

He was shot down on his 19th mission over Germany in August 1944 and was a POW until the end of the war.

A graduate of Columbia Business School in 1948, he was sent to Paris in 1954 to work for an international cosmetics company, and he lived in Europe as an ex-pat until he retired in 1982.

He and his wife Doris celebrated 50 years of marriage in 2000, and their two European educated daughters live with their families in Florida where George was beckoned by the thought of year round golf.

He writes to relive his wonderful European experiences and to help brighten his days as he tries to dismiss his physical problems.

You'll enjoy reading about post war Europe and the characters and scams that swirled around the life of an ambitious corporate executive.

Father

By George Britton

He'd rub his beard against my face as I squealed with joy when we played in bed while my Mother prepared our breakfast. I asked for the thousandth time to see his war wounds. He had fought in France for four years as a volunteer in the Canadian Army and had been shot three times. There was a star shaped piece of flesh missing from his left leg the result of shrapnel. He'd been bayoneted in the jaw, and that gave him a Cary Grant dimple. And he had also been gassed. His survival was a miracle and I was proud of him for all that he'd been through.

I used to wait for him to bring me a Hershey chocolate bar when he came home from work. He was big and good looking. For an Irishman, he was modest in his drinking, but loved White Owl cigars.

As I grew up, I slowly became aware of his shortcomings. My mother had wanted to be a school teacher in Ireland before emigrating to the

States to escape the horrible poverty there.. Here she became a housemaid before marrying my father after the war, but she projected her dream of higher learning onto me as she corrected my grammar, albeit with a light Irish brogue .

She had tried to correct my father's use of "ain't" and "youse" .He had a certain logic in his thinking since if there's more than one "you," "youse" would make this clear .She also pointed out to him that the "K" in knight was silent, but with the tenacity that got him through the war, he held onto his speech pattern, and knight came out kenight .As to pneumonia, that "p" would not be forgotten, answering my mother's correction with a "Shush, Mary, for the love of god, leave me alone."

I could forgive Russian, German, or Polish immigrants for their less than perfect English. I assumed they spoke their native language perfectly, but my father's native tongue was English and he should have spoken it perfectly. I often discussed grammatical rules with my mother, and unintentionally, my father was shut out of our conversations. The classic Oedipus complex was being played out, unknown to me, with a grammar book. . .

Although my father was bodily clean, a few spots on his shirt or pants did not upset him since he was a foreman in the long since defunct Railway Express Company. He worked with mechanics and trucks, and a grease spot or two was of no importance to him. Regarding his eating habits, it took a bit of courage to dare take the spoon out of his cup, since that was the way a man drank his tea in Ireland and he wasn't about to change.

He never hit my mother and he only hit me once. I deserved it. The principal had sent him a letter stating that my cousin Buddy and I had called a strike in school. We didn't let kids into the school building after lunch because the administration had broken its promise to let us play softball. Upon reading the letter, my mother sent me to bed early as a punishment, even before my father came home .The next morning he awakened me very early, a took me into the living room, took off his belt and strapped me a half dozen times around the legs .His duty done, he offered that worn out cliché, "Son, that hurt me more than it hurt you." I doubted that, but knew, that for him, a staunch Republican, to have a striker for a son, must have hurt

.I don't recall any overt display of affection between my parents, but I do recall the one time that my mother threw a cup of tea at him. I never knew why. But generally they behaved with Irish reserve towards each other. This was particularly evident watching them dance in typical Irish fashion, where the legs act like pistons and the arms are held closely at the sides thus preventing any possibility of touch..

A kid at school told me his family had come to America way back in the late 1700's. Here I was with my father, just an Irish immigrant, mangling the English language, careless about dress and table manners and somehow I felt ashamed. My estrangement from him grew the more I had contact with the outside world, and I perceived that we had little in common.

He did take me fishing for flounder on Long Island sound, but I felt embarrassed as we boarded the trolley car since he was shabbily dressed and he carried the fishing tackle and cloth bag which we hoped to fill with fresh flounder .

At this stage of puberty, pimples would appear on my face like wild strawberries. My father with apparent embarrassment told me that the son of his friend had some mental problems for "you know, hurting himself." I took this to mean any personal enjoyment under the bed sheets was the cause of my pickled face. This information was as helpful as his revelation, when I was 11, that storks brought babies.

There are so many conflicting memories of love and shame. I started to deliver the Bronx Home news during my high school days. On those cold winter Sunday mornings, when the snow had fallen two feet deep and each paper seemed to weigh a ton, I started my home delivery at 4am. He would say ,"Son, 'tis no problem, I'll drive you." I resented his kindness as it heightened my guilt at the shame I felt in his "foreignness" and at the way I found myself denying him as my father. On the few occasions when we went to the movies together, I dreaded his stopping at the candy stand, since I knew he would buy life savers, which he would suck loudly throughout the movie, unaware of how I was slouching down and wanting to disappear. Finally, my release came when I became a cadet in the Army Air Force in 1943.

I can't remember him ever saying he was proud of me as an officer, but I know his hair turned white when my name was erroneously printed as having been killed in a bus accident at my training base. I survived the war and matriculated at Columbia Business School and emerged with fairly liberal ideas.

. My father and I disagreed politically, about almost every issue we brought up. I praised Truman for sacking General Mc Arthur while he thought the General was our national savior. Our arguments were endless as to Joe McCarthy's red hunt. My father loved America blindly and I had fought Germans who had loved Hitler blindly. I never said that to him as he would not have understood.

My career brought me to live in France in 1954 and so contact with my parents was limited to brief visits home every few years. My family visited my parents in Florida one July. I foolishly lay in the sun too long and was tortured with a terrible sunburn. That evening my father gently soothed my burnt skin with a lotion he bought at the drug store .It was the most intimate contact we'd had in years.

When I complained to my wife that he had little to say to me at lunch when the women went shopping, she said, "Did you ever think that maybe you intimidate him with all your big words and liberal ideas that he can no longer fight ?" It had not occurred to me, but I have thought about that ever since.

In 1961 my mother called to say that. Pop had died from a heart attach. After breakfast that day, he had gone to the porch to read and they found him dead a half hour later. I flew home, of course, for the funeral.

My mother commented on how cold my hands were as we walked into the funeral home to view my father. He lay there so quietly, no more arguments, no more life saver sucking, no more anything. He was gone. I had too many mixed feelings to try to sort them out.

Irish wakes are special. His old friends came by the score .Truck drivers who had worked for him, came to pay their respects, and said, as they offered condolences to me and my mother, "He was a foine man, he was' and as honest as a gold piece." They came from all over the city. I don't know how word of his funeral spread, but he belonged to that wave of Irish immigrants that flooded in through Ellis Island at the turn of the century.—and each death diminished them all.

Irish wakers don't come only to express their condolences, view the body and then sit for 15 minutes before exiting. Irish wakers come to suffer with the family. They might leave for short breaks at the corner saloon where glasses are raised to wish the deceased a good trip to Heaven. But they return to mourn some more. The dead, they believed, deserved a few hours of respect. .

. At the end of three days and nights of mourning, when all the buried emotions had been dug up and examined and re-examined, the family is ready for the final ceremony with the minister's well rehearsed platitudes. Those present were asked to leave for the cars and the ride to the cemetery.

The funeral director came out to close the coffin. I took one last look at my father and bent down to kiss him goodbye on his brow.

I realize now what a good man my father was, and it saddens me that I can't recapture those lost years when my first generation sensitivity blinded me to his very special qualities.

⋈⋈⋈

Aunt Maude

By George Britton

That Aunt Maude loved and adored Uncle Charlie drove many family members crazy. Their unique marriage made me realize that every pot has a lid, and while others fumed about the "lazy lout", I knew that Uncle Charlie made her feel like a queen. From the first day of their marriage he told his young Irish bride that he couldn't hold a job, but that he would get her only the best cleaning jobs in town. And so it was.

He carefully checked the papers for "Daily Help Wanted ", called the clients, talked up her qualities in his lovely lilting voice and arranged the terms.

He cleaned their small apartment located on Third Avenue where he was the "building superintendent", which some 60 years ago meant washing the stairs, collecting the other tenants' garbage and exchanging a friendly word with them.

Uncle Charlie would serve Aunt Maude her three minute egg with buttered toast in bed and read her the latest news of the day as the old "El" rattled by. Aunt Maude would then dress, be briefed meticulously by Uncle Charlie on her day's assignments and be sent off with a hug and a kiss from him, telling her how lovely she looked .

He would then attack "The New York Times" crossword puzzle at which he was a whiz, always leaving a few of the simpler words for Aunt Maude who delighted in being able to finish what he couldn't. The saloon downstairs provided him with a small pitcher of beer, free for washing the windows which were covered daily with the grime from the Third Avenue El. There was no rush to dinner. Aunt Maude delighted in lighting up one of the cigarettes hand rolled by Uncle Charlie who sipped the cold foamy beer as he told her of the day's events that somehow magically happened in his little apartment building.

No event was too small when filtered through his Gaelic imagination and he was a Don Quixote, seeing delivery men having liaisons with lonely housewives, and a policeman's visit the forerunner of a coming arrest of a sought and dangerous killer. Aunt Maude probably knew it was all made up but she loved to hear him carry on so.

He would escort her out to the little dining room with the table elegantly set and a flower resting on her plate, donation of the flower shop next to the saloon. Dinner was always a surprise and only Uncle Charlie could serve a cheap chicken in one of his Haute Cuisine sauces.

Conversation flowed and he recounted the savagery of the Italian assault in Ethiopia, or the latest problems with the gold standard. Aunt Maude was most certainly better informed of world events than many of the great ladies for whom she cleaned. They sat in the evening enjoying the concerts from the old Atwater Kent radio with the slightly ripped speaker.

For all my material success, I am light years away from matching Uncle Charlie's success as a husband. I suppose the other relatives, in their self reproach just took it out on him. Aunt Maude was a queen.

The Baptism

By George Britton

Lucy, my future mother-in-law, was delighted to meet me when Doris introduced us way back in the 1950's .I was a nice boy of Irish background and, she assumed, a Catholic, an unstated but absolute requirement for marrying into her Italian family where pictures of Jesus decorated the walls, particularly over the master bed .

Months later the secret was out. I was a Protestant, with less than warm feelings towards the Pope and the Catholic hierarchy. I suppose the Humanities course taken at Columbia had increased my already inherited suspicion of them. After all, the Protestants and Catholics had been killing each other for years and as a young boy I had marched in the Orangemen parades which celebrated the victory of a King William of Orange, I had supposed at the time, over the Catholics. The historical details even to this day are a bit fuzzy, but back then the pounding of the drums and the fife's shrill sound anchored my prejudice against the priests with their black vests and white collars, and the unchallenged blind adoration that people like Lucy bestowed upon them.

She had been born in Italy and immigrated to the States as a young girl with her mother who took her to church every morning. I have great respect for this wonderful woman for all her virtues and her faults, but when Doris and I told her we wanted to marry, all I saw then was an opponent who tried to break my will. I had to sign papers agreeing that the children would be brought up Catholic. I loved my Doris and signed contre coeur as two priest gloated in the rectory at my defeat. I could understand how Gallieo felt when he capitulated to the church and agreed that the earth was the center of the Universe .

Three years later our daughter Lorraine was born in a French clinic just outside Paris. With the ocean protecting me from Lucy's wrath, I reneged on my promise and insisted on baptizing her Protestant. Doris did not share her mother's iron will and albeit, reluctantly, nonetheless acquiesced.

We asked Andre and Irene, a young French couple with whom we had become friends, and who were also struggling to get established in life, to be Lorraine's godparents. After the baptism, they gave a little celebratory party in their small house with mutual friends sharing and delighting in the pate foie gras, hors d'oeuvres and cheese dips as they made champagne toasts of good wishes. I knew that this little party had stressed their budget and I was so grateful .

I think I was ultimately influenced by Andre, a devout catholic, whom I came to love as the dearest of friends, and who often discussed religion with me. A year later I came to recognize the wrong I had done my wife. Also the pressure from Lucy continued in the many written letters (telephone calls then were so expensive}and finally I capitulated. We arranged for a local priest to baptize Lorraine catholic and again we asked Andre and Irene to be godparents. And again the godparents held a little post baptismal party in their home.

As we imbibed the last of the champagne and the guests headed home, Andre came up to me and said in his delightful French accent, "George, should you and Doris decide that Lorraine might be better off in another religion, would you mind terribly getting other godparents?"

Each family has its favorite legends that are told and retold to succeeding generations and this one is Lorraine's favorite, even as it is repeated to her own children. And the truth be told, Lorraine hasn't been in a church in the last ten years. Lucy at ninety six was still saying her daily rosary .

MMM

Bailout

By George Britton

The German fighters came in so fast I had no time to react. I felt something hit my right arm as I saw the starboard outer engine on fire. An explosion was about 10 to 15 seconds away, if we were lucky.

I never heard a bailout bell from the pilot but I didn't need one. I ran forward to open the bomb bay doors and out I went. I pulled my ripcord a few seconds later as our blazing B-24 flew on and I floated down through the wet cotton-like clouds that covered the little Austrian valley.

I quickly lost sight of the planes and suddenly I was alone in this immense sky and a horrible thought crossed my mind. What if the pilots got the fire under control and I was the only one to bailed out! The silence was eerie and I could only hear the wind flapping at my chute.

Suddenly, I heard a plane motor and turned around to see a Focke Wulf 190 fighter coming directly at me as I hung there helplessly. One small press of his finger on the gun trigger and I would be another victim of the savagery of the war. I've often thought of that one second of fate that caused him to veer off at the last moment as I closed my eyes in terror.

My brain suffered from lack of oxygen at 20,000 feet and I panicked thinking that I was ascending instead of descending, an optical illusion created by the clouds which were moving downward faster than I was.

As I came lower and the oxygen supply was richer, I realized that the beautiful mountain peaks lining the valley towards which I was headed, could be deadly. I pulled the right two risers which steered my chute away from the sharp peaks. But I had over done the pull as the chute partially collapsed. I quickly released the risers, and the chute regained its fullness leaving my fate to the wind.

I floated down into a fir tree, crushing my left shoulder as a sharp branch entered my left thigh. I cut myself down, trembling, but alive. The valley seemed to belie the terrible air battle that had just taken place and its soothing greens and sharp stillness helped calm me down. I felt terribly alone in the vastness that surrounded me. Alone and very scared.

I had never understood why I had to carry a 45 automatic in a shoulder holster. Was I supposed to fight the German soldiers who most certainly were out in numbers to catch the survivors?. I was no Errol Flynn so I threw it away along with my bombardier wings as soon as I cut myself loose. I was not prepared to be a hero.

And then to my astonishment, I ran about a hundred yards and went to sleep for an hour in a heavy underbrush. Sleep is probably the wrong word. I passed out from exhaustion and fear. When I came to, I made a vow, which I kept for ten years, to never get in another fuckin' plane. I thought of my mother and how concerned she used to be if I didn't come home on time for dinner. How shocked she would be when the War Department telegram of my "missing in action" arrived.

I knew I had no chance of reaching Switzerland which was about 60 miles way behind sky high mountains. I descended into a dirt road from the mountain slope and walked right into the path of an Austrian soldier with a rifle slung over his shoulder. There were no dramatics. I had felt so lonely and lost, like a little boy in a huge park, that I welcomed his presence. He brought a sense of reality that all this wasn't a dream. I showed him my rubber escape map and pointed to Switzerland. He just laughed as if I had shown him a joke, and indicated that I should follow him.

There was a truck with other Americans waiting below and we were driven to the local police station where I saw Larry, Bob, and Joe, pilot, co-pilot, and navigator. I was relieved to see that my idiotic fear, that they had made it back to Italy, was baseless.

Our greetings were reserved as if we had not just lived through the hell that had marked our lives. A display of joy would, we instinctively felt, demean us in the eyes of our captors. Joe was arguing with Larry and Bob as to why they had taken our plane to join the 'lame ducks' when our plane had miraculously made it through the flak-filled sky and should have stayed with the main fleet and not dropped back with the seven badly damaged B24s.

"Goddam it, Larry, if you hadn't made that lousy decision we would have made it back," hammered Joe. "With no fighter protection we were doomed."

"I felt those poor bastards needed support, and we were in good shape," argued Larry.

"Yeah," continued Joe, "and we all would have gotten medals but instead we are going to sit on our asses as the war passes us by." Joe was a gung ho fighter and felt invulnerable.

From my point of view, the war could pass me by. I had enough. A tour of duty consisted of 50 bombing runs. Since losses ran about 2% per run, it didn't require a genius to see the chances of surviving as practically zero. I felt lucky to have been shot down instead of being blown up, being killed by the flak or fighters or being burned to death as the plane fell to earth with the crew struggling against gravity to claw their way free. We were transferred to Frankfurt on the Main for interrogation. Our individual cells were small with only a cot and a thin blanket and a pee bottle. Once a day we were fed a sandwich which consisted more of sawdust than wheat but which hunger overlooked. A bottle of warm tea was exchanged for the pee bottle. - they resembled each other.

One toilet trip was allowed per day. I tried to sleep, but my mind was a kaleidoscope of thoughts. Had the 7 enlisted men survived? When would I be interrogated? My right arm was starting to hurt a little and I was wondering how my family had been informed. The time dragged by and I became restless- anything would have been better than just lying there staring at the gray walls.

On the third day, a guard came to escort me to the interrogation room. I had imagined a Hollywood room consisting of diabolical torture instruments. Instead, a good looking Luftwaffe Colonel greeted me warmly in perfect English. The room could have been taken for a business executive's. He offered me an American cigarette which I took. He even lit it for me. He then asked me innocent questions. How did I feel? Was I sleeping well? And then with professional subtlety, asked to which squadron I belonged. Without thinking, I replied the 780 th. He smiled, and the horrible awareness hit me.

All I was supposed to give was my name, rank and serial number. I felt as if I had betrayed my country and I was mortified. He saw my flushed face and laughed as he said, "Don't worry, I can almost tell you what you had for breakfast this morning.," as he waved a folder in front of my face. He knew I was small fish and dismissed me as I returned crestfallen to my cell.

Eventually we were transferred to Stalag Luft 3 near Poland. I never saw Larry or Bob since they lived in different compounds. Joe and I did meet occasionally. I was assigned to the British compound and shared a room with 5 British officers.

I developed a series of boils under my right arm pit. There were no antibiotics or anesthetics available so the series of seven boils, cut open by a South African doctor, were a cause of deep concern. How ironic, I thought, to die of infection in a comfortable POW camp.

I settled in with my room mates, who were understandably at times querulous, since several had been in "the cage" for almost five years. Tom, an older fellow with a nasty temper once falsely accused me of eating some bread crumbs. He was a trouble maker since his wife had sent him a Dear John letter .Overall life was easy, books were available and the Red Cross parcels delivered weekly kept us alive. Fantasies were not of women, but of the perfect meal. I tried not to think of the air battles that were going on.

Ingenious prisoners had built radios that caught the BBC war news that countered the German war propaganda. We were kept well informed and followed the Russian advance on the east front heading towards Germany and our camp.

Rumors grew that Hitler had given the order to kill the POWs. Air Marshall Goering refused to issue this order and they continued to keep us as hostages. I started to think that maybe Joe had been right. We should have joined up with the main force that was protected by American fighters.

The camp tension mounted and we were ordered by the senior POW officer to start a daily exercise of walking around the perimeter of the camp in anticipation of its evacuation. Dangerous days lay ahead as we prepared emergency rations, deciding on which clothing we would wear, and what we could carry in improvised back packs.

On the night of January 28 the duel between the German and Russian cannons could be heard growing ever closer. The German guards came with the loud orders Raus Raus and around midnight we formed columns and moved out into the falling snow of the coldest European winter in fifty years.

I felt helpless as I had been taken from the livable POW camp, forced out into the freezing cold and snow for a week, cooped up for three days in a railroad transport car with little to eat and no sanitary facilities. I slept in barns and fought cows for rotten potatoes in their feeding troughs, and cringed in fear in trenches outside of Nuremberg as the British and Americans bombed it day and night.

Finally in desperation, an American camp buddy and I attempted an escape to the advancing American lines. After three miserable nights and days spent mostly in hiding from German patrols, we were caught by the SS. Improbable as it sounds, they took us to a local school where their officer ordered a bowl of hot soup for us. We were then escorted back to the main body of POWs, instead of being shot. The war was winding down and even the feared SS had lost their taste for it. It was a nightmare from which I only awoke when Patton's 3rd Army crashed through and freed us.

Discharged, I spoke little of these events. Other veterans had no interest since they had their own nightmares to digest. It's been over fifty years and the memories now come alive as they carry me back to my youth and finally, to an understanding and forgiveness of the fears I've lived with ever since August 3, 1944.

Fate

By George Britton

I had met Tony at a dinner garden party hosted by mutual friends in Zurich in the summer of 1960.He was on the last leg of his six month trip around the world before returning to England the following week. He was tall and eloquent in speech with a shock of black hair with which few are blessed into middle age. I judged him to be in his fifties. .The deep lines in his tanned face were due most certainly to his chain cigarette smoking habit, at that time not socially outlawed. He regaled us with stories of the many places he had visited. He had climbed mountains with the Sherpas in the Himalayas, visited the Taj Mahal in India, walked the dangerous streets of Bombay and visited Russia when the cold war was still hot.

I learned that he was a golfer as was I, and so invited him to join me for a game the following Saturday. And then, as agreed, I picked him up for the half hour drive to my golf course called Hittnau. He enjoyed the ride through the various little towns where the window sills were decorated with geraniums and he marveled at the sense of order of the Swiss who piled their fire wood with precision into neat stacks. I had opened all the car windows since he continued his chain smoking. As an ex-smoker, I knew how obnoxious I could be, and with great effort, I managed to hold my tongue. . .

Since my wife and I had lived in England for over a year, Tony and I had things in common to discuss. Had I been to Simpsons for their succulent roast beef ? Had I seen the Mouse Trap, a play by Agatha Christie, which seemed to run forever? Had I visited the Albert and Victoria Museum?. Eventually we turned to our military service. I was excited to learn that he had flown Lancaster bombers during the war which dropped block busting bombs on the German cities at night. I informed him that I had been a bombardier in B 24's flying out of Italy. I confessed with some sense of guilt, that when my plane was shot down on my 19th mission, and I had parachuted out safely to become a prisoner of war, I was the happiest person alive. No longer did I have to fly through those flak filled skies, where I lived in dread of disappearing in a puff of smoke as had so many of the crew mates in my Squadron. To my astonishment, he replied, using a term I thought had gone out with the war's end, "Well, Yank, I understand, but I never had so much fun in my life, dropping those blockbusters on Jerry (another British term}and I couldn't get enough of it."

While flying at night made German fighter attacks less likely, it still must have been horrifying to get caught in the searchlights pinpointing the Lancasters for the ack ack guns.

I thought he was crazy or lying, but I made no comment as we drove up to my golf course. We played fairly even, with Tony slightly ahead when suddenly as we approached the 13th hole, the bright blue sky started to darken as if a bottle of black ink had been spilled over it. The temperature dropped, accompanied by a strong wind and a heavy rain caught us in our shirt sleeves. I knew from past experience that the thunder and lightning were about to put on a terrifying show. And with a note of panic in my voice I said, "There's a shelter just around the bend. Let's leave our clubs here since the irons attract lightning. We can come back later and get them."

Again Tony's behavior astonished me. He took his three iron and charged as the lightning started to strike the nearby trees, turning them into kindling wood, and waving the iron in an attack mode, he shouted as he ran, "There's no bolt of lightning in the Heaven's quiver that will ever strike me."

At this point, I had taken off my cleated shoes and lay on the ground watching this crazy man charging around like a Don Quixote attacking windmills. Suddenly the rain stopped as the clouds emptied. The lightning pin ball flashing disappeared, the black sky ink was blotted up and the heavens turned to a baby innocent blue. I stood up, thoroughly shaken, and suggested that we call it quits, return to the club house, drinks on me.

Seated on the terrace in changed dry clothes with our gin and tonics, I said, "Tony, I hope you will permit me an observation. I think you're fuckin' crazy. When you claimed happiness in being shot at on your bombing runs into Germany, I thought you were a goddam liar. But after watching you run with that three iron challenging the lightning to strike you, I think you are just a nut case."

Tony burst out laughing and said, "Yank, I'm going to tell you a tale I've never told before, but I think the time is ripe. But it will cost you another drink."

I would gladly have bought a dozen drinks to know how he had conquered normal and understandable fears. A wave of my hand to the waiter had a new round on the table almost immediately and I waited impatiently for Tony to start his tale .

"My family was fairly well to do land owners in south west England for centuries, near a little village, Westward Ho, situated on the coast with a magnificent beach where the waves come crashing in from the Atlantic during the frequent storms."

I nodded, saying I knew the village well since I had spent a most delightful week there with my family on a large farm during the summer of 56.

Tony continued. "My Dad said I should, before leaving for school in the north, pay respects to my great-grandfather and grandfather who were buried in the family plot bordering the old church dating from the 1600's. I was about 14 then and for the first time consciously noted on the headstones, birth and death dates of those two old ancestors. I was pretty good at math and quickly figured out that they both had been 55 when they died, and great-grandfather 30 when my grandfather was born, also in the month of October. I mentioned this to my Dad and stated that his birthday also fell in October. He said,' Pure coincidence, son, pure coincidence.'

I let it go at that and now, Yank, I'm going to ask you some questions. How old was my grandfather when my Dad was born? How old was my Dad when he died? And how old was he when I was born?"

I liked puzzles and could sense where Tony was heading. I didn't want to sound like a smart ass, but I reluctantly gave the correct answers despite the dark conclusions that such answers had given Tony.

All three ancestors had been born in October, had a son at age thirty and then died at age 55.

"Correct you are, Yank," he smiled, "so you see my fate is determined. I will die at 55 and not a bloody second before. I almost felt embarrassed when the Royal Air Force handed me all those medals for bravery. Shit, I wasn't brave. The medals should have gone to the poor bastards such as yourself who went up each time not knowing if you would ever get back. You guys were the true heroes. As for the lightning, I felt absolutely protected by my fate, Yank. I could tell you of other exploits where I should have 'bought it,' but survived." The English have a wonderful sense of euphemisms; 'bought it' sounded so much gentler than having been killed .In any case I would have believed anything he told regarding risk taking.

Tony wasn't crazy. He had just been convinced with the fervor of a religious fanatic that his fate had been decided in advance and nothing would change it. Time of birth, time of death, were all written down in the Golden Book of Life .

"And now I will ask you one more question, my Yank friend. .How old do you think I am.?"

"Coming up to fifty," I lied. He smiled, and said ,"You know better. Why the bloody hell am I telling you this story but that I have planned my trip to take me back to Westward Ho for my 55th birthday where I will join a Lady Shipley, my long term lover. By the way," he added "I have no children."

Our ride back to his hotel was strained as I knew I would never see him again but would carry with me a most improbable story. We shook hands and said our good-byes quickly, leaving out the "See you soon."

The Swiss summer slipped by and I thought occasionally of Tony, particularly as October came and went. Then in November, I received a small package with a note from Lady Shipley. The note stated that Tony had passed away in October and that the Doctors felt his excessive smoking led to his untimely death. She added that before he died, he had requested that she send me the little package.

I opened the velvet cover and there lay the British Distinguished Flying Cross with a little note saying, "In honor of a real hero who fought his fears."

I couldn't fight the tears that came as I realized Tony was trying to help me overcome the shame I felt at being happy to have been shot down, and as the Brits would say, "out of it."

MMM

The Bard

By George Britten

I was about forty when my dark thick hair started to fall out. I had always looked with some pity on those with shining pates, but was now forced to accept my entry into the brotherhood of "balding men." It hurt and depressed me, especially since this seemed only to be the beginning and I didn't know how far my hairline would recede. Would it keep moving back like a retreating tide? Would I become Friar George with a tight little fringe? Or would I become a billiard ball, the butt of jokes? Maybe this was payback time for my insensitivity to the suffering of others.

I tried all the hair products promising to arrest "creeping baldness." Nothing worked as the combs and brushes were covered with the black strands that I cleaned off and dropped down the toilet. I watched with a sense of sadness as they twirled around in the vortex of flushing water and then disappeared forever. .

I decided to grow a moustache. It crept in slowly but after two weeks had reached enough mass to draw comments from my friends. Some thought it attractive but others, while not commenting, probably thought

I looked like Grouch Marx. Most importantly, my wife accepted it, though at first she had said it tickled .

A General Managers' meeting was to take place in the UK the following month and the corporate president, Roster, would fly in from New York to be with us the last day when a boat ride up the Thames had been planned, giving him a chance to informally meet with all the General Managers, to chat, have a few drinks, lunch, and watch the beautiful landscape of old London architecture as we drifted by.

I knew Roster quite well from past assignments and we had always gotten along fairly well. He was a highly intelligent man with a brilliant war record and innovative ideas. He had only one problem. He became nasty when he drank and I heard the problem had gotten worse recently. Little did I know how much.

Everyone was on board when the Rolls Royce pulled up to the boarding plank and Roster got out. He had apparently enjoyed lunch since his cheeks glowed and the flush continued up through his thinning light colored hair. I moved down away from the plank as I had some trepidation about his reaction to my new look. But I knew I couldn't run away from him for the entire boat trip. I also reasoned, better sooner than later when he had poured down a few more gins.

I worked my way up to him. He saw me coming and started to laugh, really more of a sneer and said, "Good god what is that?" as he made a wiping motion with his free hand, (the other held a glass of gin) as if to say I should get rid of it. I muttered something, feeling terribly embarrassed, particularly as other General Managers joined in the laughter. And so it went for the entire trip. Roster had to make a speech and there was no way he wouldn't refer to my moustache. The group had found a theme and my moustache was it. The torture finally ended as we docked and returned to the Park Hotel for the gala dinner.

I dreaded the evening but then I recalled the only Shakespearian soliloquy that I knew. I worked feverishly for a few hours and planned my attack .I took the blade out of the razor of the Wilkinson company, which coincidently, we were negotiating to acquire, put the travel size shaving cream into my pocket and delayed my entry into the dining hall until I knew all were seated .

I took my place at my designated seat and noted that all were present, except Roster. Despite the absence of this demi-god, the English roast beef was served. But still, there was no sign of Roster as we came to the coffee cognac.

Unable to wait any longer, I stood up and took out the small travel size shave cream and lathered my face. A quiet fell over the room. I then held the Wilkinson razor as if ready to shave and began my soliloquy:

APOLOGIES TO THE BARD

To shave or not to shave, that is my predicament
Whether 'tis .nobler in this group to suffer the slings
and arrows of outraged management or take to
blades against this ghastly bush
and by shaving them, stay! To cut. To clip ,
no more, and by shave to say we mend
the heartache of these tickling lip high locks
that I have dared to.: 'Tis an abomination
truly to be dewhiskered; to cut, to clip,
to clip, perchance to cream, ah, there's the rub,
for in that clip of lips what clips may come
when Ihave shuffled off this hirsute boil
must give me pause!
your valued respect, dear sirs,
must be weighed against my own dear wife's
for who would have haired the lip and scorned the line
suffered the leader's tong, the seminar's contumely
but that this lower beard means more than death
the recovered youth of men not shorn
what I have borne! I guzzle this swill[wine]
make I no lather on these poor quills I have?
fly to Helvetia where I shall not be made fun of?
but as consumerism doth make cowards of us all
so thus the native hue of resolution
is tickled by the name of Wilkinson
shall I make this unkind cut?
what say ye, my lords?

Thus did I appease the crowd when I heard the cry: "Let the bush grow!"

Lo, these many years later, Roster has disappeared as has my once dark hair. And my wife still gladly runs the risk of a tickle from my now grey moustache.

MMM

Sucking Up

By George Britten

Mr. Carpenter, corporate vice president and my boss, said on his visit to Vienna, back in 1959, that he and his wife Ruby, would like to hear Tony Karas that evening.

Now before I tell you who Tony Karas was, let me point out that the way up the career ladder is to make vice presidents happy. Sure, sales and profits are important. Fortunately my fledging subsidiary was doing well, but experience had taught me the big shots always wanted to see something special and the local company manager had to serve up the real Paris, London, Vienna, or wherever. I called my secretary and asked that she reserve a table at the Weisser Schwan in Grinsing, where Tony Karas, was the owner and also played. It was a white wine area on the outskirts of Vienna.

Orson Welles' film, *The Third Man*, a huge success, had caught the Vienna of that period perfectly. And Tony Karas, an Austrian, had played the theme music on the Zither, a strange looking instrument of taut steel strings that had to be plucked for its weird sounds. It was played world wide and Tony Karas had made a fortune.

The Russians had just withdrawn their occupying force in the 50's and had left behind a Vienna that was gray, and the pockmarks of the street fighting were evident everywhere on the building walls. Welles had done the film in black and white capturing the shadows as Karas' eerie Zither theme music relentlessly heightened the suspense as drug dealers knifed and shot each other. It had been seen by Mr. Carpenter who was deeply impressed by the Karas Zither musical theme. I suggested the Wiener Schnitzel to the Carpenters as this authentic Austrian specialty with red cabbage and Knoedel would bring them closer to the real Austria. Grinzing was known for its new white wine, served in large glasses that also produced a terrible headache the next morning, so I drank little.

Mr. Carpenter, really entranced as Tony Karas came out later to play his Zither, recklessly drank the white wine. Somehow he would hold me accountable for his headache and that was not good for my climb up the corporate ladder. When Karas played the theme music to *The Third Man*, I thought Carpenter would have a heart attack. Frankly I never thought this old geezer, who was at least fifty, and obsessed with profits and losses, could experience such passion from a piece of music. And to my further astonishment he grabbed my shoulder and yelled, "I want his autograph for my son, Jim." He held up a paper napkin that we had not yet used to wipe away the dinner's grease, and he imperiously ordered, "Get it "

I thought of the fuckin' headache he was going to have in the morning and my only chance of surviving was to get Tony's autograph. I got up, carrying the napkin on which there was a corner for Tony's signature and my future. I went to the head waiter who stood guard at the door where Tony had exited and with a 100 shilling note bought my way into the kitchen.

In my less than perfect German, I asked the large red faced chef if I could see Mr. Karas. And then my heart dropped as I saw Tony downing a large double cognac before he slumped back in his chair and apparently passed out. "He always passes out after his show," I understood the chef to say.

. A few rungs of my corporate ladder had just been pulled out. But then I had an inspiration. I just took the napkin and signed Tony Karas and returned triumphantly to the table saying, "Tony sends you his regards," as I handed Mr. Carpenter his prize napkin for Jim .

The next morning I picked him and Mrs. Carpenter up for the drive to the airport.

His eyes were slightly bloodshot and he was quiet. I suspected he had little hammers in his head. But when we said good-bye, he said, "You did a great job in getting Tony Karas autograph."

I was promoted shortly thereafter to Switzerland and I often wonder what Jim did with that prized autograph.

July Coulter

Judy Coulter was born in Manhattan, and raised in the Bronx by her Jewish father and Irish Catholic mother.

A graduate of City College, she became an elementary school teacher.

Judy wrote a column for a magazine in Westchester County, and her articles have appeared in the New York Times, Reader's Digest. Scarsdale Inquirer, and the Gannet chain of newspapers.

She is co-owner, (with her daughter, Janie,) and President of J & J Ross Co, the music publishing company that was established in 1954, to handle the legacy of her late husband, Jerry Ross.

Judy is an avid reader and theatre-goer, and can't resist a museum or a good travel destination. Married and widowed for a second time, Judy has two daughters, a son, a grandson and two adopted granddaughters.

She lives in Harrison, New York, but is an occasional snowbird in Boca Raton.

MMM

The Invitation

By Judith Coulter

It was in late May of 1956 that the invitation for the Antoinette Perry Awards ceremony, commonly known in Broadway circles as the "Tony Awards," arrived at my home. In a bold black type that seemed to leap from the paper, it was addressed to Mrs. Jerry Ross. With little conscious awareness, my fingers caressed the name of my husband as though I could, by some magical touch, bring him back to my side. I was still in the depths of the overwhelming grief that had come with his death at the age of 29.

It was just six months after his second hit show, *Damn Yankee* had opened on Broadway. His first show was *Pajama Game,* the year before, which had won the Tony in all the most important categories. He was the toast of Broadway. After the early years when I'd watched him pick out tunes on the piano and try to further his career with little success, suddenly he had made it to the top. Our lives changed overnight, it seemed. It was somewhat like his first hit song, *Rags To Riches,* which Tony Bennett had recorded and which had topped the charts at number one. Now he had songs like *Ya Gotta Have Heart, Hey There, Whatever Lola Wants, Lola Gets, Hernando's Hideaway*, jumping back and forth between the #1 and #2 spots on the Hit Parade, the ultimate index of the best in popular music at the time. In a less than scientific survey that his retired, very proud father had done by turning the dials of his radio throughout the course of a week, we'd estimated that a Jerry Ross song was being played every four and a half minutes. He was being compared with Rodgers and Hammerstein, George Gershwin, Irving Berlin – the finest.

With his untimely death from bronchitis, a lung condition, the world had lost a great talent but I had lost my world. So I looked at this invitation at first as another grim reminder of my losses. It was only with the prodding and pushing of my family, my friends, and the people connected with the show that I'd decided to go at all.

My mother took me shopping. We bought a lovely beige evening gown, and my father drove me to the affair. The producers -- Hal Prince, Bobby Griffith and Fred Brisson -- arranged that I would sit at their table.

As I sat picking at my dinner amongst all these men busily discussing their new projects, I felt uncomfortably out of place. My shyness, mixed with my grief, and my fears that I would never be able to cope with a new life, a life without the beloved husband who centered my world, left me a less-than-desirable dinner companion. But every so often one of my dinner partners would make an attempt to converse with me.

"It should comfort you, Judy," Bobby Griffith said "to know how much Jerry gave to the world in his few short years." Nothing comforts me, I thought, but I smiled at the man politely.

"I did so love your husband," Bob Fosse, the choreographer, said. It was a knife tearing my heart, that statement. I did so love him, as well, I thought, but again smiled politely. But soon all of these men were preoccupied with their acceptance speeches, for Damn Yankees was a shoe-in to capture some of the Tony Awards that night. Each of these men -- producers, choreographer, director, and Jerry's co-writer -- all hoped to be one of the lucky winners. Many had crib notes jammed into the pockets of their tuxedoes, for they all wanted to be ready with polished speeches. As coffee was served, the ceremony began. The early announcements of various lesser categories and their winners took place. These lucky ones made long speeches, thanking all those they felt had been instrumental in their success.

And then, suddenly, the issue of time became a factor. The affair was being televised for the first time, and since this was early live television, the process hadn't yet been well refined. They realized too late that they didn't have enough time to let each single recipient address the audience. Fortunately Damn Yankees had won all the main awards so they decided to have one recipient accept the awards for everyone, thus cutting the segment to the time slot they had left. But whom could they choose? No one knew, as the whole group rose from the table to go up to the podium when Damn Yankees was announced as the winner in so many categories. As they were about to walk up to the stage, it was Bobby Griffith who grabbed my hand, saying, "Judy, come on up. You must join us, too."

Hesitantly, I went with him. We listened as Helen Hayes addressed the audience and us. I barely heard her acclamations when suddenly I recognized my own name. I was to make the acceptance speech for all of them. I was both stunned and unprepared. Someone gently pushed me into the spotlight. I walked to the microphone. Then, in an almost trance-like state but with drums thundering in my ears, I found myself speaking. Simply, I was told later, but with an eloquent sincerity, I had found the presence to thank the awards committee on behalf of all those men standing there for each category we had won, and to finish with this statement at the end: "I know that my husband, Jerry Ross, would want me to thank you on his behalf, as well, and so I must thank you once more."

I left the podium with the audience's tremendous applause resounding in my ears. From that accidental but fateful moment, my life changed. I was a person again, renewed with a new knowledge of myself and my capabilities. I would face the life that was challenging me. I would make it a worthwhile endeavor. Somehow I understood that that was what my husband would want me to do.

Attitudes

By Judy Coulter

It must have been sometime in the very early 70s, I thought, sitting across the table from Elsie, the seventy-four year old black Barbadian women who cleans my house and Jim, my seventy-five year old white Irish "handyman" who for years had been "in charge" of my household.

We were enjoying Jim's pancakes, which, he assures us each week, are the best in the entire world. At that statement, Elsie rolls her tired, red-rimmed eyes to the ceiling and murmurs "Self-praise, ugh!" and they both laugh heartily.

I join in, scarcely having to listen, since I have heard their repartee so often. My mind has taken another turn, to the time when I first introduced them to each other.

Wary, very wary is the only word that comes to mind as I review that long ago scene. Elsie had stood there mumbling an unintelligible greeting, her eyelids down covering half of her eyes, her face black. She would have appeared withdrawn except for the stiff way she was standing there. It was the stance of a woman with a large chip on her shoulder, ready for trouble at all times, a woman used to fighting with life, one who'd learned not to trust whitey.

Jim, on the other hand, was outgoing, appearing almost friendly, and confident as he assured this new "girl" that he would be of great help to her, guiding and explaining the job to her, since he knew exactly how it needed to be done in this house that he knew so well.

I wondered then how conscious he was that he was sending her the message that he was the man in charge here and if he knew how condescending he sounded. I had no doubt at all that Elsie was perfectly aware of the distinction between their relationships, although she would not have been able to verbalize it.

And so, right from the beginning, it was a stand off. Jim tried to form Elsie into his image of what he perceived to be a good servant, one who not only did what she was ordered to do willingly and well according to his directions, but one who indeed understood and was grateful to work for a great boss, who allowed her to sit at the same table with him, to eat the same foods in the kitchen, and did not send her to the bathroom down in the basement. Elsie basically stayed away from Jim as much as possible, sticking to the upstairs bedrooms and the laundry room. She also muttered a lot.

With a big house and small children, I needed both of them. I soon found my role in the triangle. I was the diplomat, the one who soothed the rough spots they regularly encountered and encouraged some sort of harmony. And perhaps because they both wanted and needed the job, or perhaps because they slowly came to understand each other's ideas and cultures through me, but also by themselves, a truce was formed.

With the peace and neutrality of their coming to terms with each other, there was a greater opening for a bond to develop between them, as well as a real concern for the welfare of each other. Often I would hear them conversing about their personal lives and I noted how they began to cooperate more fully in their household tasks. As the years rolled on, the relationship grew.

Last August, when Jim married for the first time, both Elsie and I were invited to his wedding. At the reception, Elsie walked to the podium where Jim sat with his bride, and demanded her first dance with the groom. I watched them across the dance floor, she floating with a Ginger Rogers confidence, and he barely able to move his feet at first. As the music continued, I realized how subtly she was leading him in this dance, and how willingly he was following. And noting the smiling faces of approval as I surveyed a room full of his all-white guests, I glowed with personal pride thinking back to the day they first met.

MMM

The Power of Touch

By Judith Coulter

"Touch Me," the poet says. Immediately I feel the tears spring to my eyes. A sudden sharp jab stabs at my breast. But why should these words cause such a reaction? I ponder this.

I know how important touching is! This simple act has vast meaning to all of us throughout our lives. It can determine a relationship. One has only to think of a mother and her child. A mother has an instinctive need to "touch" her child; probably a father as well. Let's not leave out lovers where touching is always a main ingredient. Husbands touch wives, grandparents reach out to hold their adored grandchildren, children grasp hands to feel their companion's warmth. In happiness, we touch; in sadness as well. In abject misery, we *need* touch. Studies have shown that babies in orphanages where they do not receive enough human touching often become ill, some die, others grow up warped in various ways

Those of us who have experienced sufficient love through our lifetimes are most fortunate. I am one of them. So why does the sudden sad tear appear, the words jab at my breast? Should not I, who have been touched, caressed, hugged. kissed and more, by mother, father, brother, husbands, lovers, sons, daughters and friends, be satiated with all the years of this blessing? But no, to be human is to want more.

So, like the poet, I yearn to have again those "touchings" that I remember, and hopefully, for the ones that are yet to come.

$$\text{MMM}$$

The Tree Limb

By Judith Coulter

The limb was large, stark and almost black, with a threatening witch-like quality. It branched out across my second floor bedroom window, effectively cutting in half my view outside. Having watched it for more than thirty years, I normally no longer saw it. But the winter wind blew it against the house in repeated knocking thumps that morning and caused me to look up at it. Quite unexpectedly it occurred to me that both the tree and I were no longer young. More truthfully we were in our "winter" years.

Indeed looking at the branch, then down to the mirror in front of me, I saw that there was no denying the fact. My pale, un-made up face showed its years and its traumas to me plainly. A shiver passed through me, chilling me. How much longer till I would look stark and somewhat witch-like? True, the tree was a good deal older than I, but trees are given many more years than humans. So perhaps we were not too far apart, this tree and I.

I looked again at the barren limb, knocking for attention with a steady drum beat and swaying with the wind against the grey sky. I felt a dismal pall settling on my cold body. I suppose I sat there for several undetermined minutes until the faint stirrings of noise in the house broke my brooding. The mirror in front of me reflected some new light which I soon realized was actually coming from the window where the sky was brightening. A large white multi-shaped cloud showed itself through the top of the window frame. It had a puffed up look about it that reminded me of a Pillsbury biscuit and it seemed to be sailing right down to me like a spirited balloon. I felt that any second it would come right into the window and plop down on my lap. I started to laugh at my wild imagination, catching myself in the mirror. The face I saw looked so much younger than the one I'd seen just before.

I thought for a minute. Ah, yes, laughter. How often it had gotten me over the rough spots through the years. And indeed, imagination is the simplest form of creativity! I waved a thank-you up to the cloud for reminding me.

Quickly I began to put on my make-up. It was time to start the new day and suddenly I just couldn't wait. There was so much to see and to do, so much to laugh about.

Luciana Duce

Luciana is a Fine Artist, Spiritual Director and Retreat Facilitator. She studied painting at New York's Art Institute and Parson's School of Design and received her Master of Arts Degree in Art, Psychology and the Humanities from The New School for Social Research in New York City.

She was awarded an internship at the Metropolitan Museum of Art in New York where she completed an extensive study on the work of the modern masters with an emphasis on the role of women in the life and art of Vincent Van Gogh.

Currently, Luciana facilitates international retreats for small groups in Versailles, France or Tuscany Italy on Praying with Art.. She also teaches six-week non-traditional art workshops, "Opening to the Artist Within"

. As a writer, Luciana is working on a series of memory "snapshots" of her family and experiences as a first generation Italian-American growing up in New York City.

First Kiss

By Luciana Duce

We were holding on to the overhead subway straps as the train crept away from the IRT Bleeker Street Station. Our 8th grade cheeks glowed a deep windswept red from the fierce winter chill and although we stood like ants on a breadcrumb we were happy to be in the warm, steamy subway.

Vinny stood with his face looking into mine, our bodies pressed close. With each jolt of the train I could feel my pink nipples tingle. I was wearing my older sister's bra, my promising Italian breasts barely filling the cups. Vinny's faded jeans were bulging at the crotch as his body rocked back and forth with the rhythm of the subway wheels.

I nuzzled my face into his blue suede jacket and sniffed the musky fragrance I later came to think of as the smell of a man. The more I sniffed the more excited I became.

With each station stop, people were struggling to get off as new faces grumbled their way in.

Secretly I hoped the subway car would stay crowded. Vinny's lean body pressing against mine thrilled my inner thighs now damp with the moistness of my youth.

Suddenly the train jolted. Stop. Go. Stop. Vinny was still hanging on to the strap and I practically fell on top of him, our noses skin to skin. He grabbed me around the waist to steady me. Like fresh coconuts, my breasts swelled against his meager ribs, my heart racing.

Vinny's lips stretched into a wide grin. His front teeth slightly overlapped and I could barely hear his words as I watched the pink of his tongue move from side to side. "I wanna kiss you," he mumbled.

"Oh my God," I thought. "If he kisses me now with all these people watching, I'll just die."

Just as the train began moving again, another jolt came. The lights flickered on and off.

Total darkness seemed to wrap itself around our excited bodies. With a quick thrust Vinny pulled me close, pressing his stiffness against my throbbing pubic bone. Strange feelings like electric sparks shot through me. I raised up on my toes, leaned my body into his and flung my arms around his waist. The smell of musk filled my nostrils and a light-headed sensation overtook me. Before I even knew I was talking, words came spitting out of my mouth.

"Kiss me, Vinny," I whispered. "Kiss me now." I shut my eyes as tight as a sealed envelope. I don't remember how long I waited before I felt Vinny's lips warm and soft brushing against mine. I held my breath. Like two mating goldfish, we puckered our lips into each other.

The subway wheels screeched to a dead stop. Our lips unlocked. When I opened my eyes, I could see the pimples on Vinny's cheeks, glowing red under the bright lights.

He tugged hard on my woolen coat sleeve and raced for the subway door. "It's our stop," he shouted, "C'mon, let's go." We ran up the subway steps. Winter's icy chill slapped against our warm cheeks. "See ya later," he said, as I watched his blue suede jacket disappear around the corner, the smell of musk trailing behind him.

Straight Up

By Luciana Duce

She was lying on the classroom floor, eyes closed, her hair black as the feathers on a raven, spilled in wild circles of curls.

"Get up, Carol!" Sr. Margaret shouted, hands on her hips, tapping her perfectly polished laced up brown shoes next to Carol's lifeless body.

"She can't hear you, Sister," I said. "She passed out."

Sr. Margaret turned her face to the rest of the class. "She's an actress, that Carol," she said. "Everything is always such a drama for her." She rapped her knuckles on the old oak desk, her gold crucifix ring softening the blows to her skin. Her eyes darted like popping corn across the room as she took a long, deep breath. When she exhaled, the words came spitting from between her short stubby teeth.

"This is the last time I'm going to tell you to get up missy. Now if you're not back in your seat in five minutes, I'll just have to call Sr. Barbara Immaculata, our very busy principal. She has better things to do than waste her time on foolish pranks."

I rushed over to the doorway and looked down the hall. Sr. Margaret grabbed me by my white cotton uniform sleeve, dragging me back into the room.

"And where do you think you're going, Miss Busybody?" She sneered, her cheeks now flushed the color of grape soda.

"But...but...Sr. Margaret," I stammered. "Carol's fainted...she wasn't feeling good after lunch...she said her stomach was hurting her."

Sr. Margaret stiffened. "Now how many times have we heard that story, my dear? She'll have to learn her lesson once and for all. I won't put up with that nonsense one more minute."

All eyes were glaring down at the floor where Carol's frail body lay straight, her breathing barely visible under her white blouse, loosely tucked into her navy blue pleated skirt.

As Sr. Margaret marched out of the room, I dropped down to my knees beside my best friend.

"Oh my gosh, Carol," I whispered, stroking her black silky curls. "If you're faking I'll kill you. C'mon, get up...she's gonna get Immaculata in here...this time they'll throw you out of school."

Suddenly Carol's body twitched. She looked straight at me and as if to let me in on a sacred secret, she winked, then slowly her eyes closed. Carol was always good at fooling me. I never was quite sure when she was playing and when she was being "straight up," which was Carol's favorite way of saying she was telling the truth.

I grabbed her by the arm to drag her to her feet but when my hand touched her, the coolness of her skin startled me.

My legs began to tremble as I remembered last year when Carol fainted in the candy store. "Nothin' to it," she explained after sniffing the smelling salts the owner put under her nose.

"Maybe that's what she needs," I thought, "smelling salts," trying to convince myself that nothing was seriously wrong with Carol and any minute she'd bounce to her feet and be sitting straight-backed in her seat before Sr. Immaculata showed up, carrying her authority over her shoulders like a long black cape.

Just as I was about to take off to find the school nurse, Sr. Margaret appeared in the doorway. She held on to the door knob making circling gestures with her right hand to someone in the hall. In seconds, Sr.Immaculata arrived, her lean body gliding like an ice-skater.. Next to Sr. Margaret they appeared as two mature trees digging their roots beneath the earth.

"So what have we here?" Sr. Immaculata asked, her deep-set eyes peering out of an olive-skinned face.

Once more I started to explain, but Sr. Margaret shoved me to the side of the room. "Get in your seat," she shouted, prodding me towards my empty desk.

The class was as quiet as a falling snowflake when Sr. Immaculata bent down and placed her hand beneath Carol's head, gently trying to lift her. Carol's frail body went limp in Sr. Immaculata's arms and she gestured firmly to Sr. Margaret to come quickly.

Without taking a breath, Sr. Margaret raced down the hall. Then standing erect, Sr. Immaculata faced the class. "You are to go straight to the auditorium -- immediately. I do not want to hear any sound other than the soles of your shoes hitting the floor. Take a seat when you get there and remain seated until Sr. Margaret arrives."

As we began leaving the room, I stopped by Carol's body. "She's my best friend, Sister," I said, the fresh tears hot on my cheeks."Can I stay with her...please," I pleaded.

Sr. Immaculata placed her arm around my shoulder. "We'll take good care of your friend," she said kindly. "Now you go with the rest of your class to the auditorium." she motioned, "and say a few prayers for her family."

With each step, I turned my head to see if Carol was moving. "Pray for her family?" I thought, wondering why she was asking me to pray for Carol's family. I said a few Hail Mary's and an Our Father but my thoughts kept drifting back to my best friend, lying helpless on the floor.

Sitting in the auditorium was the last place I wanted to be. It was noisy and crowded and the moments seemed to crawl like a night thief.

Suddenly the sound of screeching sirens pierced our thick teenage conversations. While the sirens were a familiar sound to city kids, on that day the shrill seemed headed straight for our school. "It's the police," someone shouted, looking out the small basement window.

"Oh, my God," I thought. "They've come for Carol. Sr. Immaculata must have called the police to have her arrested."

I ran to the window, pressing my chest against the glass. The entrance to the building was on the other side of the auditorium so I couldn't see anything but my heart was beating so fast I felt it could have shattered the glass. I stood by the window for a long time wearing my loyalty like a security guard at the White House.

"What's gonna happen to Carol?" one of my classmates asked. I shook my head and remained silent until I saw Sr. Margaret's robust arms motioning the class to stand up. I waved my hand like a flag in a windstorm, eager to find out about Carol.

"Everyone rise!" commanded Sr. Margaret."You are released early today. Now quietly, and I mean without so much as hearing a hair from your head fall to the ground, you are to make a single line and proceed outside. You are to go straight home. And since this is Friday, make your weekend productive."

Sr. Margaret ushered us outside and when I tried to approach her she pressed her hand on my back and whispered sternly, "Go straight home."

I didn't want to tell anyone what happened in school just in case too many questions might make things worse for Carol. Later that evening I called Carol's house but no one answered. I kept calling until midnight and by now I knew the timing of the answering machine so I hung up right before the click. Five messages were enough, I thought.

During the night I slept like a bear protecting her cubs. Just as I was closing my eyes again, the phone rang.

"Hey, girlfriend," a raspy voice filled my ears."It's me, Carol."

"Oh my gosh, Carol," the tears rolling down my startled face. Where are you? You ok? What happened?"

"Listen," she whispered. "I'm gonna give it to you straight up." A long pause and a deep breath later, she continued.

"I'm pregnant, girlfriend. I really did pass out in class. They took me to the hospital. I won't be coming back to school, you know."

As I listened closely, a foggy feeling began to wash over me. Carol's voice faded into the night's stillness.

A few weeks later, Carol's family moved away. Our daily phone calls became once a week, then once or twice a month until we were no longer in touch.

Every now and then I wonder about Carol, where she might be living and how her journey unfolded. Sometimes, I can even hear her raspy voice saying: "Hey girlfriend, I've got something to tell you...straight up."

MMM

Night Blooming Jasmine

By Luciana Duce

The exotic fragrance of night blooming jasmine thickened the midnight air as Ray and I walked across the gravel path to his studio. "Let me show you my latest efforts," he said, pressing a small fragrant bunch of jasmine flowers into my hand as we entered the converted garage. Dozens of canvases, some as big as 8 feet high, were stacked up against the cracked walls. Gallons of paint, with their labels dripping with red and yellow, orange and blue, sat on the old concrete floor now covered with thick streaks of paint.

"Watch your step," he said guiding me around the paint cans like a soldier in a field alive with mines.

"Over there," he said, pointing to a canvas that stood as high as the ceiling. "There it is." The canvas was turned with its back facing the wall so all I could see were the pieces of wood holding the frame together.

Ray began to pace in front of the painting. Up and down, back and forth, a big cat studying his next victim.

I stared, calmly at first, then after several minutes I motioned to Ray. "Turn it around, Ray. Aren't you going to let me see the painting?"

His fingers gripped the sides of the canvas and he lifted it high in the air. He began walking towards me and just as I thought he was about to turn the canvas around, he raced to the door.

"Where are you taking the painting, Ray?" I asked, but he continued walking until he was standing outside in the midnight darkness.

I took a few quick steps, following behind him. With each deliberate footstep, his breathing grew heavier. As he carried the canvas high in the air I tried to get ahead of him to get a glimpse of the painting. "Don't look" he whispered..."please don't look now."

When we reached the lake, the light of the moon seemed to throw a spotlight around the water's edge. Ray kicked off his sandals and as he walked into the lake, he gently laid the painting along side him.

My mouth opened wide as I tried to speak ."Ray, what...what are you doing?" I stammered.

With both hands, he pushed the painting out into the lake, then turned and began walking towards me. When he reached my side we stood silent beneath the moon, watching the square shape as it slowly began to sink.

"There," he whispered. "There it goes...watch it ...keep your eyes on the top of water and you'll see the image."

"Oh, my," I thought, "this time poor Ray's really gone over the edge."

"Look...look," he nudged, pointing to the middle of the lake.

I gazed into the still water. "Oh my God," I gasped, cupping my mouth with my hands. I could smell the fragrance of the night blooming jasmine that lingered in my palms as I watched pools of red, orange, yellow, purple, green and blue mix into a thousand magical shapes rolling across the water's surface.

"So, my sweet thing," Ray said, leaning his body into mine. "Now what do you think of my latest effort?"

"Oh, Ray," I said, my head twirling from the mysterious display of colors and forms dancing under the moonlight. "It's just the most beautiful painting... never ever have I seen a painting on water before."

Ray smiled and pulled me closer. "It will never sell, you know," he said. "All that paint dissolving into the water, nothing but a wet dirty canvas left behind."

"Who cares, Ray?" I answered. "And, besides, your paintings aren't made to be hung up on walls."

Ray didn't say another word as he walked me home, our hands gently touching.

All night the swirling colors drifted in and out of my sleep. The next morning I awoke to the coolness of an unexpected rain and the fading scent of night blooming jasmine.

Dorothy Dworkin

Dorothy Dworkin: I was born in the Bronx and grew up in Brooklyn but lived most of my adult life on Long Island. Now I divide my time between Boynton Beach and Portland. Oregon.

I have been writing since childhood with some success after winning a writing contest in elementary school. I've had free lance articles and essays published in the New York Times, New York Newsday, The Oregonian, various travel magazines and professional journals. I teach creative memoir writing at Palm Beach Community College and at several adult education venues in the Portland area.

MMM

Snowbirds

By Dorothy Dworkin

Like many other south Floridians, my husband and I are "birds" and like our fellow flying friends, we head south when winter winds begin to blow. Similarly, when summer heat and humidity set in, once again we take flight. But, unlike most other "birds" who fly in a northeasterly pattern, we wing it to the northwest; Portland, Oregon.

"You have the best of both worlds," our friends tell us and perhaps they are right. However, this bi-coastal life style can sometimes be disorienting. For example, shortly after we arrived at our Portland apartment from Boynton Beach, we went marketing. My grandson, who is one of our main reasons for being in Oregon, loves my chicken soup and what is chicken soup without matzo balls? I ran into some confusion when I attempted to buy matzo meal in the big Fred Meyer supermarket in town.

"Can you please tell me where to find matzo meal for matzo balls?" I asked an attendant working in the aisle. She seemed confused so I attempted to clarify my request.

"I want to make matzo balls for soup," I explained motioning their shape with my hands. She still looked puzzled but grinning gamely, she said, "Follow me and I'll show you where they keep the matzo balls."

I wasn't surprised to be getting personal service. Clerks and service people are very courteous. Often, when a customer asks for something the employee will lead them to the item. I followed the clerk but was bewildered when she led me out of the grocery department into the closet shop.

"There they are," she said pointing to an upper shelf. "There are the matzo balls you want."

I looked up and laughed. Apparently, she assumed I wanted moth balls since matzo balls were not within her realm of experience. Then, I knew I was no longer in Florida!

The dining experience also differs from coast to coast. In Boca Raton and environs, it is not unusual to itemize a laundry list of special requests when ordering dinner.

"I'll have water with lemon, fish broiled dry, salad with dressing on the side, vegetables instead of rice, hot water for my own tea bag and may I have some bread now?"

In Portland, where there is no shortage of wonderful restaurants, patrons wait patiently for service and rarely deviate from the entrees as they appear on the menu. Early bird dinners do not exist and sandwiches always include some form of cheese, often Tillamook, the local specialty.

If a south Floridian leaves a restaurant without a styrofoam box containing leftovers from the meal, fellow diners are concerned.

"You finished the whole thing?" they mock. "So much food!"

In Portland I've yet to see a doggie bag unless it's for Fido. Most portion sizes are normal and leftovers are scarce. I must confess, however, that the bagels are better in the east. It must be the water although Portland has plenty of that in the fall and winter. Residents are called webfoots and I know why.

Summers are dry in Oregon, sunny and pleasant, although sometimes the temperature breaks ninety degrees in July and August. But, even if it does, it doesn't last long and evenings are cool. There is virtually no humidity. The upside of the wet winters are the snow covered mountains which are always visible even in the city. Majestic fir trees line the highways and fill the forests, many of which are located within city limits.

There are no senior citizens in Portland. They are called "honored citizens" and receive discounts on the myriad forms of public transportation as well as in theaters, golf courses and public events. My Florida home is also geezer paradise and here, too, we are "honored."

Portlanders are avid gardeners and every street, curbs included, are filled with flowers and plants. Lawns are rarely manicured and sod is unusual. Most home gardens are lush with color and texture. The city is aptly named the Rose City and in June, the rose test gardens in Washington Park are resplendent with hybrid roses of every description. A Rose Queen is crowned in June to lead the annual Rose Parade. People reserve their space on the sidewalk the night before the parade and mark their territory with chalk and lawn chairs. It is rare for anyone to usurp the informal reservation system or remove one of the chairs.

Whereas most south Floridians have their java decaffeinated, webfoots like it strong and dark but draw the line at being caffeine purists. They are not loathe to order every kind of latte and cappuccino in the numerous coffee shops that line the streets. Walking in Portland without a steaming paper cup from Peets or Boyd's identifies you as an-out-of-towner, as does using an umbrella. "It's only misting," they say as they pull up their hooded sweatshirts.

The dress code, as you may guess, is very casual. No pastel polyester pants suits in Portland. Sneakers, jeans, tee shirts, warm-up suits and sandals are worn everywhere including the theater and work place. Most of the younger people also have a different look from Boynton Beach youth. Instead of bronzed, sun kissed skin, many are covered with tattoos and sport pierces in the most unlikely places. They are, however, polite and respectful and defer to older pedestrians on the streets. Pioneer Square, downtown, is their favorite venue. It is referred to as Portland's living room.

Exercise is a religion in both cities but Portlanders are never deterred by wet weather. They bike, jog, walk, camp, fish and hike every day of the year starting in the early morning and continuing into the night. Nike is king and their downtown flagship store is a tourist attraction with its museum quality sports memorabilia.

When in Florida, I'm never asked about my regional origins. Easterners recognize "umbreller, pizzer, wahda." In the west, I'm immediately identifies as a "Nu Yawker."

After nine-eleven, waitpersons and service people offered me sympathy as soon as I started to speak. When I questioned how they knew where I was from, they just laughed.

"It's the accent," they said. "What accent???"

Gated communities are fairly rare in Oregon although they are gaining in popularity as older Californians move north for economic and life style reasons. I have yet to spot a guarded enclave with a place name reminiscent of a foreign region: Valencia, Bellagio, Kings Point, Ponte Vecchio. Because of its proximity to the Far East, it is more likely that the new retirement villages in Oregon will have Asian sounding names: Shanghai Gardens, Mount Fiji Manor, Hanoi Haven.

Beer is the beverage of choice in the Rose City and mini-breweries flourish. The suds have unique flavors and tastes and most folks can tell what brewery bottled their pint. In south Florida, folks are more likely to sip wine (with a little ice on the side, please). An occasional Marguerita is reserved for Mexican food.

Literary events are a daily occurrence in Portland and every other resident is an aspiring or published writer. Powell's, the largest privately owned book store in the country, hosts visiting writers and large crowds turn out to hear their favorite authors. The stacks in Powell's are reminiscent of a bygone era with tall, wooden cases and old fashioned wooden floors. Readers can spend the day in the snack area and not be disturbed by employees until closing time.

When the Ducks (football team) or Blazers (basketball) are playing Rip City fans are rabid in their support. And, if the team is on a winning streak, mania takes over the city. Special events at the Rose Quarter Coliseum draw enthusiastic audiences and most touring artists make the Coliseum one of their stops.

The anniversary of the Lewis and Clarke exploration of the American West with its emphasis on the Oregon Trail, culminated in commemorative celebrations throughout the state. The local Historical Society located on the Park Blocks still has numerous exhibits and programs. The Society is located opposite the Portland Art Museum, the oldest in the northwest. Farther down the street is Portland State University with its ever expanding urban campus.

Cultural stimulation exist in both Portland and south Florida where galleries and concert halls abound in either place. On the first and last Thursdays of each month, Portlanders turn out in droves to view the latest work from established and emerging artists. On weekends, crafts persons sell their wares under the Burnside Bridge at the "Saturday Market." Summertime concerts in the park are city sponsored and picnicking .begins hours before the performances.

Sometimes I feel as if I have a split personality leading this double life. From time to time, I become confused as I make the transition from one place to the other and I begin to feel rootless. On the other hand, I'm never bored by either environment as they are ever changing and different. I meet new people in both places and on the west coast they come with backgrounds and experiences very different from my own. In the years that I've been commuting, I've learned some important lessons. I have the power to create my own reality and I am always open to changes.

When I take wing and fly west it is with enthusiasm and the expectation that new challenges await me as they do when I return east. I have begun to look forward to this double life with excitement.

Harry E. Fear

Harry Fear was born in 1929 in Johnstown, New York, He served as an infantryman with the 34th division in Africa and Italy in World War 2, and is a graduate of University of Notre Dame and the University of the State of New York at Albany.

He was in the hotel industry as a management trainee, director of sales, general manager, vice president of operations – with Hilton, Sheraton, Ramada and then operated an executive search firm specializing in the Hospitality Industry for ten years. He's lived in many cities in the United State, and in South America, Puerto Rico, Bon Aire and Aruba. His company built the first American hotel in Aruba and Surinam, S.A.

For the past twelve years, he's been working as a stipend paid volunteer Director of Stewardship and Development at St. Jude Catholic Church and School in Boca Raton.

He's lived in Florida for 26 years, when he came originally to open his executive search firm. He has four children (one deceased) and 5 grandchildren, and is writing his autobiography at the request of his children.

***

Weathering Heights and Family Connections

By Harry Fear

Each winter of my youth, I could count on the old timers to bring up the "big storm", the Blizzard of '88 (that's 1888). Some of the tales left kids like me speechless. According to their story, spring-like temperatures were in the air. but on that March Sunday around midnight, they said, all hell broke loose. Winds up to 80 miles an hour had covered Johnstown and the surrounding area with snow that piled into 20-foot snowdrifts. The mercury plunged to 12 degrees below zero. Three days later, the storm let up. In those three days 21 inches of snow fell.

That's the way their memory recalled the "Blizzard of 88". My old school chum, Jim Taub, reminded me of a storm in 1943 that would make those old timers forget about '88 He thought it was about February 17, 1943, often referred to as the coldest day in the history of Fulton County where Johnstown was the county seat. The recorded temperature was 44 degrees below zero. Jim and I were high school juniors. Upon arriving at school that morning we were told to go home because the ancient boilers in JHS could only get the heat up to 35 degrees. Jim and Red

McGuire hitchhiked to Gloversville and went to the movies at the Hip (Hippodrome) where a banner flying outside stated that the theater was "air conditioned." The temp at noon that day was minus 24 degrees. I even remember that the movie was "Commandos Strike at Dawn," starring Paul Muni..

Jim observed that the odd thing about that cold snap was that it was quickly followed by an exceedingly warm two weeks of February in which the thermometer soared as high as the mid 60's.

In 1947 the December storm saw 26.8 inches of snowfall in the county in 15 hours. And yet, that Blizzard of '88 has grown into fantastic proportions.

It was during the storm of '47 that I was to face up to the fact that all men are not created equal, at least not in the eyes of some of the city's south end "Brahmins." For their entire wealth, the rich people living in the south end of the city could not prevent a power outage that forced them to make concessions in their daily lives. Many moved into the hotel where I was working as a desk clerk. Beverly was a particular friend of mine, a year behind me in school. Her family moved into the hotel where her father was president. He was also a leading national leather goods manufacturer in the city.

Someone organized a sleigh ride and I asked Bev to be my date on that occasion which she accepted. When her father learned that she was going out with me, he made her cancel and she begrudgingly gave me the reason. It embarrassed her, but she told me, "You're not one of us".

I never forgot that and I never forgot Bev, We remained friends, and I saw her often until the day she died. Ironically, her sister and brother in-law turned out to be some of our closest friends and are til this day. As for her father, it took me maybe 20 years, but I did become "one of them."

Managing the after effects of a large snowfall was a problem. First of all, snow removal equipment was limited to two plows for the entire city.

It would take days and even weeks to remove snow from all parts of the city. There were no snow blowers as they have today.

Manpower with shovels, and plows with wooden blades pulled by horses, acted as a snowplow for many areas. Ice storms meant that many people would strap an item called creepers to their shoes, and that would help prevent falling on icy sidewalks and roads. Ashes from coal burning stoves in the home would be scattered on icy sidewalks to help prevent falling.

Kids of all ages loved to collect icicles; some as long as 6 foot that formed on homes, barn and garages. Snowball fights of course were the order of the day after a snowfall, as was a game, played in the snow, (preferably on someone's snow filled yard,) called The Fox and the Goose. Sleighs, homemade toboggans and garbage can covers that served as sleds and were put to good use during the winter months. Sometimes cardboard boxes were broken down and they were used to slide down snowy hill slopes.

Skating too was popular on Scrivers Pond. We had the type of skate you slipped your shoe into and then tightened with a key. No fancy shoe skates like today and there were no ski boots, or skis with harnesses, just a strap. Some even made their own skis out of barrel staves. No Olympic prospects were ever found in Johnstown but like most of Upstate New York, it was a winter wonderland, the kind that probably doesn't exit anymore.

I have been thinking as I write these pages, that I have gotten to know myself better, just by the stories I have been telling. These stories have illustrated life, describing how things were, way back when. Some stories I tell may be hard to believe, but they do embody my memories, beliefs and emotions. I write about family, friends and the nature of life when I was a youngster. Stories, I have found, can affect us for better or worse. They can bring a family closer together.

I remember that during the 1946 newspaper strike in New York, Mayor Fiorello LaGuardia read the news over the radio, and made a point to read the comic strips aloud for the children.

The Mayor understood the power of uplifting stories, even of the simplest kind, for keeping people connected and that's what I am attempting to do with my story telling. Keeping the family connected.

What's in a Name

By Harry Fear

What's in a name? To paraphrase Gertrude Stein "A rose is a rose is a rose etc." And so I say, "A street is a street and by any other name would smell as - Well, would smell."

In my early childhood, I lived in a small town in Upstate New York on Pleasant Avenue. Was this someone's idea of a joke? Pleasant? The street was originally called Mill Street and it should have remained so, for it was the home of 2 coal yards, 4 leather tanning mills, a blanket mill, a knitting mill, a wood yard and a trucking business. In addition, at various cross streets along the way there was a chemical storage plant and a nearby railroad for freight trains to keep us alert with it's whistle and smoke. The mills, the train and even the power station had their own special fragrance that they freely shared with the folks on Pleasant Avenue. Whatever "fragrances" were not emitted onto that street come out as raw waste dumped into the Cayadutta Creek, which of course morphed into its own fragrance,-one that would have been of no interest to Estee Lauder.

Pleasant Avenue, nee Mill Street was unpaved, but every other year or so the town's city council would authorize a covering of tar over the dirt road bed, to make things even more "pleasant", I suppose. I don't recall anyone complaining about his or her neighborhood. They were "pleasant" people, happy to live on Pleasant Avenue. The kids played as kids might play anywhere, with one exception. There was no playground in the area. Actually, we didn't really need one, with so many fun things to do in a coal yard or a knitting mill, not to mention the fun we had dodging the trains that choo choo-ed their way across Mill Street, or rather Pleasant Avenue.

Winter was the really "pleasant" time of the year. Mill Street, I should say, Pleasant Avenue was always one of the last streets to be plowed, but kids didn't care even if their parents did. The snow covered a multitude of sins on Mill Street, oops, Pleasant Avenue. Even though the temperatures would often drop to 20-30 below and snowfalls could reach 2-3 feet each time it snowed; it was very "pleasant." for us kids. One of our favorite games was collecting icicles. Some were 4-5 feet long and could be found on area barns and garages. We couldn't conceive of anything that might be more fun for us.

Now that I have had a chance to reenter my life and reclaim in part what has been lost in time and circumstance, living on Mill Street had been positively "pleasant."

Food, Glorious Food

By Harry Fear

During the "Great Depression" which President Hoover had called a recession, claiming that "recovery was just around the corner." Johnstown New York was a poor place to prepare for the struggle of the 20th century. Somehow, however, it was a great place to spend a childhood. And although many families were bereft of material possessions, food was still, if not plentiful, in seemingly sufficient supply to answer the basic needs of our neighborhood.

I can remember very vividly the many delicacies that made their way out of the neighboring Slovak kitchens; and yes, all of them made from scratch. There were no frozen foods or pre-packaged items and I don't believe any of our delicacies would be on your "calorie counters" short-list of favorite food items today. Come to think of it, the word "calorie" had not even entered into our everyday conversations. Obliviously chubby old Noah Webster, the father of our modern day dictionary, hadn't heard of it as yet, either. It wouldn't become an accepted part of his word collection until 1939. It was mainly used in scientific language.

Of course, other nationalities had their favorite dishes, but to me, the Slovaks were the undisputed champions of milking the most out of whatever raw foods and vegetables were available to them. Time has away of erasing even the most cherished of memories. As a result I no longer can remember the Slovak names of all the foods I enjoyed back then, but the reminiscences, if not the names, will last forever. Most families grew their own vegetables and many had grape arbors and made their own wine which was especially welcome during Prohibition. The wine caused many a hangover in the neighborhood. We attributed that to "the wrath of grapes."

On Sunday mornings after Mass, the kids were expected to go to the Slovak grocer who was also the local bootlegger. to pick up freshly baked poppy seed rolls as well as a bottle or two of booze; "homebrew," as it was appropriately named.. Prohibition or not, this homemade booze still flowed freely and not just for the Slovaks. It seemed everyone was making homebrew, but it didn't happen at my house. Mom wouldn't allow it, her Irish heritage not withstanding. Homebrew and Moonshine could be bought off the back of trucks that rolled through the neighborhood.

All the clubs -- Moose, Odd Fellows etc had it available for its members. No Elliot Ness ever came to clamp down on those illegal sales. My mother often decried the men who with what little money they could earn in those days of depression went for flings in our neighborhood grocery store, where Mr. Kuchy gladly ladled out his moonshine into Mason jars to all who had the money to pay for it.

Holidays, particularly Easter and Holy Week were a time for great food and fun times as well. The men traditionally would weave a braided switch like whip from the pussy willow plants that were so plentiful in the area. These were given to the children to visit neighboring Slovak homes and demand food (preferably pastries) with the implied threat that if they didn't get it, they would use the switch.. This was similar to the "trick or treat" thing that kids do today. Of course that switch was never used.

One pastry name I do remember is Buchty (pronounced book tee) a hands down favorite of everyone. Buchty is a Slovak yeast bun They are small pieces of raised dough, stuffed with sweet cottage cheese, poppy seed and plum jam. When they are fresh out of the oven they are sprinkled with confectionery sugar.

Another insight on unusual Slovak customs; was their habit of leaving fully decorated Christmas Trees up until Easter. They were kept in the front living room, just as they were on Christmas Day, because the living rooms remained unheated and closed off. The season's frigid temperatures allowed the trees to hold up surprisingly well. I meant this to be a gastronomic salute to the Slovak community of my day. Contrary to cooks today who demand easy to follow recipes, suitable for quick everyday or entertaining, the Slovak families, way back then, made a production of every meal. Whether the event was to be fancy or casual, all meals were time consuming to prepare and carefully planned. They enjoyed gathering with family and friends for exceptional meals, having guests for a special occasion or just a quick Sunday family breakfast before Mass. A guest at a Slovak meal would have left the table singing, "Food, Glorious Food," had the famous song been written at the time.

MMM

Kings of the Road

By Harry Fear

Back in the early 60's, Roger Miller composed and recorded the hit song, "King of the Road". As I thought about that song recently, my mind slipped into reverse and I was able to recall the kings of the roads of my youth. In the 1930's they were called hoboes.

Hobo is a word you don't hear much anymore. When I was a kid, hobos were a part of the fabric of America. So what was a hobo? I quote from someone who should know. A one time King of the Hobos, Rambling Rudy said a hobo is a man, who travels in order to to work, as different from a tramp who travels and won't work and a bum who doesn't travel, and won't work.

The word probably is derived from the days after the Civil War when traveling men carried hoes, with them and hence were called "hoe boys". These were the men, and many teenagers too who spent their lives hopping freight trains to everywhere and nowhere, asking for handouts of food and/or money on street corners or knocking on doors in cities and towns everywhere. Johnstown, New York, my hometown was no exception.

The *Fonda Johnstown and Gloversville Railroad.* was our local freight lines. This was no mainline railroad, yet, the hobos found their way to my little town. With a third of America out of work, historians have estimated about 4 million people crisscrossed the country on freight trains in search of work, food or adventure, or more likely all three. In addition to the hobos, we had a collection of Gypsy's that always came to town and left their "calling cards" Things always turned up missing when they visited you in your home or property. They usually set up their camps on a farm in the east part of town.

My father never approved of feeding the hobos, but my mother felt otherwise and treated them kindly, offering them sandwiches and coffee when they crossed her threshold. "I do this and it makes me feel better" she would say when he asked why she would give handouts when she was hard pressed to feed her own family.

My father once told me. in a kind of a whisper, that after seeing my mother chatting with a visiting hobo at our kitchen table, he thought my mother had Irish brains that were softer than soap. We later learned that our hobo guests left an unique mark on the curb or elsewhere in front of hospitable homes so other hobos who might be passing would recognize this distinguishing symbol and would know where they would be welcome.

Hobos were not the only ones who were on the receiving end of my mother's hospitality. Many times, particularly during cold winter months if she saw men from the power and light company or city crews, working outside her door, she would gravitate towards them and invite them in for hot coffee and a snack and when I delivered hot cross buns on Good Friday mornings, people would leave their doors open and while they slept and I would enter their homes about 3-4 am and quietly place the buns in their waiting hot ovens.

Hey, times were different then.

Arachibutyrophobia

By Harry Fear

The period from 1929-32 was known as the Great Depression Era when the entire country was on the brink of economic ruin. At first many thought the country just had a "flat tire", but we soon learned it wasn't a flat, the "damn wheels were coming off". Hundreds of thousands were out of work. Breadlines were a common sight.

While the Depression was supposed to be over in 1932 when Franklin D. Roosevelt was elected, it really continued in one form or another right up until 1942 when it took America's entry into World War II to right the economy. At a time when the country really needed a drink, it couldn't get one. Prohibition.

Americans, then as now, like to think of themselves as patriotic. They have been saying as much to pollsters for years; men, women, old people, young people, rich people, poor people, white, blacks, urbanites, farmers. Nearly everyone says the same thing. My mother scorned all polls except those that supported her views. When FDR said that it was patriotic to try to do something extra to earn money rather than go on Government Relief as it was called in those days. Mom took up the challenge. She was then employed as a hemmer in a Glove Shop. The Shop was a typical sweatshop of that period. It was three stories tall, wooden frame, one set of stairs, no elevators, no fire escapes and only one exit. The hemmers worked on one floor; maybe 50-60 machines all lined up in a row. The noise was deafening. In the spring the rains came and left a calling card beneath each window that made rivulets of water everywhere in the building. As the seasons changed the winter made the shop cold, and the heat of the summer made the building even less inviting. The other floors were occupied by men who were labeled cutters. They cut and fashioned the skins into the shapes of various styles of gloves for the hemmers to sew together. My mother would sit at her machine and sew ten hours a day, eating her lunch at her machine as she continued to sew. She noted that many of her co-workers were coming to work with no lunch and that gave her an idea. Here was her chance to display her patriotism. She would be the "Lunch Lady".

Cooking was never one of my mother's strong points, although I didn't realize that until I was married. For some reason, long forgotten, she felt she could make meatloaf that would make all diners step up and cheer. The Smullens family who lived downstairs had a mixed breed mutt named Pete, who spent much of his time upstairs with us. Pete would eat your shoes if you let him, but he wouldn't touch my mother's meatloaf and come to think of it, neither would my father.

While making sandwiches isn't cooking, that's what my mother decided to do. Make sandwiches and sell them; and not just any kind of sandwich. She would create a special kind of sandwich, available nowhere else. The sandwiches main ingredients were her own special egg salad (lots of onions), pimentos, green peppers and peanut butter. This was the only sandwich she would feature and she had it on sale every day. So how many times a week can you eat the same sandwich, Depression or no Depression? I am sure those ladies had a depression of their own when that sandwich showed up every day. That was not the only reason, however that sales reached a new low in only the second week. The problem was the heavy use of peanut butter in the mixture; it was sticking to the roof of their mouths and attaching itself to the dentures of others. Sales dropped because the ladies had a fear of that happening and they didn't want to have to deal with it.

Nearly 70 years later I was to learn that fear had a name. Its called "Arachibutyrophobia". So, on the big stage of sandwich makers, Mom came up small. Soon after my mother abandoned the sandwich business and began selling homemade aprons. This time kismet was on her side. It would become a business that would prosper for a number of years. FDR would have been proud.

Tova Fischtein

Born in Tel Aviv, Israel in 1958, Tova grew up with two younger sisters. She and her husband Zvika (Harry) Fischtein opened an electronics store. Her first child, a daughter, was born in Israel in 1980.at a time when the Israeli economy was in a very deep recession. They decided to move to Toronto to provide their children with greater opportunities.

In Canada, they sold apparel and accessories. Over a decade later the company expanded to sell cosmetics to stores across Canada and the United States.

Tova's next three children were boys and once they were all old enough to go to school, she became a real estate agent while working with her husband in the cosmetics company But in 1999, the Canadian cold was reason enough to move the family to Boca Raton, where Tova received a teaching license. She is currently a Hebrew teacher..

She always loved writing stories especially tales of her remarkable family history, as a twelfth generation Sabra (born in Israel) on her mother's side and a first generation Sabra to a holocaust survivor on her father's side. Her in-laws were also holocaust survivors. Tova is writing her family history for future generations.

She also has two dogs, a cat, and a bird as if four kids were not enough.

She is a very active volunteer in F.I.D.F. a non-profit organization that supports the emotional, spiritual and mental needs of the Israeli soldieries.

Recently, she and her husband became motorcyclists and they are out on the road with friends about once a week. A good restaurant, an Israeli nightclub and an evening of dancing keep her spirits floating .

Family comes first with Tova. Her life philosophy is to enjoy every minute and regret none. She works at what she loves and loves what she works at. She believes in working hard to achieve her dreams and never giving up. Failure, she believes, is not trying, rather than not succeeding.

I Am Sorry, My Son

By Tova Fischtein

Until the day she died, my grandmother Esther kept apologizing to my uncle Chanina. Throughout his life, she gave him whatever he needed or wanted..

Germany 1938: My Grandmother Esther, a tiny young woman with two small boys, had been walking for days from village to village in the snow. She was looking for her missing relatives. The boys were hungry, and cold and cried constantly. They wanted their papa, who disappeared a few weeks before, along with Esther's six siblings and her mother. Grandma Esther cried too, but only at night when the boys were asleep. In front of them she was strong, singing marching songs to distract them from their sore feet.

Every night she prayed to God to help her find her family, especially her mother, with whom she had been very close. But sometimes she worried that she might be asking too much of Him. "He is busy now with sick and injured people," she thought, "Everyone must be praying."

It was not easy taking care of the two boys all alone with no income, no food, and no shelter. So when she arrived in the village near the river, she thought her prayers had been answered. She could not believe the news. She heard that her family had already arrived on the other side of the river, and that the last boat would be leaving to meet them that day. "And the timing," she thought to herself, "one more day and she would have been too late to catch the boat."

"Just a little longer," she told the boys, "we only have to get to the river and then you don't have to walk any more. We are going on a big boat. Do you know" she continued, cheering the boys to walk a little further. "who we will see after the boat ride? We will find Bubbie, your uncles and aunts; the whole mishpuche will be there."

"I am so lucky," she thought to herself as her size 5 feet walked faster. "Wait mama," cried out her 5-year-old Chanina, "I can not run so fast and Hershel is still back there." He pointed his finger at his three year old brother, my father, standing all by himself and crying. Esther ran to Hershel and scooped him in her skinny arms, shifted him to her left hip, extended her right arm to Chanina and said, "Let's go, fast! This is the last boat, so we must hurry."

Near the docks at last, she put my father on the ground and stretched, "Look, Boys. Look at the big ship over there. We have a little time, so let's play Patti Cake, Patti cake."

They played and pretended to eat some cake. The boys knew this was pretend. They had already received their food for the day, and they knew there would be no more until tomorrow. .

."O.K, it is time to go," she said rising from the damp grass, brushing her skirt to shake off the snow. "Come on, Chanina, let's go," she said. But the child did not move. She bent over and touched his shoulder, "Chanina honey, lets go." My uncle shrugged his shoulder and shook his head from right to left and back. She tried again. This time he only shook his head. Then her tone of voice changed. "Let's go please, now!"

"NO!" he said, in a very firm voice. She was shocked by his stubbornness. He had never behaved like that.

She was desperate. The boat was about to leave and almost everyone was on board. So she picked Hershel up and told Chanina, "Okay. If you want to stay here, you can. But we are going to get on the boat. Hershel and I will see Bubbie soon. She has lots of food there. You know, real cakes, Challah, choolent and chicken soup. G'bye, Chanina. Be well, and I hope you will find a new mama to take care of you." And she started to walk towards the dock. When she turned around, she expected to see Chanina run after her just as he had done so many times before. But this time, he sat there, exactly as she had left him.

Now she was enraged He could not have picked a worse time to be so obstinate. She took a deep breathe and let out a long sigh. "Okay, Hershel. Your brother won. Let's go back and beg him to stop acting like a mule." She tried to make a joke to relieve her own stress. My father was only three years old and didn't know what a mule was and he could not recognize a stressful smile when he saw one.

And so my father and my grandmother turned around and went back to where Chanina was sitting. She expected him to run to her but he did not move. As they came closer, Esther looked at my uncle's face. He had a very strange look. She had never seen his eyes so cold and blue. A chill went down her spine. She trembled and said, "Okay Chanina. Come on. Let's go." She extended her arms but he only shook his head.

"Let's go!" her voiced pitched higher. She had never raised her voice to her kids before. Still his answer was, "NO"

She felt the blood rushing to her head. She had never been so angry in her life. "Come on!" she yelled, "You cannot say no to me. I am your mother. When I say go, you go. Understand? Now let's go!"

Unaccustomed to hearing his mother yelling or seeing her so agitated, he started to cry. She forcefully picked Chanina up despite his weight, knowing that Hershel would follow. Time was running out. She had to get on the boat. but Chanina was struggling in her arms, waving his legs and arms violently and screaming at the top of his lungs.

"No! No! I don't want to go on this boat, Mama! No!" Esther was only 4 foot 10 inches tall. Chanina's weight was too much for her frail body. She did not have a proper meal in weeks, had walked hundreds of miles, and had no strength left. Her grip became looser and Chanina used this moment of weakness and freed himself from her grip.

The commotion was unbearable for her. Hershel was crying, people were running towards the ferry and Chanina ran the other way as fast as he could. She was afraid that he would get lost and so she chased him while dragging my father behind her. She caught up to him and knew that she was losing control. At that same moment, a very loud horn pierced the air.

"The ferry! The ferry is leaving! Come Chanina! Come now, I said!" She yelled. Her face was red and her whole body was shaking. But Chanina stood still.

She looked back towards the river and saw the ferry moving slowly away from the dock. She was frantic and she turned around, and slapped Chanina across the face. Her hand slapped his left cheek and then his right. She was never sure how many times she struck his flushed face. All she could remember was the child's cry for her to stop. For a moment, she did not know where she was and then she realized what had happened. She had lost the only chance she had, to be reunited with her family. She felt the whole world getting dark and she collapsed on the ground, crying hysterically.

When she came to, it was dark and light snow was falling. The children were sleeping from exhaustion on the ends of her skirt, each holding a small piece close to his chest. Chanina's right arm was lying on Hershel's left shoulder. A smile came across her face when she saw her kids, so sweet and innocent.

But then she remembered where she was and what had happened and she. turned her head to the sky and cried out, "Why are you doing this to me -- allowing me to hope, making me think that you answered my prayers, bringing me so close to my dream and snatching it away from me. What have I done so wrong that I deserve such punishment? I have always kept Shabbat and when I had a home, it was always kosher. I have served my husband well before he went off to the war and even though it has been months since I heard from him, I have always kept faith and hope. Even here, now that my babies and I are homeless, hungry and cold, I never questioned your actions. I always kept my faith in you. You allowed the Nazis to take away our money our homes and our lives but I fought to keep my spirits high, and now this! What sin did my poor babies do? I know that I am not suppose to talk to you this way. I know that God works in mysterious ways and a poor woman from Galitzia is not supposed to question the Creator of the universe. I am sorry, I am so sorry."

The next thing she remembered was her boys standing over her, calling her in a soft voice. "Mama, please wake up. It is morning, mama please." She awakened with puffy eyes but she had to go back to the village for food.

If only she had some jewelry left she might have found someone with a boat to take her across the river. But she had traded all she had weeks ago, for food and shelter. Now she had to beg for whatever she could scrape together.

They started to walk back. The wind slapped their faces and their spirits were low. She had no strength left to cheer her boys. They saw the big barn as they approached the village. It was the one with the big brown doors and the broken lock. They had slept there two nights ago when the kind old lady allowed them to rest the night after she had given them some hot soup. It was the night before they were to go to the ferry. Esther never thought she would see this kind lady again.

When they arrived, the lady was very surprised to see them. She hugged Esther and pulled her indoors to the main house with the boys. She was crying, laughing, and talking all at the same time. Esther could not make out what she was saying. A few minutes later, the lady's daughter came in and told my grandmother the horrifying news. The Nazis attracted as many Jews as they could, promising jobs and free ferry rides to the other side of the river. Overnight, they burned houses, and barns killing everyone.

Esther sat there in deep shock. She couldn't even cry. The Nazis had killed her family; her brothers and sisters, aunts and uncles and her mama. "Mama is gone forever. They are all gone forever." It was all beyond comprehension.

The boys were playing quietly beside the fireplace. My grandmother got up, walked in their direction, and hugged them. Chanina put his head on her shoulders and said, "I love you Mama." She was shaking with emotions, kissing him all over his face, his head, his arms. She could not stop. She kissed him, cried, and apologized. And she continued apologizing for the rest of her life.

Great-Aunt Esther

By Tova Fischtein

"For us she is dead, Sara, our Esther is dead." Oved shouted. His face was red and his lower lip shook with anger. "Tear your dress woman," Oved screamed while tearing his own shirt. "I am sitting Shiva, and you are sitting with me." Sara's wailing carried out to the street, through the open door and windows. She sounded like a wounded lioness. Sara slapped her face over and over crying out to G-d to take her away. She tore her hair and scratched her cheeks with her nails. Thin lines of blood covered her face. "Imma, stop it." Her oldest daughter called out. She tore her mom's hands off of her face and they fell onto each other's arms and cried.

The youngest children Eli and Mazal sat in the corner looking at their parents and siblings. They were very confused and scared. They held each other and did not dare to make a sound. Frida, their 13 year old, extended her hand to them and whispered. "Come let's go outside for a while."

The children had spent many hours in this yard, running and hiding between the huge sheets that were hung to dry on the lines. They had chased the chicken that Grandpa bought on Erev Yom Kippur (the day before the day of Atonement) and used it for Caparot, (A Jewish ritual). They rode the goat that Grandma milked every morning. As they came to the back door, their grandmother who stormed into the house, knocked them down. Her large hips were usually a source for many games with her grandchildren but this time they got in the way and she dropped tiny Mazal to the floor.

"What is going on here?" she screamed as she rushed to the living room. "In G-d's name what is wrong?" She looked at her daughter's face and her son in-law's torn shirt and froze. "Mama" Oved started to talk, "Your grand daughter Esther, married an Arab today."

He swallowed the tears that choked his throat and continued. "She is moving to his mother's home in Lebanon. We are getting ready to sit Shiva." His voice became weak and he went down on his knees, bent, over and banged his fists on the floor. He blamed Sara for giving Esther too much freedom. He blamed the Arabs for mixing in with the Jews. He blamed Yom Tov, Esther's older brother for not watching over his sister. He also blamed himself for producing "such a child." His cry became louder with every accusation until his vocal chords gave up and he sounded like a violin in the hands of a child.

The room was quiet until, like thunder, a large bang broke the silence. Oved was still on his knees, his body was still curled up, but now his arms supported his body weight and his elbows were bending every time his head banged the floor.

The commotion stopped for a moment and every one looked at Oved but no one talked to him. Sara, his oldest granddaughter ran into the room, free from her aunts who were holding her. "*SABA, SABA, STOP! STOP!!!*" she screamed, running to her grandfather. She placed her arms around his neck and they both sobbed.

Esther walked down the street, her head looking down, when she heard the screams from a distance. She knew that she would never see her father again. In her hand she held a small paper bag that her mother had given her just before she left. "Take this." Her mother had said, "I baked them this morning. It's something to hold you on your long trip."

"How did I allow myself to think that he would understand? I should have known better," Esther mumbled to herself. Small drops of rain fell and with each step they became larger. She felt as though the universe were crying with her.

"Esther, Esther." She thought she was hearing voices. "Esther, wait." Her eldest sister was calling. Esther saw Simcha, hopping with her one short leg as fast as she could. They fell into each other's arms. A moment later Simcha pushed Esther gently and wiped her face from both the tears and the rain.

"I have to go back before Abba finds out that I left, but here, take this" And Simcha shoved a white handkerchief into her sister's hand. "It is not much but that is all Shlomo and I were able to save, and I want you to have it. I love you. Take care of yourself."

Before Esther had a chance to react, Simcha turned around and walked back down the narrow street towards the house." I love you too, Simcha, thank you."

Esther yelled after her, but Simcha kept walking just as fast as before. It took every ounce of strength for her not to turn around, but she had already disrespected her father by running after Esther and she had to return.

Achmed had been waiting for Esther in the back of the local theatre. By the time Esther reached him they were both soaked. He saw her walking from a distance and his heart ached. Her steps were slow, her back was arched and her head was not visible to him as it hung down towards the floor. Achmed waited anxiously for Esther to get closer. Then he jumped out and wrapped her like a blanket in his arms. She did not have to tell him what had happened at her father's house. He saw it in her eyes. A moment later Achmed led Esther to the back of the theatre where he took out the bag had placed behind a rock. He helped Esther to get into the black mantle. She wrapped her head, face and neck with the black shawl and looked at him with scared eyes.

"You look wonderful" he said, answering her unspoken question. He kissed her forehead and added. "You couldn't have looked better if you were born in my village. Come let's go home." A faint smile came upon Esther's lips and they walked together to the bus stop.

*****

"It's been three years," Simcha whispered to her mother "Do you think he forgave her? Can she come to the house yet?" "Tfu, Tfu, Tfu". Her mother "spit" three times to the floor. "Don't even mention her name beside him. He is a sick man and I am scared to get him upset. We will wait until he goes to work and the little ones are at school and we will let her in. You can not say anything about it to any one, not even Shlomo."

Esther hid behind the theatre, just as Achmed had done the first day she left home. She removed the black shawl, revealing her delicate skin, and peeled her black mantle. She fixed her hair and placed all of her Arabic articles in a bag. She hid the bag behind the rock and took a deep breath. Esther was wearing the same outfit that she had on the day she left. She did not own any other clothes, and she had no use for them in the village, where Galabias were the feminine attire. She liked wearing the comfortable long shapeless embroidery dresses.

Esther walked towards her parents' home. Her steps were small and rushed. She was careful not to be seen, so the word would not get to her father that she was in the area. She knew how dangerous it would be both for her mother and sister if anyone discovered their secret. Both of them would face possible expulsion from home by their husbands. They could be sent away without money or clothes and with no chance of ever seeing their children again. "It is so ironic" Esther thought,"The culture is so similar, so is the food, language and customs, yet they are two different worlds with an ocean of deep hatred between the two people."

As she arrived at the house, the door opened and an arm scooped her in. "My daughter, my beautiful daughter" her mom cried on her shoulder in Arabic." I missed you too Imma," Esther replied in Hebrew. Although she spoke Arabic fluently she missed speaking her native language. Her mother had prepared her favorite dishes. Esther ate until she felt full.

"When you eat for two you need to eat a lot," Sara said. Esther's mouth dropped, and she blushed. "How did you know?"

"A mother knows," said Sara and gave her a huge warm hug. "Mazal Tov, Esther" said Simcha.

"I was going to tell you, Imma" Esther said. She took her mother's hands in her hands. "Mom's hands are so cold," Esther thought. She looked at her mother's face and found the same warm brown eyes she remembered and longed for, but the face that surrounded the kind eyes had too many wrinkles. Esther knew that many of these wrinkles appeared in the past three years. She felt responsible for them. Sara sat beside her daughter, and stroked her hair. "Come on Sweetheart, tell me how you are doing. Are you happy? Is your mother in law treating you right? How is his family...?"

"Mother," Simcha laughed, "Let her talk".

"Well," Esther said in a low voice. "I am not sure where to begin," and then her eyes lit up. She grabbed her purse from the coffee table and pulled up a small envelope. "Open it Imma, this is a gift for you."

Sara opened the envelope slowly. She pulled out a piece of paper with a mix of a few red lines and three or four blue circles. Sara lifted her eyebrows in confusion and Esther smiled. Her hazel eyes looked like two shiny almonds. "Ok, I give up," Sara said. "Tell me who sent me such a unique gift?"

"Your grand son, Imma" As she said these words she handed her mother a picture of a toddler. "Meet your grand son, Abraham."

. An enormous smile came on her face. The wrinkles almost disappeared," She thought. Sara extended her hand. "May I please see my grand child?"

"It's time to go, Esther," Simcha said after they finished their coffee and had eaten a few of Sara's home made salty round cookies. "Abba will be home soon".

"I know, I know" Esther said.

"Can I keep the picture, Esther?" Sara asked.

"Sure Mom". Esther replied. "You can keep the picture and the drawing. It might be worth a lot of money one day."

The women were laughing all afternoon,

"I will walk you to the bus stop, Esther," Simcha said. "I have to pick up Sara from school. She is in first grade already."

"I am so overwhelmed from all the news that you and Imma told me." Esther said. "I know that we have a large family, but I never realized how many births, weddings and even deaths can occur in three years."

"Please send me a letter when you give birth, Esther," Sara said. Her eyes filled with tears. She took Esther's face in her wrinkled hands and kissed her forehead. "May G-d be with you," she said and shoved a large paper bag in Esther's hand.

"Take this home for little Abraham".

"His full name is Abraham Oved." Esther said and the tears covered her cheeks.

"After everything your father did, you named your first born after him?" But Esther did not hear her sister's question. .

*****

Sara kept four piles of pictures and drawings under her mattress, one from each one of her "Arab "grandchildren. She covered the piles with newspapers, so if Oved ever looked under the mattress, he would never know.

"Imma," Simcha said one day. "When did you hear last from Esther?"

"Now that you mentioned it, it has been a long time since a letter came from her." Sara replied.

"I am worried" Simcha said. "The last couple of times that she was here, she looked pale. She looked like she had lost some weight and she had dark circles under her eyes."

"Let's wait another week or so," Sara said. "And if by next Shabbat no letter will come, I will go to the butcher's wife and ask her to open Esther's luck in cards or coffee."

*****

"I haven't spoken to my mother for so long," Esther thought to her self. The night was bright; the shining moon seemed to be smiling. "I know," Esther smiled back at the moon, but her smile was sad. "You have been kind to me throughout the years. You have watched over me many times when I traveled to Israel and back."

"Esther" She heard her mother in law calling. "The water is boiling and your husband is calling you."

Esther shook her head. "I am day dreaming again." She poured the hot water quickly into the white round enamel bowl, and carried it to the back room. "I will clean his wounds, mama,." Esther said, while bending on her knees in front of her husband's bed. His weak trembling hand moved so very slowly towards her face. He stroked her face gently and she kissed his palm. "I am so sorry, Esther," he said in a frail voice.

"Sorry?" Esther asked. "For what, Achmed? What are you sorry for?"

"I know how much you miss your mother." His voice cracked and tears rolled down his cheeks.

"Because of me and my stupid illness, it has been so long since you went to visit your mom." They both knew the end was near.

*****

"Esther," her mother in law said on a windy winter morning." It has been forty days since Achmed died. The mourning period is over and you have done your duties as a wife."

"I know Mama,." Esther said. "I will never be able to love another man like I loved. Achmed".

"What I am about to tell you, is not easy, Esther," Achmed's mom said. She took Esther's face in her hands looked into her eyes, and continued. "I love you like my own daughter. I have loved you from the first day Achmed brought you home. You loved my son and gave him four sons to carry his name."

"I love you too, Mama." Esther said, extending her arm to hug her mother in law, but the woman placed her finger on Esther's lips.

"Hash ya bintie". The woman continued. "As much as I love you, it is time for you to go."

"Go? What do you mean? Go where?" Esther was confused.

"You have to go back to your father and mother." The old woman said. Her black veil hid most of her face but her red, shiny eyes gave her away.

"How can I go back?" Esther asked and without waiting for a reply she continued. "My children do not speak Hebrew at all, they are too old to start living their lives as Jews, and too young to lose their father."

"I am glad you understand, Esther." The woman said softly. "Your children are not going anywhere, you are leaving alone."

"BUT..." Esther cried. "No but, Esther, this is the way it has to be."

"Those children are Arabs. They are the only thing I have left of my only son."

"But I am their mother!" Esther cried out. "Those are my babies, they need their mother."

"I will be their mother, and my brother will be like a father to them. You are a young woman, Esther. Go back home, find another man and have new babies with him."

The old woman took a deep breath and continued. "I packed you some food, and here is some money for the trip." Achmed's mom took a small handkerchief out of her bosoms that dangled close to her waist. She handed it to Esther. "Today you will not have to walk to the next village to catch the bus. I have arranged for my brother to borrow a car, and he will drive you." Esther felt as if a lightning hit her. She was numb and could not speak.

It was a little after noon, when Esther finally reached the Lebanese Israeli border. Her legs were sore and the old boots were full of rainwater and mud. She walked through the Christian villages many times before, but the trip never felt so long and the walking was never so difficult.

The five mile walk to the nearest bus stop inside Israel took Esther about three hours. "But at least it stopped raining," Esther thought to herself. She took the "Eged" bus number 500 to the Tel Aviv central station. Her eyes felt as if they were on fire. "How many more tears is my body going to produce?" She asked herself. "I thought I ran out of tears in the first two weeks after Achmed died."

She closed her eyes. "Tel Aviv," she heard the driver yell.. She looked at her watched and knew she had missed the last bus to her sister's house. She would need to walk across town.

*****

It had been a wet week. The rain did not let up for four days, when Simcha heard light tapping on her window. "Is this storm ever going to stop?" She mumbled and turned around in bed. "Hey, you are pulling my blanket," Shlomo said. "I am cold", Simcha answered, "What time is it anyways?"

"It's too early for us to be talking, woman," laughed Shlomo and wrapped Simcha in his arms. But what sounded like rain- drops tapping on the window before was defiantly knocking. "Shlomo, I am scared," Simcha said sitting up in her bed. "Please go see what it is. Maybe the window got loose."

"Ok, princess" Shlomo said. "Just remember you owe me big, getting me up in this nasty weather to close a window".

"Simcha, come quick!" Shlomo called. As Simcha jumped out of bed, she grabbed her flannel housecoat and ran to the living room. Shlomo opened the front door and there she was. Her hair was "glued" to her face; her nose had been dripping water. Her brown coat was so big and wet it lost it's shape.

"Esther!" Simcha screamed. "What happened? What are you doing here in the middle of the night, in this awful storm?" Simcha asked while stretching her arms towards her sister

"I will put some water on the fire," Simcha said

"NO, no, you sit down." Shlomo said. "I will make us all coffee." Baby's cry sounded from the next room. "I got it." Shlomo yelled from the kitchen.

"Simcha" Esther said as she sat on the love seat that was covered with jelly stains. "My life is over"

"Esther, please" Simcha begged. "Calm down, please tell me, what happened?" Esther could not stop crying until Shlomo handed her a glass of water which she drank quickly.

"It's good to see that our family's old customs did not die despite the resemblance to our hated Arab neighbors,." Esther said, with a bitter smile.

The sun was up by the time Esther finished telling her story to Simcha and Shlomo. "I guess I have to go face Abba now," Esther said. "Do you think he will allow me back to his home and heart?"

"You never left his heart, Esther," said her sister, handing her dry boots.

*****

"It has been a year since you came back, Esther. "Oved said to his daughter one day. "It is time to look for a husband."

"I met a nice boy named Yacov,." Esther said bowing her head to the floor.

"So, why don't you invite him for Shabbat dinner Esther? So your father can meet him."

"I will Abba, one day I will. "

"Esther! What is the matter with this boy?" Oved's moustache looked much bigger when he smiled. "Why don't you want your father to meet him? He is Jewish Esther, isn't he?"

"Yes, Abba he is". Esther answered in a quiet voice. She felt as if she were five years old again, and got caught breaking her father's favorite ashtray.

"Ok, then tell me what is so wrong with this boy, that you are afraid to let your papa meet him?"

"Well," Esther began to answer. He is --.He just came from… He was born in Poland." She finally plucked up the courage to say.

"A voosvoos!"(a nick name for a person from a European decent) Oved's laughter was heard throughout the apartment and Sara came running from the kitchen, wiping her wet hands in a checker towel. "What is going on here?" She asked, but when she saw Esther's smiling face she relaxed immediately. "This Shabbat you have to prepare the food with 'Rachmoones' on the spices." Sara's face was puzzled and Oved continued. "Esther is bringing her voosvoos boy friend to Shabbat dinner tomorrow."

*****

"Esther..." did you hear what I said?" Yacov asked his wife of 22 years.

"No, I am sorry." she said, "I was thinking."

"What is the matter?" Yacov asked, noticing her shiny eyes. "I spoke to Rivka today." Esther said

"And how is our oldest daughter doing? How is that skinny husband of hers?" Yacov asked.

"Well, the army drafted Ze-ev today. His unit is serving in the northern border near our son Sammy's unit.."Esther's voice was as fragile as the political situation in the Middle East. Yacov wrapped his arm around Esther's shoulders.

"They will be ok. Both of them will come back home," he tried to assure her.

"But..." Esther looked up into Yacov's blue eyes and she whispered, "But do you think my children are shooting at our children?"

MMM

The Neder: A Promise To God

By Tova Fischtein

Some family stories remain in our bones forever. This one about my great grandmother has shaped the person that I have become, giving me a deep respect for G-d and my faith.

My great grandmother Sara was at the end of her 8th pregnancy, and when she went to see the doctor, she knew this would be her last visit before giving birth. As he placed his hands on her stomach and felt the fetus, his face darkened like a winter cloud. "I am sorry Mrs. Chadria," he said, and continued to jolt her stomach as if he was trying to push the baby around.

"What is the matter? Is the baby dead? Talk to me, please," Sara begged. The doctor asked her to get dressed and come into his office. "We have to talk" he said in a somber voice.

As he approached his office, he heard her praying. She was standing near the wall, facing east. Her eyes were closed, her hands were hugging her stomach and she was benching, rotating from side to side. He placed his hand gently on her shoulder and helped her into the chair beside his desk. "There is no easy way to say this Sara," his voice rattled. "What?" she yelled. "The baby is not dead. I can feel it. Look! Come, put your hand here and feel him kicking me." But the doctor did not get up from his chair. Instead he leaned forward and said in a soft low voice. "Please listen to me Sara. The baby is alive, but his position is -- well, his head is not where it should be. The baby turned and now it is stuck". He came around his desk and placed his hand on the left side of her stomach, "There is his head," he said and placed his other hand on the other side of her stomach "and those are his legs".

" So," said Sara, "when he wants to come out, he will turn back."

"No Sara, he is too big. This is a dangerous situation. This is very serious. I need you to go home and talk to your husband. Is he here or in America again?"

"In America," Sara said, lowering her eyes to the floor in shame. "Well," said the doctor. When a decision like that has to be made…"

"What decision? What are you talking about?" interrupted Sara. She was anxious and confused. The doctor sat in the chair beside hers and held her hands in his.

"The position your baby is in is, called bridge. Medicine is not yet so advanced that we can have a safe delivery. So…" He took a deep breath and continued "… what I am trying to tell you is, that I am expecting a lot of complications. I need you to tell me if things get really bad whose life should I save? Yours, or the baby's? In my experience I will not be able to save you both."

Sara's mouth fell open. She could not believe what she had just heard. She sat there frozen. The doctor's hands were still holding hers and he kept petting them. After what seemed to him like eternity and to his surprise, my Great grandmother got up slowly and left the room without saying a word. She was pale and her legs were shaking.

The next morning she called my grandmother, her oldest daughter. "Simcha, I need to speak to you".

She told my grandmother about the visit to the doctor in great detail. My grandmother was shocked, and tearful, but she did not dare interrupt her mother. "… Last night." Sara continued, "In my dream, I saw Elisha the prophet. He told me that if I promised never to leave this land, both the baby and I will be fine." My grandmother hugged her mother and they both cried. That same day, Sara had a healthy baby boy and named him Elisha. .

About fifteen years later, Sara received a letter from her second born, who had moved to Argentina years before. In the letter he told her how well he was doing financially and asked her to come be with him for a while. "You deserve it," he wrote. "You worked so hard your whole life. It is time for you to rest…" My great grandmother did not forget her dream and the promise she made to God. She went to ask the rabbi for advice. "The way I see it, you fulfilled your promise. You are a good woman Sara. Let me make a special prayer and release you from your obligation," said the rabbi. And so it was done.

A few months later Sara was ready to go on her trip. Her children drove her to Haifa, where the ship was docked.

"Before we let you on board, you must go through a medical examination, Mrs. Chadria" she was told by a crewmember. She stood in line and was seen by a nurse. "I am very sorry Mrs. Chadria, "said the nurse. "You have an eye infection and can not join us on this trip."

"But I don't have any pain," Sara insisted. The nurse had already called the next person in line and my family went home overcome with disappointment.

The following year, Sara was on her way to Argentina again. This time she went to her family doctor two days prior to her trip, and received a clean bill of health. After going through the medical and passport checks, she boarded the ship. This was the first time she had ever left her homeland. She knew she would miss her children and grandchildren. But the thought of finally seeing my great uncle Yomtov and his family made up for the loss.

When the ship arrived in Argentina, Yomtov was waiting for her. He brought a limousine with a driver to take her to his home. My great grandmother stepped off to the docks and Yomtov ran towards her. She opened her arms to hug him but lost her balance and fell to the ground. Yomtov ran to her and tried to pick her up, but she was too heavy. He sat there on the floor, holding her head in his arms and crying for her to respond. She did not react .An ambulance was called and took her to the hospital. Her whole body was paralyzed.

Yomtov hired private nurses, and the best doctors he could find, to try to discover what went wrong with his mom. He could not believe it. He had waited all those years to see his mother and they hadn't even been able to visit each other when this catastrophe occurred. He had always known his mother to be a strong woman. She had given birth to nine children and then raised them all by her self...

When Sara was released from the hospital and moved into Yomtov's home, there were nurses around the clock and the best physiotherapists in town. Although they all worked with Sara for more than a year, she achieved very limited movement in her body and the cost of his mother's illness took its toll on Yomtov's assets. He went into heavy debt and then into bankruptcy. Still he continued to pretend that he was a wealthy man paying his bills with checks that the bank did not honor.

Finally he decided to send his mother back home. He was afraid she was dying and she was feeling the stress of being away from all of her other children and grandchildren, and away from the land where she was born and raised. He knew how important it was for her to go back home. With money he did not have, he purchased a plane ticket for her and notified the family to pick her up at the airport.

After she boarded the plane Yomtov turned himself in to the police, knowing that he would be jailed for fraud. His debtors had a meeting and when they heard his story they were so touched that they decided to allow him time to pay back his debt, with no jail time. For many years thereafter, Yomtov paid all of his debt but he was never able to become wealthy again.

Meanwhile confined to a wheelchair, my great grandmother returned to Israel, with a stop in Europe. Instead of being escorted to the plane to Tel Aviv she was taken to a small room to wait. The planes were over booked because of the Passover and Easter holidays. A few hours later an air line representative approached her. "Mrs. Chadria," he said. "We have a problem. There is a war going on in Israel, so there are no flights going out in the next few days. We are going to give you a hotel room until it is safe to fly there." He was probably thinking, "This old woman is going to Israel to die. The rush will be over in a few days and we will get her on the plane then. No harm done,"

Back home my family had not been notified of her detention. They expected her to arrive on time and went to the airport to greet her. They saw all the passengers coming out one by one and finally realized that she was not on the plane. Their frustration intensified when they learned that the airline representative had left for the night. Some of the men in my family waited at the airport while the women and children went home. In the morning the men went to work and the women continued the airport vigil.

For six days my family continued this routine, each day hounding airport officials for information. Finally my great uncle Elisha decided to take matters into his own hands. He marched into the executive office, past the secretary who tried to stop him, but there was no stopping Elisha.

As soon as he walked in, the manager stood up. He saw this small framed young man not even five feet tall and very skinny with a very angry face. Elisha climbed on the manager's desk and grabbed him by his neck. "I am going to kill you right now," he screamed. "Tell me where my mother is. Did she die in Europe? Where did you dump her body? Tell me now or,"

Cold sweat covered the manager's face. He knew Elisha was serious. He had been brushing him and his family off for almost a week now. "Ok sir. I think I know where your mother is. Let me make a phone call. Just give me another minute. Please." said the frightened manager in a high pitched voice.

My great grandmother was on the next flight to Israel.

Finally at home, Sara was surrounded by her children and grandchildren. She lived for another 10 years but never walked again, accepting that, as her punishment for reneging on her neder- her promise to God.

Cassandra Hancock

A native Floridian, Cassandra N. Hancock earned a B.A. at Rollins College (1966), an M.A. at Florida Atlantic University (1977), and a PhD. at the University of Miami (1989). As a young graduate she worked first as an editor in the Presentations Department of the Martin-Marietta Corporation in Orlando. During those years she taught high school and she and her husband raised three children.

Cassandra studied fiction and playwriting both at Florida Atlantic University and the University of the South in Sewanee, Tennessee, at the Sewanee Writers' Conference which was funded by the Walter E. Dakin Foundation, which Tennessee Williams established before his death. She is a two-time winner of the Stageworks Competition in Tampa ('03, '04), and she has had two productions mounted by her parish drama group at the Chapel of St. Andrew in Boca Raton: *Fresh Bread from Bethlehem* (2000), and *Fabian the Foosh* (2001).

Self Portrait

By Cassandra N. Hancock

She is home spun. She wears a cotton chambray shirt and cotton twill pants, with cotton stretch socks and denim suede shoes. She carries a crossword puzzle to work at traffic lights, bridge delays and railroad crossings. She carries an extra pair of cotton underpants to put on after she swims laps and showers off. She carries a *New York Review of Books*, in case she solves or loses patience with the crossword. To protect her eyes, skin and hair from the sun, she wears dark sunglasses and a tightly woven Tula palm hat with leather chin strap. She always carries enough money to buy a bottle of water, or else she carries a glass of water. She is constantly observing the nouns and verbs around her. She prefers to think of herself as a verb, but admits to her nounness. She is a wife, a retired school teacher, a retired mother, a writer, a beach jogger, a long distance swimmer, a beach surfer, a bulimic reader, a gourmet cook, an expert in nutrition, a sex enthusiast, a practicing Christian, a liberated liberal, a choir member, and underneath, a half-skilled soprano, half-skilled pianist, cat lover, orchid grower, aquarium keeper.

MMM

Florida Childhood

By Cassandra Hancock

My early childhood was full of silences. For my family, it must have been torture that their little girl would not speak. I communicated with nature's creatures with ease, but the world of people struck me dumb.

I liked to watch the pelicans fly high in formation and dive head first from the sky into the glistening water, or skim low over the water surface, looking to catch silver bait fish in their dark throat pouches. Among the quiet v-shaped flocks of brown pelicans, I might see one we had found when it was small, with a hook in its mouth. It had tried to scoop up in its bill a bait fish that was hooked to a deep-sea fisherman's line. The flock left it for dead. Doc spied it, stooped down. You could see his hairy bulge up between his legs but he didn't care. We were amazed to see the pelican slowly waddle towards him on its webbed feet, leaving little pie shaped footprints in the sand.

We watched Doc carefully take out the hook. He gradually nursed the poor flightless creature back to health. It was a long time though before he would be able to fly again. It thought Grampa Doc was its mother. That grey-brown pelican, "Bellican," he called it, toddled behind him everywhere, around the putting greens, up and down the shuffleboard courts, and grew to be almost as big as I was. His huge elastic throat pouch, I thought, could swallow my arm whole, maybe even my head with it, if I was brave enough to stand up on the wooden Adirondack lawn chair and hold the fish Doc gave me over its open bill.

Later I got courage when I spread my arms out to the flocks of soaring pelicans to see if one would dip its wings at me. And if it did, I knew that was "Bellican," who didn't want us to forget about him and wanted to reassure us he was doing fine, and hadn't forgotten us. Sometimes he would simply feed away from the others, as though to show off for us while he was swimming on the water, scooping up a fish, then shaking his head to drain the water out of his pouch before swallowing. On a good day Grama Lois might give me her stale bread to take to the laughing gulls, who were always starving. I worried about them because I often saw them feeding on crabs and shrimp, trash and insects. Before I gave it to the gulls, though, I pulled a chunk off for myself to see how good the bread tasted. I thrilled to feel the gentle fanning and brushing of their white-tipped wings around my head, to see the direct look from their shiny eyes, and feel the wildness it awakened in me. They greedily took every scrap I tossed them in their black bills, sometimes catching their bread fragments in mid air, and constantly calling for more: "Ha, ha. Ha, ha!" It was a kind of Holy Communion, and I felt very loved by God in those moments. I turned my face to the breeze and felt it lift my hair from my shoulders and blow it back behind me. It made me feel pretty.

One gull that had only one leg had a hard time competing with the others for the scraps that fell in the sand. While they took the bread and ran with it down to the surf to soften it in the salt water, I made sure he got his share. He was my peg leg, and I watched out for him. I could see he had to fly more than the others did, to get around, and I knew that though he might have only one leg he would have stronger wings for it.

"You sure have those gulls trained," my grandfather said. I let him think that, because it seemed to delight him so much, but I knew they weren't really trained. They were just hungry. I knew I'd get the cigar ring today, without my sister and brother there. But the stories were not nearly as much fun without them. What I wanted more than anything was the box the cigars came in, with the pretty lady dancing on the cover, for my shell collection. But I was too scared to try to ask.

On one such beach wandering, I made a cheerful discovery. When my sister and brother went off to school and I was stuck home with my mother, I was allowed to listen to a record player, to stay out of her hair. We had decent recordings of Gene Autry, of the "Bozo the Clown" story, of many of A.A. Milne 's poems well read and sung, as well as my favorite, my father's fraternity glee club songs. I could listen to those recordings all day long if I didn't scratch the record or play it too loud. My mother was an avid gardener whose ability to enlist my enthusiasm for weeding was limited. She spent all day gardening, to the point that her back bore the imprint of her bra where the sun's rays streamed through the sweatshirt she wore to protect her skin. "Wasn't she getting lonely?" I might ask myself when I looked out the window to see her puttering around, repotting periwinkles, purple, pink and white. I went out to check on her between records.

"I lose all track of time in my garden," she said, rubbing her forehead with the back of her wrist with her sleeve. Meanwhile, that year, I was getting a full education in children's poetry and glee club songs.

On my solitary beach walks I thought about those stories, songs and poems. My memory of them was company to me. I could think about the stories and turn cartwheels to my heart's content at low tide, when the sand was firm and level. I could try to talk and no one would laugh at me because no one could hear me. On one glorious day I discovered that though I couldn't talk, I could sing! Then it became a challenge to learn the songs and to sing them to myself as I walked on the shore. Eventually the speaking of them came to my tongue as well, and I screwed up my courage to use their words in front of family. I found I could keep them in astonished knee-slapping laughter for as long as I wanted. "You *can* talk!" my sister said on the first such occasion. "You've known all along. You've just been faking it." I had become the family jester, but to speak for myself was another matter altogether. The words still got stuck in my throat.

It was not long after this that I decided I wanted to become a writer when I grew up. Early on, this became my sole purpose, my dominant inner drive. Writing was what I was born to do and what I lived to do. I breathed, I thought, I lived, I loved to write. I was determined to share some of the joy I gained from the spoken word with others.

At five I typed on my mother's typewriter the entire text of Clement C. Moore's "*The Night Before Christmas.*" I thought that made me a writer. "But those aren't your words, are they?" my mother said when I proudly showed her the pages I had labored over all day. I felt as crushed as the crabs that blanketed the streets near the ocean, when we drove home from the beach. I couldn't believe how mistaken I could be. Chagrined and dismayed, I felt very dumb.

"How dumb can you be?" asked my sister.

My Love Life In A Nutshell

By Cassandra N. Hancock

I'm lucky I was pretty. I could seduce any man I wanted, During my junior year in College, I seduced the wealthiest man in the county and bore him his only child, our daughter. All he wanted to do was cruise and travel, and all I wanted to do was be with our daughter.

After our divorce, I decided to sow my wild oats, or rather, having discovered the pleasures of sex., I was unable to resist sowing wild oats. I needed to prove to myself that I was desirable.

I seduced the best tennis player at the racquet club, a Davis Cup champion, the dethroned King of Spain. He thought he was impotent, but I helped him discover he wasn't. He took me to Madrid, where everybody bowed to us. I liked sleeping on silk sheets but I didn't like being revered. I knew I was no better than the woman who scrubbed the front steps at the Ritz, but I did feel desirable..

I threw him over for a former boy soprano whom I had idolized throughout my childhood, and who now had a beautiful trained baritone voice that made me weak in my knees, as I am now, simply writing about him. He was just back from Viet Nam, and so shell shocked that all he could do was sing in church and do lawn work, but my daughter loved him, so we were together for a good year. He helped me feel more desirable, but I needed to find someone more suitable.

When my ex-husband's lawyer called to ask if I were still unattached, I said I was. At the time I didn't know that the family had kept on a retainer fee, and so officially, he was still working for my ex-husband. Ours was the joy of forbidden sex. He always presented me with a fresh gardenia when I opened the door to him. Both my daughter and I were crazy about him, but he was allergic to my perfume. Every time he came to the house, he'd start sneezing and asking between sneezes "Are you sure you don't have a cat around here somewhere?" It was only years later that I realized I drove him away without meaning to.

Then I thought it might be fun to seduce a bishop, a great theologian. He had been a widower for several years and was older than my father. He paid me pastoral visits from time to time, assuring me that I should get on with my life and that he would grant me an ecclesiastical annulment. He was a saintly man, and I was lonely. I often put him up in the spare bedroom downstairs. When I decided to tiptoe downstairs to see if I could arouse him, I found he was really good in bed. Ours was the joy of spiritual sex. After each visit he would say "It'll probably happen again."

Then I decided to seduce an old boyfriend from my high school and college days. We had shared an ongoing summer romance working at the same resort, but we had never slept together. He was in the Navy and out of the blue, he called from his ship that had docked in the Port of Palm Beach. Before he had a chance to identify himself, I recognized his voice and asked "What took you so long to call me?"

I hired a sitter, put my afghan hound in the front seat beside me, and drove up to Palm Beach to meet him. I think I took his virginity. The idea of it was fun, but the reality, a bit disappointing. During his long hours at sea, on watch, he had become a versatile poet. He wanted me to come live with him when he finished his tour of duty and went for his Ph.D. I liked the idea, but I didn't want to yank my daughter out of kindergarten. School was the only stability she had. Later, his wife, whom he had met in graduate school, made him burn all my letters but I still have his.

Then I had a chance to seduce a famous baseball player, but I felt sorry for him because he was an innocent, and I decided not to. He deserved my mercy. I decided to try to be chaste for a while. Quit while I was ahead.

Soon I met my husband, my angel, who drew me up out of the world of unenlightened sex, and to whom I am, gratefully, still desirable. My daughter calls him her father and our sons are her brothers. People say her son, my grandson, bears a strong family resemblance.

How Nine Eleven Touched Me

By Cassandra Hancock

I was the youngest of three and almost ten years old when Clark, "the love child in our family," was born, nine months after the night I heard my mother cry out to my father, "You're turning me into a pretzel!"

Born with a golden glow that he retains to this day at the top of his shiny bald head, Clark had no idea how much his arrival meant to us as a family. We were torn and tormented by the conflict we witnessed in our parents' marriage, the union of a Yankee and Southern belle, but Clark brought us all close together, with our delight in him. By the time he was old enough to have much in common with us we were out the door and off to college and careers.

When she was alive, my mother kept in touch with him and shared stories of his life in the northeast, but in the last ten years, though often deep and passionately caring, our communication has been scant. I have shared with him some of my writing, and though I know he is an avid reader, if I have to pester him for comments, well, that doesn't speak well of my writing, does it?

I was sure my Clark, who I knew did volunteer rescue work in the New York City area, had been involved in rescue efforts after the twin towers came crashing down. For a while I wasn't surprised when I did not hear from him at all.

After several weeks I became concerned. I studied all the lists of the deceased I could call up on my computer. No Clark. My students and I all wrote notes to him, telling him how much we admired his and his co-workers' efforts and hoped he had survived the ordeal. I called his office time and time again only to hear his voice promise he would return my call, but he didn't. I studied an article I had saved about him from the New York Times: My brother--an expert in the field of noise abatement, in his area.

After several months and much prodding by my idealistic teen-age students, who were baffled by my situation, I found sense enough to call his secretary, who told me he no longer worked at the Teeterboro Airport, but he could be reached at the Westchester County Airport. When he finally called back, my voice was full of angst, "Clark, are you all right? I've been very worried about you."

All he said was, "Yeah, I'm all right. We have on our runway here, ten refrigerated semi-trailer trucks loaded with bodies and body parts waiting to be identified. There is no one I know who hasn't lost a loved one. The airport is patrolled by soldiers dressed in fatigues and carrying M16 shot guns. Yeah, I guess you could say I'm all right, as much as anybody can be, living with the stench of decaying bodies, wondering where the hell the family members are who should claim the bodies. I guess some of them are dead, too."

I have not pursued him or heard from Clark since. There was nothing for me to say. I felt as though I was part of the noise he needed to abate.

I don't think he liked hearing himself talk about his feelings either. I realized he may have been experiencing what the Army calls survivor's guilt. I thought perhaps my concern and my call added to his survivor's guilt, or he might want to spare me my survivor's guilt.

I could sense he was depressed, not only in the brusque clip to his answers, but also in what he did not say. I wanted to hear a story about a loved one he had lost. I thought I might be able to share the burden of his grief. I think he was so deep into his sadness that he couldn't talk about it without crying, and although he surely needed to cry, he did not want to cry over the phone, and surely not to his sister. No one likes to cry in front of an audience, except an actor. Words could not serve his sense of loss. It wasn't just the loss of the people who were killed, that he mourned; it was also the loss of their beliefs and faith in the potential of the American dream.

I should be grateful that he told me all he did. What he said did help me accept my son's decision to enlist in the army, soon bound for Iraq. He had became inspired when subsequently, he heard his Uncle Clark's voice as the call-in expert on a CNN in-depth study of the aftermath of 9-11. The depth of my brother's grief reminded me of the core values our parents' post World War II generation imparted to us. Considered by some to be the greatest generation ever in America, theirs left us with a legacy of challenging ideals to enact.

It was the thought of unclaimed bodies that saddened me most. That might mean, as he suggested, that the victims' loved ones had perished too, or worse, that they did not know or care about whom they had lost. When I read recently that half the dead were unidentifiable and that what is left of the Trade Center is to the families of the victims a cemetery of crying souls, I realized that's what I heard my brother's soul crying out with the unidentifiable dead.

I respect the fact that he never calls me. He is entitled to his distance, his space from me, and his space from immediate family. He doesn't want to be worried over. We were just strangers growing up in the same house, thrown together for a few years, taught to share the same dreams.

Thinking about him is a good exercise for me in powerlessness. I see his face and that golden glow on the top of his head every day when I pray, "Oh God, I entrust all who are dear to me to your never-failing care and love, in this life and in the life to come, knowing that you are doing for them better things than I can desire or pray for."

MMM

Candy Wrappers and Secrets

By Cassandra Hancock

"What should I do?" asked my friend Lil, with whom I walked the beach, under a Wedgewood blue dawn. She liked to walk with me in the summer months when we might find turtles nesting. The veil of concern and fear on her face was like the grey mist on the face of the ocean. This wasn't like her. She is usually one who rambles on about her pride in her children.

I hadn't been paying close attention to what she said. On a day as steely calm as this I knew I stood a good chance of finding fresh, nesting tracks in the sand. "What does a mother do when she finds empty candy wrappers is the corners of her child's room?" She repeated.

"I don't know," I said. "Tell her to pick them up and throw them away?"

She was worried about where her child got the candy. She wondered if Toni brushed her teeth after she chewed the candy. She remembered how she used to do the same thing, and her mother never said anything to her about it. She wondered if the housekeeper had found them first, and her mother never even knew about them. "What should I do? I remember that's how my bulimia got started."

Our footprints left white haloes in the sand. "Is this about you, or about your daughter?" I asked.

"I don't want to project myself into this," she said as she bent over to pick up a shell. "But I know secrecy breeds bad decisions. Should I call the pediatrician?"

She threw away the shell as though it did not meet her standard of perfection.

"Yes, see what he says."

"I thought about asking advice from my mother."

"If you ask me, there are many worse things to find in the corners of your children's rooms than candy wrappers," I volunteered. "Like what?" I reminded myself that some people can't think without talking.

I said, "You know, I just need you to be quiet for a little while so I can collect my thoughts."

"Yes, I need to do that once in a while too," she said. "Like what else?"

"Like empty alcohol bottles, drug paraphernalia, pictures of your children sitting around with friends getting high on dope. Candy wrappers in the room of a five year old? What's the big deal?"

She stopped in her tracks and looked at me as though I had deliberately set about to arouse in her undue concern about her child. We were both overreacting now. I had made matters worse. But yet I knew I had just articulated her worst fears. I realized I needed to model quietness, to be what I wanted her to be.

"They say we're only as sick as our secrets," she said in a take charge voice.

This was a challenge for me. Lil and I often disagree—about the merit of a movie, mall shopping as opposed to catalogue shopping; fiction as opposed to nonfiction, political leanings, and so on.

"Secrecy is a symptom of what?" I asked. "Isn't that the concern? Toni feels afraid of how she might look to you if you saw her consuming the Hershey Kisses. Why shouldn't she have a secret life?"

"Because secrecy alienates people. I don't want her to grow up feeling alienated."

"Think of it this way. She sees you giving the puppy treats for good behavior, and so she starts to reward herself for good behavior."

"I hadn't thought of it that way," Lil said. "But the puppy's just a dog. A child shouldn't have to be rewarded for everything she does right."

"No, but isn't it human to appreciate reward?

"Yes, I suppose."

Isn't it also human to be secretive?"

"Maybe so. I don't know."

"Doesn't nature keep secrets?" I could see schools of bait fish churning the waves, but still no turtle tracks.

"In what way?" she asked.

"Think about it," I said.

"Well, yes, if you mean laws, like gravity bending light and all."

I love her scientific bent. "Secrets always come out in the end, don't they?" she asked. She pulled the bill of her sun visor over to the side of her face nearest the direction of a path of sunlight bouncing off the water.

"Who can ever know the answer to that question?" I asked.

"I guess I'd be fooling myself if I believed that, wouldn't I?" she asked.

"But you know how much fun it is to eat bread in secret," I said, "especially that first slice, after you've smelled it baking all afternoon!" She had me going.

"Do you think God may send us messages through our children's secrets?" she asked.

"It's possible," I said. "Are you saying you think you ought to examine Toni's secrets for what light they may shed on your own secret life?"

"I suppose," she answered. "My mother always said that secrecy plans pain."

"Come on. You read too much into things. Even a rider and his horse keep close secrets. Why do you think Smarty Jones is always smiling?"

"I don't know. He likes running maybe."

"Or, he's having fun leading the other horses to think they stand a chance to win the race this time."

"You got me there," she admitted.

"Why not be straight forward with your daughter? Open rebuke is better than secret love, no matter how deep. Can't you just say to her, "Hey, Pal? Catherine our house-keeper found empty candy wrappers in the corners of your room; what's up with that? Don't you know where the wastebasket is?" Couldn't you let go of your worst fears for a moment?

"I don't know how she'd take it," said Lil. Toni can't laugh at herself yet.

"So let her have her little secrets. The wind has secrets!" I stretched out my arms in the soft morning breeze. "I have secrets, don't you?"

She stared down at the sand. "Maybe you're right. I think it was the secretiveness of Jesus that made him so great. He didn't go around touting who he was." Even the bible says it's good to give alms in secret.

I remembered how much she loves the bible. I admire her for that capacity because I find it so boring. "Yes," I said. "Even happiness has its secrets in my feelings of desire and admiration that I don't express. Luck has its secrets too."

"How so?"

"Luck can bring good when I think it is bad, because it may change me for the better."

Lil contradicted me. "Or luck can be just pure luck, neither good nor bad."

"Secrecy is like luck, isn't it?"

She picked up a flat mollusk shell, raised her arm like a major league pitcher, and skipped the shell several times over the flat surface out towards the increasing sunlight, where the turtles might be mating and waiting. I counted six skips.

"But secret, in terms of Mystery, really belongs to God," she said. "Even God has secrets."

"As far as I can know," I conceded. "Sometimes it is better and safer (particularly in strange and new situations) for me, not to speak my thoughts, but simply to listen with a quiet open mind." I began to realize she could not take a hint "Then you're keeping the secret of who you are from people."

"You could call it that," I said, "It's my business isn't it?"

"Death has secrets," I said "Yes, there is a lot we don't know about death."

Somehow, sooner or later, it seems we get on the subject of death. I'd rather walk alone than discuss something I don't understand. But I often feel a need to share the mystery of the beach I have access to, to make it more real for myself at the least. Just like Lil, I longed to find the beauty that lay between my experience of the moment and my projection of myself into it.

"I have a secret to share with you," she said. "After I say my prayers I like to meditate for a few minutes. Yesterday, I had a vision of you and your son. You were holding him in your arms. He had just sacrificed his life to save several other soldiers, by holding his helmet over a smoking grenade, but he was dead. I didn't know if I should tell you or not. There it is. Do with it what you want. I have no idea what it all means."

I felt stunned but I held my tongue. It seemed now that she had shared this, the burden of its reality for her now rested on my shoulders. I wished she hadn't told me, but I said, "Thank you for telling me. It must have been hard for you."

Finally, she asked, "Do you think I shouldn't have told you? Would that be honest? I would have felt foul inward if I had not said anything about it. It would have been a sin for me to keep it a secret."

"I don't know," I admitted. "I don't have to know all the answers."

"I think so," she said. "I think guilt catches up with us sooner or later."

I tried to imitate her toss and threw a flat shell out towards the sun, but it simply sank. Where were the turtle tracks? I wondered.

"Foulness and sin eventually reveal themselves," she remarked. I thought she was being too precious. What did this have to do with candy wrappers? Maybe she'd been going on and on about her daughter to try to keep from telling me about her vision. I thought about how Auden observed that there are always secrets in songs, in paintings, in voices, in scents, in sporting events, in handshakes, even in coughs, and in kisses, and I said, "I think secrets are wonderful." I tried to put on a brave face.

I realized at this moment I should shake off my fears and ask myself how I am like Lil and her daughter, instead of trying to set myself apart, but I couldn't think how. I identified more with the child than with her mother.

"Some feelings (like love) can be more pleasurable when they are kept a secret than when they are revealed," I said.

She kept going back to judgment. "I couldn't help it," she said. "I felt morally responsible. The bible promises that God will bring everything we do into judgment, including everything we do in secret, the good and the bad."

I didn't mind her having the last word, but I didn't want the conversation to end there. What was so bad about candy wrappers? It seemed so trivial in contrast to her vision.

"I think we will be surprised that he is more lenient with us than we may be with ourselves or with each other."

"Do you?" she asked. "I wouldn't be too sure about that."

"I know I have no secrets from God. The danger of secrets for me is that I have to be careful how I use secrecy, that I don't fool myself, or let others forge it into a sharp-edged tool to use against me. It takes up energy in that sense and drains me from having to perform all that guard duty."

"Secrecy is at odds with democracy," she said as she pulled the hair away from her face. I was glad to hear her let up on the hell fire and brimstone. "I probably have lots of secrets I keep from myself that I'm not even aware of."

She looked at me with surprise that seemed to cut through her veil of concern and fear when I said, "My secrets reveal themselves to me in dreams--often, no, usually, by surprise, when I recall them. I have to be careful whom I confide my dreams to." I picked up the inside of a spiraling shell to admire the progress it had made. It felt like a miracle in my hand. "Don't you think the sand is harder and flatter than usual today?"

"What causes that?"

"I think it has to do with whether the tide is coming in or going out." We trod on through a few moments of silence. I felt as though I walked right where divine secrets stand outside the boundaries of place and time. It was good to share this space with Lil, who might be comforted or gladdened by it. Shared secrets to happiness can be more valuable than gems.

"I guess everyone has secrets," she said.

"Fish know the secrets of the ocean," I said.

"How do you know?"

"Just think about how the turtles return to find the same beach where they were born, to nest. It's a mystery!"

"I guess it's up to me to figure out for myself whether to keep a secret or not."

"All you can do is role model for her how to follow your own conscience," I said. "Like my son has done for me. Your vision simply reveals to me the cost of raising children with strict ideals."

In the distance we could hear thunder revealing itself to an anvil cloud. I wondered if that was why we did not find a turtle nest that morning.

Steve Kates

New Yorker Steve Kates earned his B.A. in Medieval and Renaissance French and English History from the Johns Hopkins University. He then earned his MBA ay Columbia University.

After a career in the advertising agency business, he and his wife Linda moved to Boca Raton, Florida in 1989 where Kates expanded his career horizons by filling several executive positions in corporations, the last as a COO of *Fit America* in Deerfield Beach. His daughter lives with her family in Boca Raton while his son and family reside in suburban New York.

After retiring from business in 2000, Steve became involved with the Institute for Learning in Retirement (ILIR) and was subsequently elected to its Board of Directors, as well as editor of its newsletter. He is also teaching a one semester course on Short Story Writing there.

Kates is the resident film critic and freelance feature writer for the *Boca Raton Observer*.

A frustrated writer for many decades, he has finally consummated his first love – words and the English language, which continues to keep him young.

A Father's Study

By Steve Kates

I tiptoed into my father's study. I swore I heard the old man say, "You might have had the courtesy to knock, first."

How many times had that same scenario been reenacted, me walking in, and my father remonstrating my lack of manners.

"Sorry," I murmured, surprising myself, since the room was empty. The study was dark, book-lined, claustrophobic, and the air was heavy with the residual smoke from my father's Havana cigars. What light might have crept in was effectively blocked by thick floor to ceiling drapes, which covered the four windows, as though to protect a religious shrine from the prying eyes of infidel intruders.

I pictured my father, seated at the carved partner's desk, explaining that he would soon die. "There's nothing they can give me now except painkillers. I expect you'll find me somewhat mellower over these next several months." Mellow? There was no narcotic in the world which could mellow my father even moderately, I had thought, suddenly feeling guilty at my insensitive reaction.

My father had been a commanding figure of authority for over twenty years, doling out punishment, criticism and humiliation. Ours had been a relationship based on mistrust, grudging but silent admiration, intellectual competitiveness, and a mutual devotion to my loving mother.

Just returned from the gravesite, I hastened to revisit my father's study, leaving my mother upstairs for a few moments while I bade a private goodbye. It was dry-eyed and brief, but deeply satisfying. As I scanned the sepulchral library, I was confronted with memories of tender and thoughtful gestures made by my father. The years of abuse and pain retreated from my consciousness, and I was able, for the moment, to mourn my father with love, rather than recrimination.

I knew this revisionism of our history would not last, but for this instant, it felt unaccountably good.

Uncle Louis - Savant

By Steve Kates

My great-uncle Louis was not a bright man. He might charitably have been characterized as a plodder. Of the five brothers and six sisters in his family, it was the boys who lacked the spark and imagination for achieving financial success. On the other hand, in an ironic genetic twist of fate, all of the six women were extremely successful, either by reason of their wits and talents, or by the directions and business acumen they provided for their husband's enterprises.

Also, they all had great legs.

Louis married early, had three children, was widowed young and lived to 91. I don't know what he did for a living in New York, but early in the twentieth century, he met a man there named Marcus Loew. They became fast friends and ardent pinochle playing buddies

One day, Loew came to Uncle Louie with a business proposition. He was investing in movie theaters, which, he said, would become a big profitable business. The film industry was dawning, and Loew saw this as the road to fortune. Uncle Louie gave this much deep thought, and justified his ultimate refusal with the rationale that no sane man would spend a Saturday afternoon in a dark room watching pictures, even ones that moved, when he could be out in the park or at the beach. This was typical of the corporate farsightedness of my uncle and, probably, his brothers, as well, and thus was a major family fortune unrealized.

I had heard this story many times across family dinner tables, and it was always told with a slight snicker and a rueful sigh of resignation. But my teenage imagination ran riot with the fiction of Uncle Louie having been shrewder and actually becoming a co-founder of Loew's, and thus an owner of Metro-Goldwyn-Mayer studios.

In my adolescent fantasy, I could have been S. Gordon Kates, boy Hollywood tycoon, a nepotistic triumph, producing major films, exhausted from fighting off eager starlets, cosseted and excessively well paid for life. I could have been the successor to Irving Thalberg! Of course, that was twenty years before I was even born.

Also, it never dawned on me for a moment that I totally lacked the compulsive venality imperative for survival in the film industry. I just knew about the glamour and the money, and it was a heady fantasy.

But, if Marcus Loew had befriended my grandmother, instead... hmmm.....

Edited by: Emily Rosen

Taking Care

By Steve Kates

My father died of a massive stroke at 83. Up to then, he had been in quite good health until the incident, which mercifully lasted only a week. Then he was gone, just like that. No contact, no tearful farewells, simply gone.

About a year earlier, he had taken me aside, and said, "If anything happens to me, I want to know that you'll take care of mother." I was struck by his obvious low opinion of me as a son, to think that I would do anything other than take care of my mother. But, given the sensitive topic and his penchant for sparring, even battling, I replied that, of course, I would, and let it go. As I look back, it never occurred to me to ask if something was wrong with him (there wasn't). Perhaps he entertained a particular petulance and resentment at my omission.

My mother went into a complete withdrawal after my father died. They had been married for 66 years, and, despite their overtly cool relationship, they were deeply in love. They had enormous respect for one another, yet they disagreed on almost every conceivable subject from raising a child to what kind of summer home they would like to own. He had a violent temper, and she was the moderator between my father and me in our seemingly endless disagreements. I think that acquired role aged her prematurely. Certainly, it could not have been pleasant.

I had always harbored the notion that my mother would not mourn my father very much. It was nothing she had ever said, just my own intuition that she would be, in a way, liberated by his death. Perhaps the timing was just off. She was 81, and already in either a deep depression or suffering from dementia. At any rate, she was not liberated. She just died emotionally when my father did.

I attempted to get her some help through a social services representative at the hospital, who was also a friend's daughter, but my mother would not even consider it. I thought she might want to go on a cruise, or to some place she'd never visited, but that, too, was out of the question.

She lived comfortably in her apartment, with her maid of many years, who was gentle and solicitous, and whom my mother trusted totally. After a few weeks, my mother would go to the hairdresser and get a manicure, but nothing else seemed to matter. She was taciturn in phone conversations, and chose to respond monosyllabically, giving (I think) what she thought were answers I wanted to hear ("did you eat dinner?" "yes"). I made it a practice to visit her at least once a week to see how she was faring. Our get-togethers were empty – no longer could I hold a conversation with my mother, and the things I wanted to discuss were, by now, beyond her capabilities.

Occasionally, my wife and I would take her out to dinner, but it was so difficult, and she responded so little, that we gave up on this form of diversion.

One time, my mother announced that she wanted to take piano lessons. "From whom" I asked. "From Hedy Spielter," she replied. "She's been dead for almost thirty years, now." I told her. Spielter had been my piano instructor when I was a child. "Besides," I added, "You don't have a piano." "I'll buy one," she said. The matter rested there, unresolved yet finalized, but I suddenly realized that this sad revelation, this fantasy probably represented a repressed childhood wish of my mother's, never fulfilled, but acted out in her grooming me to be a concert pianist.

My wife and I had gone away for a long weekend one summer, to visit the children at their camps in Maine. On our return, I called my mother, but when she answered, she moaned, totally unresponsive, as though drugged. I drove down to the city and went into the apartment. It was stifling. She did not have the air conditioning on, she was soiled and obviously in great physical distress. I called her physician, who sent an ambulance and we went to the hospital. She had been dehydrated, overheated and unfed. Clearly, she could not live alone as she was.

The doctor observed that she had been taking much too much of her medications. Presumably, she would forget that she had already dosed herself, and simply ingested more (I did not even want to think that this might have been deliberate, rather than merely absent-minded).

For better or worse, I was determined that my mother would not be relegated to a nursing home. I thought that, in her lucid moments, she would be more comfortable and content surrounded by her possessions and familiar things. I could not see her reduced to a statistic spending the rest of her life in a commons room in front of a television set.

The doctor, an old family retainer, got me to the social services people, again, and I arranged for round the clock live-in help for my mother, in addition to the maid.

On her return home, my mother had clearly deteriorated. She did not want to get dressed, she needed to be fed and bathed, and she sat in one or two chairs, seeing nothing, externally, and not speaking. She was fragile and shrunken, and very thin.

I alerted the practical nurses to make sure my mother got up and walked frequently, if only to avoid blood clots and get circulation going. They did this religiously, and just as religiously, gradually removed much of my mother's jewelry from her home.

"Take the jewelry out right away!" said my cousin, whom I though was just being venal and overly cautious. Would that I had listened to her. By the time my mother died, about 80% of her antique jewelry was gone. Because she did not go out, she no longer wore it, so there was no reason to notice its absence. I had no legal recourse, because there were three shifts, as well as substitutes when one or another of the women returned home to Guyana for a visit with family (no doubt bestowing lavish gifts of jewelry!).

Apart from the (at that time undetected) theft, the arrangement with the practical nurses seemed perfect for my mother's needs, and mine. She was bathed, fed, and generally well tended. There were a few incidents that were a bit unnerving, though. One night, at about 2:00 AM, my mother awoke and rang for the elevator. The elevator attendant alerted the nurse, who took her back in. The next day, we installed a very high bolt lock which my mother could not reach.

On some occasions, we brought our children to visit their grandmother, but she didn't even recognized them and, in retrospect, it must have been chilling and frightening for them to be so obliterated from someone's memory. We would bring in a dinner – chicken soup, hot dogs, easy stuff to accommodate the apartment's small galley kitchen.

My mother, generally a picky eater with little appetite, devoured the food we had brought. Only later did the doctor tell us that it was, of course, all the salt. She was on a salt-free regimen, and so things had little taste for her. The meals we brought in were laden with sodium, and so she rediscovered her taste buds. The doctor admonished me not to provide this sort of fare; I felt that at 82, if my mother enjoyed it, and given her deterioration, who cared?

My weekly visits were more duty-inspired than enjoyable. I paid the help, did the bills and paper work and checked on anything the household might need. But that was administrative and not emotional. The lump in my throat rose when one of the nurses showed me how she and my mother played "this little piggy" with her toes after her bath. I wanted to sit down and weep. I did not want to see my mother, who had been dynamic, witty and so intelligent, reduced to a blathering infant, miming some nonsense verse. This was not my mother; I did not even belong there any more.

I resented my mother for slipping away like this. There were so many things I wanted to tell her, to ask her, and to have her explain to me. With all of the family animosities and betrayals, I still wanted to tell her I loved her, and to hear that she loved me. I would never hear those words from her, again, as I did as a child, when she would sing a bedtime lullaby, or when I had done something especially pleasing for her.

The visits became shorter and more perfunctory. I would kiss her hello and goodbye, and hold her hand, but there was no outward sign of recognition. Mother was a shriveled specter, sitting in her navy cashmere robe, with thick, cataract eyeglasses that magnified her green eyes to an alarming degree. She was waiting to die, and I was waiting for her to do it.

At last, she, too, suffered a major stroke, and was hospitalized. The doctor told me that the hospital could not provide the kind of nursing care she would need, so I arranged for private nurses to attend her in the hospital, to turn her every few hours, adjust the feeding tubes, bathe her, and the like. That was in January. I went every day to pay the nurses, and to watch my mother disintegrate even more. Inwardly, I cried each time – I held her hand, hoping that she might return just for a moment to recognize me and smile, knowing that this would not happen.

Having been told that my mother would never recover, I gave up her apartment and had her things moved to my home. It was then that I realized just how much jewelry had been siphoned off by the undeserving and cynical caretakers. But they were things and at such a time, I no longer cared about them. My wife would have less, but these were fairly meaningless, though desirable, artifacts.

The doctor called to tell me what extraordinary nursing care my mother was receiving – without it, she would have already been dead. It was a bitter reminder of my struggle regarding pulling the plug or waiting it out. I could not pull that plug, nor order it done. I knew intellectually that it would have been sensible, even humane, but to me, it would have been matricide.

Finally, in March, the call came in the middle of the night that Mother had died. I don't know if I wept more from relief than grief, but at last, it was over for both of us.

The Walking Woman

By Steve Kates

She became, for us, part of the landscape, blending with trees, streets, shrubbery and ponds as she walked the roads of our hilly suburban community.

She was a slim, lean-legged woman, immaculately dressed, with gray blonde hair tied back into a long braided ponytail like those on the horse paintings of George Stubbs - something akin to knotted breads. In cooler weather, she wore a hat and a trench coat, and her face was always heavily made up, with jet-black eyebrows and bright red lip-gloss on her broad mouth.

Her footgear almost never varied from the flip-flops she sported, and no matter the outside conditions, she never carried an umbrella or, for that matter, a purse, but I do seem to remember a headscarf in colder or inclement weather.

When we had first moved to Larchmont, we noticed the woman only as a diligent exerciser who was up at the crack of dawn walking the town streets and roads, with routes extending to communities several miles away. Only little by little did we realize that her walking was not confined to a morning constitutional, but was, instead, a compulsion that had her on the move all day long, every day.

Once attuned to the obsessive ness of her behavior, we began to seek out other little characteristics of her long journeys. She never looked at her surroundings, but was focused, straight ahead, on her pathway. Nor did she even turn her head slightly to glance, once in a while, at a passing or oncoming car. Her pace was purposeful, but not terribly rapid - a fast saunter.

How many times did we pass her in our car and casually suggest that we stop and talk to her, to ask where she was going, or if we could give her a lift? But we never did. Instead, we began to fill the vacuum of her existence from our own fantasies and fictions.

Was she a jilted spinster who now roamed the countryside, unable to stop and come to terms with her rejection? Miss Haversham on the road? Did she find solace in the outdoors from a difficult or warring family at home? Did she live in a house or an apartment? Did she actually have a home?

When could (or did) she attend to the normal necessities of daily existence - food shopping, using a bathroom, bathing, bill paying, banking, even purchasing her heavily used cosmetics?

Was she an outpatient from some obscure mental facility who was allowed to walk by day as a means of dealing with her demons? Had she any family, friends, or even caretakers, in her seemingly barren life?

Our inventions grew ever more bizarre and fanciful. She served as a springboard for our collective imaginations and storytelling instincts.

Gradually, over a period of years, she became a fixture, and, thus, somewhat boring. Our commentaries were now merely redundant, and we had run out of scenarios and even concern.

We have been gone from Larchmont for fourteen years. On occasional visits back, we have seen our walking lady, like a fondly remembered animal at the edge of a wood, and the only response she elicits now is one of comparative satisfaction that she is still there and hardy, rather like a memory chip from our years in the community. She is a link to part of our past, but of no other personal interest to us.

What richness of communication did we miss by not making contact with our lady? What subtle social service might we have performed merely by stopping to chat? And of course, what would have been her response to any of our overtures? These are answerless questions, but the curiosity still lingers, for how long, we do not know. But surely, it will be with us after our walking lady finally comes to a halt, and vanishes forever.

John Kenney

John Kenney started his technical career in 1969 with System Development Corporation (SDC) of Paramus, N.J., as a technical publications analyst, responsible for abstracting information from technical publications dealing with computer technology and acting as the resource person for information needed by various SDC personnel.

SDC, a spin-off of the Rand Corporation, .was one of the firms with a contract from Advanced Research Project Agency (ARPA) to develop a communication system for North American Air Defense Command (NORAD). Out of much of the work, the Internet was formed.

From 1969 to 1987, Mr. Kenney worked for IBM in the Components Division in Fishkill, N.Y. In 1978 he was transferred to Boca Raton, Florida where an independent IBM unit developed the first IBM Person al Computer. Mr. Kenney's title at this time was Information Developer, and he was a member of the design team that developed PC-DOS.

During his IBM career, Mr. Kenney received an area manager's award for his initiative in installing the first Script Text Processing system used by the IBM publications department at the Boca Raton facility.

He also received an award for solving some particularly difficult problems that arose during the production of the Version 2.1 PC-DOS software manuals

After taking an early retirement from IBM, Mr. Kenney was hired by Florida Atlantic University from 1989 to 1994 as a database administrator.

Since 1994 Mr. Kenney has volunteered to teach computers at Senior Network

My Mother

By Jack Kenney

My mother's girlish figure and classic features are apparent even in the black and white photographs of the time. Because the nuns liked her, I thought her beauty and provocative way of dressing were okay.

As a boy, I thought it was a big plus that my mother never kissed me. This way I did not have to submit to the taunts and jeers the other boys went through after coming back from visiting their parents with lipstick all over them. Nobody was ever going to call me a sissy.

My mother was widowed in 1930 after my father died of tuberculosis. Shortly after, I contacted polio when I was four years old. I dimly recall seeing my father visiting us at home from Saranac Lake. I can recall him taking me to the circus, combing my hair. In photographs he is usually smiling and appears to be well built, athletic, and handsome. Several of the photographs show him carrying either me or my brother when we were babies.

There are also many photographs of him, my mother, and other young relatives and friends dressed in swim suits at Coney Island or Rockaway Beach. My father had a big family, but I never met them.

Whenever I asked my mother about my father's side of the family, an iron curtain would fall. There was no contact between the two families after my father's death. During this time, we lived in a series of Brooklyn apartments as my mother continuously sought lower rental units, mostly in two-family houses. I can remember her banging on the pipes for more heat in the winter. I distinctly recall the (NRA) National Recovery Act advocates staging big parades with huge flags in support of President Roosevelt's anti-depression measures. I can remember Roosevelt's CCC and WPA, young men begging in the streets, a salesman pleading with a customer to buy something. These memories will always haunt me.

Our family at that time consisted of me, my two-year-old brother James, my grandmother, and my mother. Often we shared our apartment with a male boarder who would rent one of the rooms. I was suddenly introduced to my sister, Cecilia, one day in 1931 when my mother carried her home, put her down on the front porch of our upstairs apartment, and said, "This is your little baby sister." My sister was then eighteen months old. As was her habit, my mother never did give us a credible explanation of where my sister had been all that time. This was a presage of things to come.

My mother was one of the fortunate few who had a job during the depression when the unemployment rate was about twenty-five percent. She told us years later that employees felt sorry for her because she was a widow with three children and her mother to support.

Under Roosevelt's share-the-work program she was able to get a job as a part-time telephone operator working twenty hours a week and sharing it with someone else who worked the other twenty hours. Later she worked full time .

My grandmother had some money which my mother eventually inherited. My Aunt Joe and Uncle Jack lived on Bergen Street and I would often visit them by trolley or when they were within walking distance. My Uncle Jack ran a speakeasy in his cellar and sold homemade beer and wine to cops and politicians. After prohibition was repealed, he had enough money to live on for the rest of his life.

My mother made no distinction between fiction and the truth when telling a story. She said times were rough during the depression, and I believe that to be true. From 1930 to 1933, I was confined to New York hospitals for periods ranging from one to several months. She would take me to a hospital for a physical, and then surreptitiously walk out while the doctor was examining me.

Either she or my grandmother would visit once in a while and I held on tight to my mother's hand. But she would pull away from me and leave. In my loneliness I wanted to hang onto anybody or anything from outside the hospital walls. I can recall waving from a fourth story window for hours at people walking on the sidewalk below.

I did not know it at that time, but St. Charles Orthopedic hospital in Hicks Street, Brooklyn, was a staging point for children being sent to St. Charles hospital in Port Jefferson, Long Island. The Hicks Street hospital consisted of two wards, one for boys and one for girls

The boys ward was a long, rectangular room that accommodated about fifty boys ranging in age from about seven to fifteen. I was in bed most of the time, but some of the children could get around on crutches or wheel chairs. I was then seven years old and the younger children were subjected to much bullying by the older boys.

A nun would show a motion picture in the ward on a Friday night. She would hold her hand in front of the projector during kissing scenes. Sometimes she would remove her hand too soon and all the kids would yell. Aside from that I do not remember any other fun things about that hospital. I don't recall the last time I saw my mother before I was bundled into the car on that cold December night in 1933 for my trip to Port Jefferson, about one hundred miles away.

Years later she told me she could not afford my medical treatments and St. Charles in Port Jefferson, Long Island was the best place for me. I always thought that one day my mother would send for me. I did not have any more surgery or medical treatments after 1937, my last four years at the hospital.

The nuns would send a postcard to my mother's Brooklyn address telling her that I was recovering from an operation, and what a brave little boy I was. I did not see her until her next monthly visit. It was only after I came home in 1941 that I found out the entire family lived in an affluent home in suburban New Jersey., and that lack of money was no longer a problem to her. Shortly after coming home, she told me that I had been a lot of trouble to the family.

During her visits my mother talked with everyone--parents, nuns, and children--in the outgoing, vivacious manner she was so capable of assuming. I don't know exactly when I first noticed a change in her behavior.

In the fall of 1936 on one of her monthly visits my mother was accompanied by a man she called Frank. He appeared to be about thirty-five or forty years old. No introductions were ever made, and I did not know his surname or what to call him. Affable and good looking, he usually wore fashionable sports clothes and always drove a new car. He was trim, of medium height, and dressed in a jacket, tie, white shoes, gray fedora, and trousers that appeared to be slightly crumpled after a long drive. He incessantly smoked cigars, but I didn't mind that. I liked the smell of cigar smoke. I was quite pleased to go back to the hospital ward with the smell of cigar smoke clinging to me. I felt like a real man.

My mother and Frank would park their car about a half-mile away from the hospital and walk through the hospital gate leading to the main entrance. My mother cautioned me to not to tell the nuns about the car. If they asked, I was to say it was owned by my grandmother. Whenever the receptionist in the parlor asked in a friendly way if they had come by train, they always said yes. My mother seemed increasingly vague when answering questions. She commented with some asperity that the nuns were very nosy.

We often went for a ride in the car. After their visit, Frank would drive the car to a point about a hundred yards from the hospital gate and drop me off. I always walked back to the hospital entrance alone, even when I was on crutches.

Occasionally, my younger brother and sister would come to visit. I was frequently annoyed at their evasive and indefinite answers to friendly questions from the nuns. Sister Thomas, the school principal, once asked them what school they attended. They gave different answers mentioning different schools. Sister Thomas questioned me closely afterward as to whether they really went to Catholic school. To the nuns it was a disgrace for any Catholic to go to a public school. I was embarrassed and irritated. I had always been proud of the fact that my brothers and sisters went to Catholic schools.

I was beginning to feel a bit uneasy. Something was going on, but what was it? I was sure my mother was behind all this. She was beginning to act like the mother I knew from the past. I tried not to think about some dark secrets that still lay half-buried in my subconscious.

MMM

Impure Thoughts

By Jack Kenney

The nuns were obsessed with sex. Never once did they write or verbalize that particular word. Impure thoughts are what they talked about, day after day, as they lectured us during catechism class. Never once did they ever give us a specific example of an impure thought. The chaplain with his heavy French accent gave numerous sermons about "dirty 'tings" as he called them. After hearing all this, I had to make up my own mind about impure thoughts We were told that an impure thought could come unbidden into our minds, but if we deliberately held on to the impure thought for longer than a minute or so, it was a mortal sin.

I constantly worried about impure thoughts. Did I look at that kid for more than a minute when I accidentally opened the bathroom door? I giggled and laughed when another kid farted. Had I committed a mortal sin? The priest said that even perusing a modern newspaper was a perilous adventure for the soul. We were only allowed to read the sports pages, but what about that picture of the sexy girl in advertisement? Was I allowed to look and did I look away fast enough? That older kid told a dirty joke. Was that an example of one of the dirty things the priest was talking about?

We only saw two or three religious movies during my entire childhood. They once showed a movie called King of Kings. Before the showing of the movie Sister Thomas talked to our sixth grade class warning us by saying, "The impurities, oh!" While viewing the movie, I tried to connect the dots. I could not figure out what she was talking about, unless it was about the actress who played the part of Mary Magdalene. I found her to be bewitching and delightful. If watching her was impure, then why did they show the film? I decided that, since it was a religious film, there was no sin in watching it.

The nuns would also complain that the radio played nothing but love songs. This was cited as an indication of what a depraved world we lived in.

We also had to be careful of words. A mild expletive was a venial sin. But we were informed that certain words were mortal sins. We were never given a list. The nuns would not let me keep a cowboy book that someone had given me because it contained the word, "darn."

One day our class teacher, Sister Thomas, gave us a lecture about girls out in the world who wore their skirts three inches above the knees. What these girls didn't realize, apparently, is that people were sinning all around them. I suddenly thought of my mother.

It was always the same. Once a month on a Sunday, someone would shout out my name and I would look up and see a cluster of nuns waiting for someone to emerge from the parlor where visitors first came through the hospital door. The nuns in their Dutch-cleanser uniforms reminded me of a bunch of penguins. That meant only one thing. My mother was here! The nuns did not cluster together like this for anyone else's mother.

I raced toward the parlor in my eagerness to see her. My mother was completely oblivious to the fact that all the nuns were watching her. I think they were fascinated by this woman, so unlike them with their drab uniforms and regimented lives. My mother appeared free and uninhibited.

She was taller than all of the nuns and walked in confidently, not at all conscious of the sensation she was causing. She had a slender body, shapely legs, and wore her colorful silk skirt several inches above the knees. Her movements were graceful and natural. One of the nuns had once told me she liked the fact that my mother did not wear rouge or lipstick. But, my mother's cheeks were always a bit rosy and her lips were a beautiful red. Her eyes had a greenish tint and she flashed her dazzling smile as she passed by the nuns in the waiting room. When she spoke, everyone went silent, not wanting to miss a word as she greeted the nuns with a charm that she was capable of adopting for the occasion.

Even as a child I realized she was very different from the other mothers. Invariably one of the nuns would shake her head and mutter in her French accent: "Young girl, vah!"

After my mother visited me, I wondered about all the impure thoughts floating up to the heavens and how the good Lord was keeping track of all these sins for the final judgment day.

Friendships

By Jack Kenney

True friendships among boys at St. Charles were not all that common. Two or more kids would form a group and sit together sharing sweets or cookies from their parents. These friendships were especially precious, and I was sometimes invited to join a group. I felt privileged to participate—candy, cookies, or sweets were a special delicacy since they were so unavailable. Despite the many kids around, I needed someone for support. Also, some kids banded together for protection, like tribes. Friendships at St. Charles were often long-lasting.

A large majority of the boys and girls at St. Charles were white and Catholic. The state paid some of the cost, so the hospital admitted black children and those of other religions. Race and religion played no part in determining who would make friends with whom, however. Isolation had a few advantages. We were not infected by the prejudice that we found in the outside world after we came home. Once we got used to it, skin color became a characteristic that had no more significance than the color of one's hair.

Randall Harris and Richie Brodie were two black guys I knew fairly well. I regarded Randall as a genius because he was a good mechanic who could fix almost anything.

He came to St. Charles when he was about eleven years old, so he knew a lot more than the other kids. He could mimic anyone on the radio, he could also imitate the sound of a bugle to perfection, and he could play the harmonica. Carmine DeMorey, a blind guy, was his best friend.

Carmine, a big, strongly-built boy, could see shadows. He would walk with his head slightly inclined toward the ground while glancing back and forth. He resembled a bear. I can still hear his deep voice imitating Amos and Andy as he and Randall would laugh together. I envied Carmine's ability to read books at night in the dormitory when all the lights were off. He knew Braille.

Randall was a good carpenter. One time he made a sled from an ordinary wagon by taking the wheels off, fastening runners onto it, and altering the steering mechanism in some way to steer it.

When the first snowfall came in December they were eager for a sleigh ride. Carmine wanted to steer. For the trial run Randall chose a steep hill leading from the chapel to the yard. Reluctantly, he yielded to Carmine's entreaties and let him steer.

With Carmine at the helm, the homemade sled hit a tree. Carmine suffered a broken nose, but fortunately Randall Harris was not seriously hurt. Randall's injuries could have been especially serious because he had soft bones due to rickets.

The nuns never got over talking about that incident. They did not understand how Randall could let a blind guy steer. I admit that at the time I thought it was the dumbest thing I ever heard of. Years later, I asked Randall about this incident after meeting him at an alumni meeting. He smiled sheepishly and said he had hoped nothing would happen or he could intervene in time. He did not have the heart to tell Carmine that he could not steer.

The other black guy, Richie Brodie, was in my class and also suffered from polio. Richie's school grades were good, but his best subject was religion. In fact, he got the highest marks in religion every year. The trouble was that he was a Protestant. The nuns taught us that most Protestants would go to a place called limbo when they died, but many would not even go there unless they sincerely believed theirs was the one true religion. Since only Catholics practiced the one true religion, most Protestants would probably go to hell. Father Rondon, the hospital chaplain, was very concerned and made it his mission in life to save Richie Brodie.

The hospital chaplain was always dressed in black clerical garments. He appeared tall when standing next to the nuns and projected a formidable image. He was stern and uncompromising about most things, but particularly matters of religion. During Masses, he gave many hellfire and brimstone sermons. However, he fancied himself an intellectual and many of his sermons were incomprehensible to us.

After each meal of the day he smoked exactly one cigarette He never varied his routine of three cigarettes a day. When one of the boys said that his father could not give up cigarettes, Father Rondon bluntly replied, "That's because he has no will power."

Father Rondon was a stamp collector, as were many of the boys. This is how we found out about his genial side. We soon learned to be wary of trading stamps with him. He took great delight in getting the better of the deal. This is when his stern visage would miraculously change as he savored his victory with a smile of great satisfaction.

Another thing he liked to do was ask trick questions in the hope we would give him the wrong answer. When we did, he would say, "Hah, you fell into my little trap." He would then flash a triumphant grin and laugh out loud with a mighty "Ha, ha, ha!" His seeming victory was lost on us most of the time. We assumed he must be very intelligent and that's why we couldn't understand him.

Often he would walk up quietly behind a boy and flick his ear with his finger. When the boy would turn around muttering an imprecation, Father Rondon would laugh in delight at the boy's discomfiture. He also took great pride in training a new altar boy. If the boy first served at morning mass, Father Rondon came down to the yard during recreation with a long list of mistakes which he would meticulously review with the boy. He seemed to enjoy these sessions very much.

Father Rondon took a personal interest in Richie Brodie. That's when he again revealed a genial nature. He seemed to genuinely like Richie and wanted him go to heaven. Also, he thought it was a shame that a Protestant got the highest marks in religion every year.

He desperately tried to convert Richie to Catholicism. The priest talked to Richie's mother one visiting day. But much to Father Rondon's chagrin, Richie's mother, a strict Baptist, adamantly refused to allow her son to be baptized a Catholic.

I can still see Father Rondon shaking his head in sorrow on the day Richie went home, and asking us all to pray that Richie Brodie's mother would relent and let her son become a Catholic. I had never known Father Rondon to take such an interest in a child.

After seven years at St. Charles Father Rondon became seriously ill, and his superiors decided to send him back to the Holland where he was born. He refused to allow any farewell reception. However, on the day he was leaving, one of the nuns hastily rounded up all of the children to wish him a parting goodbye. He did not appear pleased. "You should not have done this sister," he said testily as he walked slowly toward the car. He took off his glasses to wipe them and that's when I noticed his eyes were moist. Only one other time had I noticed the merest suggestion of a tear. That was on the day he told us that Mrs. Brodie had refused to let her son become a Catholic.

Irene Kessler

Irene was born and brought up in New York City. She is the mother of three and grandmother of four children. She attended Performing Arts High School in the drama department even though her musical talents appeared at a very young age. The Eastman School of Music at the University of Rochester honed those talents during her studies there. During the next few years, music studies continued at the Third Street Music School in New York under scholarship. Vocal work, opera coaching, and opera workshops for performance skills filled these years. Irene went on to sing with many opera companies in the United States and Europe. A life-long interest in psychology resulted in a return to school where she quickly completed her Master's and PhD degrees. Years of working with a predominately female population peaked her interests in women's issues, particularly the oppression of women and the feminine. Irene's dream is to produce a book and a play addressing how this oppression is perpetrated in different countries around the world and its effect on women's feelings and behaviors.

In My Own Voice

By Irene Kessler

My time in this realm is growing shorter and although my intention, which I laid claim to when I learned to subtract, is still to reach age 100, I don't know how long it will take me to write this, so I've decided to get started. There is a lot I "have" to say.

My mother was called to school when I was in first grade. I met her at the principal's office not knowing why I was summoned. The principal offered me a chair. I didn't know whether to feel grown up or sink down in it until I disappeared. He spoke to my mother for a while. I have no idea what they talked about; I was too scared to listen to grown-up talk. Then he turned to me. "Why do you talk so much in class," he asked. I took a moment to consider his questions and replied, "Because I have a lot to say." That moment went down in the family history book. My father always said that I was vaccinated with a phonograph needle. For those of you who do not know, a phonograph was the first invention used to play recorded music and sound. It had a round turntable and a needle you placed on the record. My father had a very dry sense of humor.

I have entitled this *In My Own Voice* because that is the essence and the reward of my life's journey, the journey of growth from a child who was able to tell the principal her thoughts, to one who learned not to speak up.

I have spent most of my adult life trying to recapture the little girl who could express herself. I want my children to really know me as a person, not just as their mother. I also want my grandchildren and those who follow to know about the times in which I lived and how my life was influenced by those times.

It was not until my grandparents passed away that I realized I had so many questions I wanted to ask, and that I never really knew them. They made perilous journeys from Europe as teenagers traveling alone, or with brothers and sisters, to reach this country and they never talked about it. I am really sorry I let that opportunity pass and I don't want that to happen to my progeny..

My journey was not from country to country but in many respects it feels the same in the end. Mine was not the shock of a whole new life but a slow and fairly steady path as if I were being pushed and prodded from an unknown source. I am not denying that there is also this need in me to write all of this down. Perhaps it will give me more insights and understanding of my life for it has certainly been quite a trip!

I can only tell this story from my own experience, through my own eyes and so it may sound like I am blaming. There were many years when I was angry and I did fault others. I now know that it is a waste of time and energy to blame, and that in the end I must take full responsibility. I will try to explain what I learned from my many encounters with life.

The only thing I know for sure is that I don't know. The more I learn, the more questions I have. The more I learn, the more I want to learn. I want to know everything, to understand everything. Most of all, I want to know myself, heal myself and complete this journey a better person than when I started questioning.

I believe that life is about growth, growing by learning. As Lao Tzu, the man who wrote the Tao said, "That which is perfect is dead." I think he was saying that if you are perfect, there is no more you have to learn and without the need to learn, there is no reason to live. I certainly have never been nor expect to be perfect. All I can do is to continue to make myself a better person.

MMM

Always In My Heart

By Irene Kessler

I wanted to scream "STOP". But she had already thrown out all his stuff. "What are you doing?" I yelled.

"I don't want anything around. I don't want anything left in this house," she replied.

It was too late. His clothes and personal items were already bagged, tied, and sent to Good Will before I'd even arrived at the house.

I plunked down on the bed. She had done it again, thrown stuff out without asking if I wanted any of it. The one thing I managed to salvage was his shirt and only because I was so hot when we returned from his funeral that I went into his closet and pulled out one of his short-sleeved shirts that went with my skirt.

"Is that the only tangible thing I will ever have of his?" I thought. I needed to touch and feel and smell the scent of my father. I wasn't ready to let go of him just yet Even eighty-seven years was not enough.

Two months later my brother called and asked "Would you like to have Dad's watch?"

"So that's where all the stuff went," I thought. It was OK to give it to the male in the family. That figures!

"Of course," I cried, tears streaming down my face. "Mom didn't save anything for me. I would love to have it."

One year later I was visiting in New York City and while walking, I tripped on a raised portion of the gutter, and went flying into a fire hydrant. Luckily, I was not hurt, except for sore shoulders and arms that had braced me, but the watch was shattered.

Now, all these years later, I understand that having him in my heart has proved to be enough.

MMM

My Brother

By Irene Kessler

I was eight when they brought this ugly looking thing home. And they put it in my room. There it was, wriggling, squirming and crying--- in *my* room. It belonged to them. Why wasn't it in *their* room? Was I being punished? Did I do something wrong? Was I a bad girl?

During the next few weeks, my room was invaded by visitors spending hours it seemed, gawking at this thing and making the stupidest sounds I had ever heard.

That would not have been so bad except for the fact that the room was very small. Having visitors in the room practically pushed me out the door. My mother was able to fit my bed and my brother Jay's crib across from each other on the two long walls and a tall chest of drawers on the short wall to the right of the door as you came in. There was a large casement window on the other short wall which allowed us to not only check the weather, but look down twelve stories to see what was happening in the outside world. To the right of the chest was a small closet in which my school skirts and blouses were neatly hanging, and my two pair of shoes were lined up on the floor. My coat was in the closet in the entry foyer to the apartment.

If I thought he was a pain in the neck when he was born, I had a lot to learn. It was not long before he figured out that if he held his bottle by the nipple and twirled it around as hard as he could, the nipple would pull out of the bottle, sending the bottle flying, with the result that my bed and parts of the room and floor were splattered with milk. I would come home from school to the smell of soured milk because sometimes the bottle landed on my bed so quietly that my mother never noticed it.

Jay worked hard at figuring out his next great trick. First he learned to pull down his diaper. He worked at it for weeks, finally freeing that squirming little body from its imprisonment. Thank goodness that took a while, because his next discovery was that he could pee between the bars of the crib.

While performing this wonder, he laughed heartily. I would swear that he was trying to reach my bed which was directly across from his, and I was thankful that he was never able to accomplish that feat. So now, cleaning my bedroom floor was added to my list of household chores.

As a toddler he was no less of a terror. Learning to climb out of the crib was the beginning of the end. On Sunday mornings, when the rest of us were trying to sleep late, he would quietly sneak out of the room and go to the kitchen. The routine went something like this: the rest of us would wake up and go to the kitchen for breakfast to find Jay sitting on the floor surrounded by anything he could get his hands on. The list included silverware, pots, pans and covers, ajax, brillo, ink, cereal, newspaper, soap, etc. while the cabinets and the floor and Jay himself, were covered with his modernistic artwork.

My mother would then yell at me for allowing this to happen. But this was one of the few times in my life when I yelled back. In my loudest voice, I told her that I had the right to sleep on a Sunday, and he was her son, not mine.

The kitchen had to be cleaned before we could eat, so my father and I would get dressed and go out to get breakfast goodies. If I could, I would have encouraged my brother to do this more often because that was a special time I had to be alone with my father, something that did not happen very often.

Jay's next trick was a dangerous one and included the screened casement window in *our* --- yes, I finally had to admit that he was here to stay --- bedroom.. My brother could not reach the upper part of the windows but he did figure out how to open the bottom portion. My mother walked into the room one day to find him sitting on the open bottom window with his little feet pushing out against the screen as if to loosen it from its bindings. It was as if he were determined to escape from the controlling elements in our household and fly away.

Considering the fact that we lived on the twelfth floor, thirteenth if you count the lobby floor, this could have been disastrous. I am amazed that the fire department didn't hear and respond to her screams. My father tried a number of ways to secure this part of the window but my brother always seemed to find a way to undo it. Finally he tied it with a thickish rope which he then wrapped around the bottom of the radiator and my brother's plot was foiled.

I wish I could say that things improved as he got older. Even now, at age 61, he still gets into trouble. These days it is with the stock market.

MMM

Depression

By Irene Kessler

Dear Erik, Ira and Sue,

We have never talked about those Sundays. Do you even remember them? You were so young. I cannot picture what it must have been like for you because I am unable to picture myself or my actions during those periods. I know what they feel like now, so I assume it must have been similar back then.

My body feels heavy, enclosed in a prison whose bars are so near they do not allow any movement of my limbs. My mind is dull with no desire or energy to focus on anything. My emotional faculties are numbed and vacant as if I am in a trance. There is a hole, an empty place where my stomach belongs. Every once in a while the hole becomes a tornado with wrenching and spasms over which I have no control.

When I was younger I could force myself to come out of it, especially when you or your Dad needed me, but now it gets harder to break through to the real world. Although my bouts with this other self are now rare, when she does takes over, I have little desire to push myself to come out of it and fewer reasons to want to. While I can sense somewhat what I am like, I can not imagine what you saw and felt.

One of the vivid pictures I do have because it happened on a regular basis is Sunday mornings when we were summoned to spend the day with either set of your grandparents.

I always felt tremendous pressure to have everything just right. I knew the expectation was that we were all supposed to look as if we just stepped out of a perfect picture with every hair in place. As I write this I wonder if things would have been better when I was a child if I could have stayed in that picture forever. Always aware of the weight of the demands I felt, but not understanding their source, I would start the washing and dressing routine with you, Sue, my baby. Since you were the youngest, and a girl, my notion was that you would be least liable to get into trouble and ruin my efforts. I would always smile when I put the pink bow in your hair, which you had to have from the day of your birth. It signified 'female' to the world. In the meantime, your Dad was reading the Sunday New York Times.

Ira, you were next. You always wiggled and squirmed when I had to dress you but you never stayed still in my womb either. I was positive I was having twins. Grandpa even took out twin insurance with Lloyd's of London just in case. Clothes were not important to you. Foremost in your mind was what you were going to play with next. You hated when I combed your hair and you would take your little hand and mess it up as soon as I was finished. In the meantime, Dad read the newspaper.

Finally, it was your turn Erik. You were last because I knew I could depend on you not to get too mussed up. As the oldest, you seemed to have some understanding of the need to get cleaned up and get some clothes on so we could go out. You were so handsome in your man-tailored long pants that your great-grandfather lovingly made, and your bow-tie. I don't think you liked all the fuss. You were just willing to put up with it. In the meantime, Dad took his shower.

Now it was time for me. While I showered, put on makeup, did my hair and got dressed, the three of you did a great job of being children. You played, cavorted, jumped up and down, took out every toy you collectively owned, fought over them, raided the snacks and generally had a terrific time. In the meantime, Dad got dressed.

By the time I finished primping and preening and convincing myself that I was now ready to face the eyes that would tear me apart looking for any flaw, you were all a mess. I took each of you in turn in an effort to try to resurrect your previous perfection. In the meantime, Dad was finishing the newspaper.

During the time it took to redress all of you, I would feel myself slipping into another state. My head would begin to ache, my stomach churned, my ears rang and all of my senses became dull. Without planning it or even being aware, I would slip away from the present and find myself in different state of being. In my head I removed myself to find refuge and safety in numbness, even as I was getting you all ready to leave the house.

Memories Milestones and Memoirs

By the time we got to where we were going, I had little connection to what was going on around me. I would wonder if I were acting in a normal way. No one ever said anything so I assumed I made sense and was able to hide whatever this weird thing was that was happening to me. In the meantime, Dad was...somewhere.

I Love Chocolate

By Irene Kessler

Don't let anyone tell you they have no secrets. Everyone has both big and small ones. Here is one of mine that I have never told a soul even though, looking back, it doesn't seem to have been such a terrible thing. I guess I am still carrying the shame and guilt of my ten year old self.

I started to gain weight after my brother was born. I am not blaming him, but I do think the two are connected. I was the first child and first grandchild and so I got all the attention in the family until I was eight and one half. All of a sudden I had to share it. By the time I was ten, my mother became very concerned with my size. Her solution was to hide all the cookies. Of course, I found all her hiding places.

This hunt for sugar and chocolate changed me. I even started eating sugar right out of the bowl. I would wet my finger with saliva, dip it in and lick it off. My weight continued to rise and more stringent measures were undertaken. My mother thought she won the power struggle by not buying sweets unless we were having company.

My cravings were so great that they were painful. All I could think about was eating those forbidden things. My mother would send me to the corner grocery store, which was in the middle of the block. I would look at all the things I loved and price them. I had no money of my own, since I did not get an allowance, but I wanted them as I had never wanted anything else. So I started taking money from my parents.

I would wait until the day I knew I was going to baby-sit for my brother and I would buy a chocolate cake mix and a small can of chocolate frosting. That was the cheapest thing I could find that would satisfy me.

I went through a rash of feelings while waiting for my parents to leave. The shame and guilt were easily offset by the imminent excitement of my adventure and the anticipated ecstasy of filling my body with the pleasures of chocolate. My baker's hat was on my head before the front door closed.

Out came the mixing bowl, eggs, water, butter and pans for my masterpiece. I carefully mixed the ingredients and got it all ready. I put the cake in the oven to bake. I had to be careful because I could not afford to make a mess in this kitchen that was cleaned from top to bottom and had the wooden countertops waxed with a machine on a daily basis.

I would then clean up the few things I used, put them away and turn to putting my brother to bed. The waiting was excruciating for the cake had to cool before I could proceed. After it cooled, I would apply the frosting as quickly as I could, first on the lower layer and then on top and down the sides, and then at last, I sat down to savor my lopsided success. I stuffed myself until I could not eat any more and took the rest to the incinerator, the place where they burned the garbage. The remaining utensils were cleaned and replaced in their appropriate spots and I got into bed completely happy.

One night, after I went through my baking routine, I came back to the kitchen to see if the cake was ready to be frosted and there were bugs all over the kitchen. I panicked. I could not figure out where the bugs were coming from. I frantically started cleaning them up fearful of how I could possibly explain their presence in my mother's pristine kitchen.

With horror, out of the corner of my eye, I spied them coming out of the cake. As fast as they appeared, I killed them and down the sink they went. It seemed like an eternity before they finally stopped. Yet again, I put the kitchen back in order but a bit more carefully this time. Then I sat down to consider the cake. All the bugs were gone. The cake had to be perfectly fine now. Should I throw it out? How could I possibly deprive myself of the treat I looked forward to all day and worked so hard to make? Could I take a chance that I would eat bugs? Would I taste them? Would it be dangerous? Would I get sick? It didn't matter. None of it mattered. I had to have that cake. And I did.

This was the power struggle I had with my mother and I felt that I had to win even if I ate bugs. I now realize how my feelings of deprivation were connected to my life-long battle with food and weight. This was the secret I had kept even from myself.

Perhaps it took too long, but I was finally able to face up to my sweet secret. It took a lot of digging and talking before I could wean myself away from the need for chocolate. Today I can eat it in moderation because I now understand what triggered my addiction and I have learned how to handle all the destructive thoughts that want to bring me back to that old self.

And now that I've lost all that excess weight, I certainly wouldn't want to eat bugs --- er I mean – all that bad stuff again.

Joan Krukewitt

I grew up in a small community in Ohio. I am number nine of twelve siblings. We lived in a two bedroom house with a path to the outhouse. It's taken me many years to look past the hardships of my childhood and come to appreciate the self reliance I was forced to develop.

I married at 18 and for more than 25 years. I was a dutiful wife and a devoted mother to three daughters. I divorced at age 44 and began a new life. I went back to school, began to date again, traveled much of the world and eventually remarried.

My husband recently retired and I'm enjoying my new freedom – golf, grandchildren and writing.

MMM

What's In A Name?

By Joan Krukewitt

"What's in a name? A rose…"

I could just say my name is Joan but it isn't. My name is Joann but with one "n".

I didn't attend kindergarten (I don't know if they had them back then). I started school in the first grade with no knowledge of letters, not even enough to spell my own name.

My first grade teacher, Mrs. Beath, taught me to spell "Joann" with one "n". So much for Mrs. Beath's command of spelling.

You are probably wondering how Mrs. Beath got to decide the spelling of my name. It's simple. I was born at home, delivered by my grandmother, number 9 of 12 children and there was no birth certificate, no record of my birth until I had one made at age eighteen.

Mother, and older sister and family Bible accompanied me to the courthouse as I recorded my birth. I now had proof that I lived--Joann but with one "n".

"What'll we name this one?" must have been the question asked that frosty morn in January.

My oldest sister, Pauline, got to name me. (She would have been about 13 at the time.)

"Let's name her Marjorie for Aunt Madge, and I like the name Joann." So Marjorie Joan it was.

I doubt that they knew or cared what a pain-in-the-neck that name would become.

Marjorie--is that spelled with an "ie" or a "y'? "And you say Joann but with only one 'n?' Let's go over this again."

To add more confusion to the issue, I never use my first name unless it's on legal documents. "No, Joan is my middle name, Marjorie is my first name that's "ie" not "y"."

Thankfully my maiden name was rather common--Rodgers. Well, maybe not so common, it's spelled with a "d".

In my first marriage. I got "Boggs" for a handle. That name, like its' owner, bogged me down and I finally submerged after 27 years.

Nine years ago I acquired a new name. "Krukewitt." What a mouthfull! Now I get to spell that too.

Yes, Marjorie is my first name, but I only use it on wills. That's spelled with an "ie" not a "y." Yes, Joann does only have one "n." That's "K..r..u.. k"--no, not "K..u..r..k." The pronunciation is like "crew cut." Yes, that's "K..r..u..k, then an "e" that sounds like an "a" and "w..i..t..t--that's wit as in "dim" or in "nit".

MMM

Growing Up Number 9 In A Dozen

By Joan Krukewitt

The humor, the tongue in cheek wit, the good natured banter is what I love to remember about growing up number nine of a dozen. How wonderful to be surprised, to be pulled off balance by wit, to know you've just been zinged or put in your place--and to know at a deeper level you only zing or tease people you love.

Now that I'm grown, I know this is how we showed our affection for each other because we were never outwardly demonstrative.

My mother was quite reserved--she was still a virgin although she'd given birth twelve times. She was a lady and found no humor in anything off-color.

Dad delighted in shocking Mom. He'd look slyly at us kids, sometimes wink and then say something completely outrageous. Mom would recoil as if slapped and then give him the "you are nothing but dirt" look down her nose. He'd howl!

So innocently, so nonchalantly he'd say things like, "You know, you can always tell the size of a truck driver's dick by his belt buckle. The bigger his buckle, the little'r his dick!"

To this day, big buckles make me recall Dad's theory.

Mom was often funny without trying to be so. I remember vividly, I was grown, married and about seven months pregnant. Dad, my younger sister, Linda, and I were at the kitchen table having coffee. Mom, as usual, was up waiting on us and Dad lit a cigarette.

"You know you shouldn't smoke. You know it's bad for your health!" she preached at him.

"You've never smoked in your life and you've had all kinds of lung trouble!" he snapped back. (Mom had survived T.B.)

"Well!" full of indignation, "maybe I should take up the habit!" And with that she grabbed one of his Lucky Strikes and crammed more than half of it in her mouth and lit it up, She took a big puff, fire and defiance sparking from her eyes. The spectacle was so ridiculous. It was Eleanor Roosevelt in a thong bikini roller skating. It was Queen Elizabeth hunching and bumping a dancing poll. It was Mona Lisa climbing out of her frame, wiping that insidious smile from her face and gesturing 'up yours' with her middle finger. It was my stoic, peace at any price- pray-for-your-enemies mother, fed up and mad as hell, being childish; being human!

She pulled from her mouth the soggiest, most disgusting looking cigarette I've ever seen. I gasped and doubled up! I feared I'd give birth on the spot! I exploded. I cried with laughter.

I can still see her with that cigarette between her fingers and it still makes me laugh.

As amusing as I found my parent's idiosyncrasies, I find nearly as much humor in the way their off-spring took after them.

My brothers are most like my mother, perhaps because she always used Dad as the example of how not to be. They are real gentlemen and although they enjoy a good joke, they never laugh if it's told in mixed company. My oldest brother will change the channel if TV gets the least bit racy. (He's still a virgin, too, although his history belies it!)

I've never seen any of my five sisters naked. My husband laughs at how I lock the bathroom door even though just he and I are home.

Modesty is about where it stops with me. It used to bother me when relatives would tell me I'm just like my Dad. Now I know it takes all kinds and he was the kind who was human---and I'm that kind too.

My childhood memories are precious now, although while I was living with them I wished things could have been different--it wasn't all laughs and good times.

As a child, the 'saint and sinner' parenting was often confusing. The living in cramped quarters with so many people with so many personalities (all of them seeming to want to change mine) was challenging. Pig pens in the front yard, outhouses, hand-me-down clothes and my father's weekend drinking binges are some of the things that make me appreciate the life I have now.

Looking back, recalling the past is bittersweet, the best recollections are humorous. By the way, Dad's belt buckle was rather small.

MMM

Pig Killing

By Joan Krukewitt

The girls were forced to stay inside during the killing. I find that strange now that I'm grown and decades removed. My father, a man not given to respecting females, thought us under-beings too fragile to witness the shooting of the pig.

The pen was to the front of the property, a kind of 20 by 20 protrusion, pushed out front of the otherwise square acre lot. It must have smelled awful in the summer, but I was just a kid and I don't remember it being offensive to me.

Piglets purchased in the dead of winter sometimes got to share the warmth of the house if temperatures dropped below zero. They were fed mostly slop--a mixture of table scraps and grain, purchased for pig feed.

I remember the pride of my parents…"our pig was never served dishwater as some people's pigs were." (Soap residue couldn't be good for a pig and ultimately us!)

In addition to the slop, there was a special weed (I doubt I could recognize it now) known only as 'pig weed' and one of my daily chores was to pull this weed and feed it to the pig.

It was a yearly, fall ritual--the day to butcher the pig. And it was quite a festive event with neighbors coming to help and a big bonfire made to boil the water that would scald the pig in the huge barrel .

I heard (remember the girls were not allowed out of the house) "You must shoot him so square between the eyes that he doesn't even squeal!" my father's instructions on the art and science of pork shooting. Squealing the pig was not a good thing!

The animal killed and gutted, the girls were now permitted to go outside to witness the event.

A contraption like a tall saw horse held the crucified pig, it's head hanging down limp, its' body sliced from neck to privates gaping open, exposing its lack of insides. There was a hanging period--time allotted to let it bleed.

A very large tin barrel much like an unlabeled tomato juice can with rims around the top held the boiling water. The animal would be dipped into this to loosen his hair. All the neighbor men were vital at this point to muscle the pig into the hot water. The scraping came next to remove any excess hair not removed by the scalding.

It was quartered, eighted and so on until the pieces could be washed and later salted down.

Each neighbor was given a piece of meat--payment for his help for the day. I remember talk about how, after everyone was paid, there was little enough left for the real family of the pig.

Butchering day was an exciting time. It was a time of fellowship and accomplishment, a gay event, a party atmosphere while serious work was done. The pig would provide food for the whole winter.

The morning after, was special also. Mother would fry tenderloin (filet mignon of pork) and make gravy and biscuits. It was a feast!

Men's work was done, women's work had just begun. The sausage had to be ground and seasoned. The head was made into mincemeat, feet were pickled. The strips of fat were cut into cubes and rendered down for lard and the residue made cracklings. (pork rinds). The rest was salted and spread out on tables in the adjoining unheated back porch. The salt was a preservative when winter temperatures rose above safe refrigeration levels.

My two older sisters (teenagers) Betty and Lillian complained that the rendering smelled and the stink got in their hair and clothes. It must have smelled awful but I was just a kid and it wasn't offensive to me.

Brother Jack

By Joan Krukewitt

"God must love the common man. He made so many of them.." I thought of Lincoln's line when the minister at my brother's funeral said, "Andrew lived to be 70 years of age, the allotted, average life span."

Andrew-- Jack we called him, had his allotted shot at it--at life. I wish it had been longer and I wonder if he thought it fair or enough.

My brother was the first to die of twelve siblings. We all wondered (at least I know I did) how long our streak could last.

Mother had no miscarriages, no still births. She gave birth to six healthy boys and six healthy girls, their ages now ranging from 52 t o75 years. Jack was number three in the sequence. I am number nine.

There's something about knowing that someone you've shared a womb with has died. It brings death up close and personal and you're forced to look it square in the face. This is what it looked like to me.

Jack had shown signs of Alzheimer's starting at about age 65. I ignored the signs and actually wondered if his wife didn't relish telling everyone about how bad he was getting. She's the kind who knows the answer before the question is asked and she decided early in their 40 year marriage that she needed to wear the pants.

Jack served his country, fathered and raised two children, worked every day and did what he thought was right--always. He had a black and white view of what was right and he'd correct you, bring you back into focus if you erred into gray areas. He was known as a smart-ass.

His condition progressed until he was no longer manageable at home. He was placed in a nursing home on Valentine's Day of 2003. My sister, Betty, and I went to see him as soon as I returned from Florida in April.

He didn't know us. He knew he was Andrew Rodgers and that was all he knew.

"He looks awfully healthy. This could go on for years," said Betty.

The call came about 3 am on June 25. Jack had been taken to Mercy Hospital and they thought he'd had a heart attack.

Just minutes later my husband and I entered the hospital through the emergency room and I asked about Jack at the desk.

We were shown to a small room across the hall and I didn't notice the sign on the door. My husband did, and later told me it said 'grief counseling'.

Jack's wife, son, brother and sister-in-law were already seated in the room. They gave us the news. "Jack is gone. It was a massive heart attack."

I felt calmer than normal, like my body was there but I was somewhere else. I felt detached, merely an observer.

I was trying to process the information just given me when a nurse came into the room. I soon understood that she was to be our "grief counselor."

She had no neck, was fat and unhealthy looking. She was disheveled, tennis shoe clad and would have looked more appropriate behind a McDonald's counter.

"My God," I remember thinking, "is this the best you've got? Doesn't death deserve more dignity than this?"

"…how sorry she was…was he sick long?" she asked. Niceties disposed of, she got down to business. "Who is to be the mortician?" And she left.

Then came another nurse. This one was wearing a dark print smock over the white uniform and she looked neat, trim and efficient. "Does anyone want to see the body?" she asked.

"Yes, I do." I said. I didn't know why but I did.

Jack's son, Kelly, and I followed her out the door and through a couple of rooms with usual hospital paraphernalia. "We have not done anything to him yet. He's still got the tube in him where they were trying to revive him," she explained as we walked toward his bed.

"Mr. Rodgers, you have visitors," she quipped as she pulled down the sheet.

There he was. I don't know what I expected. I'd seen many people in coffins but never a new corpse.

He indeed, did have the awful tube taped in his mouth. His eyes, half open, were blank and staring. His skin was a blotchy gray and lavender.

I'd seen enough. I remember thinking, "This isn't real. He isn't dead. There's more to this than I know, now."

The viewing and the funeral were pretty uneventful. The mortician did a good job. Jack looked youthful, healthy and I'd never noticed how pretty his hair was, a full head, sandy with very little gray and it glistened.

I finally broke down when they brought the casket out of the mortuary. The sight of my remaining five brothers and Jack's only son acting as pall bearers was just too much.

My youngest brother is 58 years old, graying, and the rest of my siblings have the typical senior citizen look.

"Who's next?" I couldn't keep from wondering.

It's only been four short months since my brother's death. It seems much longer, perhaps because he started to leave us years earlier with Alzheimer's. I know the suddenness of his actual death seemed like a blessing.

My brother's life was rather average and unexciting from my point of view. But could it be that even in death, he was being the common, decent man he'd been in life? He was in no pain in his fog. He must have known how much it pained us, his family, to see him in that condition and so he decided to do the right thing…as always.!

Boring Dinners

By Joan Krukewitt

I've been here alot. These restaurants that make the desserts look like works of art. It was enjoyable the first time and maybe even the second but the rich food, the expensive wine that tastes like the cheap stuff to me, seems ridiculous. I want to say, "I'll just take the money! Keep the food, the wine, the fancy desserts and give me the money!"

There is an expression that my husband's Irish friend often used. "Larry, can I buy you a drink" he'd say, "or will you just take the money?" This was his way of manipulating Larry into having another drink.

But back to this boring dinner with these boring drunks who have a bad case of the "I's".

"I" did this and "I" have that and "I", "I", "I"."

"I" have heard these same stories hundreds of times and they become bigger with each telling. Could their offspring really be the Christ child in disguise? Do they know, do they care that they repeat themselves? I must drink more to endure this evening.

I'm remembering words from Emerson on 'society' and the cost of membership, words about pasting on smiles to cover up boredom with dull company. I'm doing that now--pasting on a smile, trying to be polite and "nice."

I hate 'nice!' 'Nice' is a four letter word---overused, lukewarm, certainly unexciting. But I'm being as 'nice' as I can possibly be.

I'm being nice because my new husband is the host of this little party. I'm playing a new role as a wife of the Pres/CEO. A role that has me feeling insecure as well as angry.

I feel insecure because I certainly do not want to be an embarrassment to my husband. He's worked hard, proven himself and deserves my support. I feel angry because I feel dishonest.

"She never bothers with people she hates, that's why the lady is a tramp."

I'm no tramp but I don't bother with people I don't like and I'm not 'nice.' I'm kind. I'm loyal. I'm honest. I say what I mean and expect others to do the same.

"Why do you work so hard, line their pockets and have to kiss their asses too?" I ask. "It seems to me you could do one or the other but not both."

"You must learn to play the game, Joan." says Larry.

I'm playing the game as best I can. I'm smiling, charming their pants off and longing for the evening to be over, longing for retirement, longing for the day when I can boldly say, "I'll just take the money!"

164

Lucia Leao

Lucia Leao was born in Rio de Janeiro, Brazil, in 1963. She has been living in Florida for 13 years, where she works as a translator. Her first book of short stories was published in Brazil 2001. She holds a master's degree in Brazilian literature from UERJ (Rio de Janeiro, Brazil) and a master's degree in print journalism from University of Miami, Florida. Leao is married and has an eight-year old son.

MMM

Veranda

By Lucia Leao

I dreaded the perfume of body powder and of the prospective of the sunset that I felt every Sunday at my grandfather's house. The veranda where he used to sit with his radio to listen to the soccer matches faced the mountains of Rio. At the sunset, the lights of the modest houses around us could be seen in the distance, coming up slowly from behind the trees and behind the day that was leaving us. Back then, there was not what we now call slums, but the presence that breathed in the mountains told a story made of samba and blackness, of rivers and music, of life and death.

The black-and-white tile that formed hexagonal patterns on the floor had cracks that seemed to grow every week. On my grandfather's neck the white blotches of powder made me uncomfortable. Was he a baby or an elderly man?

There was a sense of accomplishment in the almost evenings when I saw him there. The week that was behind had been another challenge that we had all faced together. And together we stayed, in the family.

When I was a child growing up very close to my grandparents, Sundays were the days when the structure of the family was more visible. My grandfather was the successful businessman whose house was the center of energy for all of us. He was a tall man, with Italian ancestors, and a sweet tooth. He had a big forehead and a big smile. There were special desserts for him, who would take a nap after lunch and wait patiently for the soccer game to be broadcast through his portable radio.

He didn't wear glasses, and I could see his eyes fixed in some indefinite point as he sat on his chair with his ear glued to the small round speaker, on the radio. Sometimes he would look at the floor for so long, I would think he was sleeping with his eyes opened. But he was only listening.

The swinging motion of the hammocks where I sat in the big and long veranda made his profile tremble, as if the face were a sound and the waves could be disturbed by my movements that tried to change his routine.

Maybe it was the repetition that bothered me, and the way he distanced himself from the rest of us.

He seemed to become a statue with an empty brain and an empty mouth on those Sunday evenings. He would not talk with anybody until the game was over. It was not that I wanted his attention, it was something else that I wanted, maybe to alter his profile. I was about six and I loved his loud, easy laughter, and his height. He seemed to be above everybody else in the house.

There was an agony of things coming to an end on Sundays, especially when the night came. We would go back to our house, my sisters, my parents and I. It would be hard for us to leave my grandparents again, as it was clearly difficult for my mother to separate from her parents. There was a tragic feeling in the air, as if life were too short for families to live apart. We lived one hour away from them.

My father would in a few years replace my grandfather, since he was the one that my mother had chosen to fulfill this role in her life. This would come much later and we needed first to experience the power that grandparents can have if life allows them to.

The diabetes changed my grandfather's life completely the day he woke up blind. I was eight years old. He was 55. He would live almost 30 years in the dark, relying on sounds and on the recognition of shapes to move around.

Later, after retiring, he would rely on the radio for having contact with the world, and more and more as he got older. There was no surgery that could give him back his vision. And he never showed any kind of despair.

For us it was painful and embarrassing to have him around, as time went by. He wore big sunglasses to hide the eyes with no expression, and he had to be attended to as a child does. We helped him around every time he came to visit or when we went to his house. But the embarrassment was related to the way he showed a happiness that didn't seem to be consistent with his condition. He behaved like a child or somebody too naïve most of the time, as if not aware of the seriousness of his disease and of his condition. There was something bewildering about his behavior, as if he had made up a faith in life or as if I was the one, for instance, who needed to make up one for myself.

I had teary eyes every time he touched my face, my hair, and smiled, trying to figure out how I looked, since I was growing and he couldn't see me. He did it to all of us, to my two sisters and my brother. And I wanted to run away. His lack of desperation puzzled me.

But before his blindness, on the evenings on the veranda, I felt a restless need to do something, as if old age and the passage of time were already too close to me. I felt a need that I now recognize as the need to know what to do with the melancholic waves coming from everywhere around us at the end of those Sundays. Life seemed to inspire a longing for something else that was maybe far away.

Some say the presence of slaves can do that to a people, reminding them unconsciously of the need to get free, of the sadness of being bound to a world to which they don't belong, of separation and loss. The end of the day would bring the certainty that there are chains that need to be broken, but haven't been broken yet. Isn't love some kind of imprisonment? Isn't family love the biggest captivity of all?

The idea of a prison that stays inside the culture after slavery is finished is a symbolic one, and it brings the longing for an undefined freedom. My family had, as most people in my country, a past full of sad chants that the slaves had brought from afar. We had inherited maids who were part of that past, black, mulatto, poor, and in a subordinate position. Some of us heard the sadness in their history, in their chants. Others heard the mysticism, the poetry, and a different musical rhythm, but we were all surrounded by them one way or another.

So, maybe it was a life bigger than mine that influenced my vision of my grandfather and shaped the question his existence seemed to draw in mine. Maybe it was the net of family blood and genes and stories weaved throughout the generations. But I will never forget the sound of the soccer games, the screams of "Goooooooooooooooool" coming from the radio, muffled sounds distorted by my grandfather's ear against the speaker. I will never forget the purple sky, the open veranda, the voices coming from inside the house, the dining room lights being lit, the smell of food for our last meal together that day. The agony of things about to end or that have already ended.

The last time I saw him in Rio, I had taken my three-month old son there especially for my grandfather to hold. Soon after that he died, and I couldn't go to his funeral. I was away, already living abroad.

In the Backyard

By Lucia Leao

When I heard the screams, I tried to run to the maid's quarters. The single blue wooden window was silent, closed, and the door was locked. I forgot it was Helena's day off.

I looked for my sisters in the backyard, among jasmine trees, and I saw my grandmother's ancient turtle looking for a hideout as slowly as I was, but not so nervously. I could barely move.

My sisters were screaming somewhere and there was somebody else screaming. Suddenly there was a forest of shouts around me. A hand came and grabbed my dress so fast that I couldn't see it was my mother's hand, and that her mouth was closed. She was the only one who didn't scream when it happened or that is how I remember her that day.

"Come quick," she then directed my youngest sister, whose big eyes were searching for the source of all that noise.

"What is it?" she asked, more brave than I. But I didn't want to know what was turning our Sunday afternoon into a dark mystery, a memory of childhood full of female fears and loss.

It had to happen at my grandmother's house, of course. It had been there that I had lived my first years, there that I had learned to walk in her corridors, running towards her, looking for her in the kitchen, in the garden, always looking for her. The mystery of all femininity, that was my grandmother, more than my mother. It took me many years to understand why.

But the screams were now accompanied by a loud laughter that seemed to approach us.

"Come," my mother took my hand, and ran with us to the house.

Helena's quarters were in the back of the house, a bedroom and a small bathroom. On the side, stairs led to an empty area in which I used to play with my two sisters and my cousin until they called us for a snack or to say it was time to go home. Further back were banana trees, bushes, the neighbors' houses that we never saw, behind all the green. That Sunday afternoon, one of the neighbors came to greet us.

He had jumped from high up, lost his balance and had fallen heavily on the ground. The first scream came from one of my aunts, as soon as she saw him standing up above Helena's room, his mouth full of blood, an aura of craziness around him.

The first scream was hers, I would learn later. My mother had gone to get us and my grandmother had probably stopped making her famous meringues and looked through the window. I imagine her moving her small hands to her mouth and praying for a few seconds before screaming too. She was very Catholic and the vision of a man bleeding against a gray cloudy sky, his bare chest and his disheveled hair must have reminded her of other sufferings and miseries.

After falling, the man went down the stairs, crossed the backyard, growled at the dog that was tied to its leash and to its dog house, and went straight to my uncle's house.

They lived on the first floor, my uncle, his children and his wife. It was a complete house that they had, but it was so close to my grandmother's that I felt at home there too.

He went downstairs, a fugitive, a runner, a young man escaping from his first delusions. More screams came when they saw him, blood and all, entering their living room and ruining the afternoon with his blazing and scared stare. I think he realized that their screams were worse than his own fears, and he locked himself in my cousin's room, trying to silence all the voices inside his head.

They tried everything to make him open the door. They didn't even know exactly who he was. The whole spectacle had happened too fast for any real recognition.

"Open it!" my uncle shouted, still holding his glass with beer and unable to hit the door as he wished.

"Open it!" he repeated, but the silence seemed to be his only answer, heavy as the terror that had invaded our Sunday.

My aunt came and spoke gently, but with no results. Everybody tried a trick, a strategy, but anger was soon becoming the man's most feared opponent. My uncle had finally forgotten his beer and was trying to put the door down, hitting it faster and stronger so he could bring the show to an end, go back to the TV and watch the soccer game.

"Wait," said another aunt, my mom's sister. They all respected her. "Let me handle this."

Her nun's clothes were still new to the family, and to herself. But the compassion she had must have been in her genes since she was born.

Another silence came, bringing with it a lack of air. It would be a match: her compassion, her knowledge of human nature, her faith in her faith. All this against his fear, his strength, his escape, his lack of reality.

They never told me what she said, how she said it and what his face looked like when his sister came to take him back to their house and, later, to a hospital. They never told me how I mixed so many versions and created mine.

In my mind, there was a quiet afternoon, and a deserted backyard. The children's world was suddenly shaken by a man in love, desperate to see his loved one who had abandoned him to dedicate her life to God, to live in Christ.

He had come to claim an engagement ring of a cancelled wedding. He was furious and sad, madly in love with a woman who couldn't see in him any value that would prevent her from joining the big community of the Church. She had chosen to be away from all men, to join the idea of mankind, and had refused to give her life to him, an ordinary man, in flesh and blood.

"No!" my mother laughed when I told her the story. "You got it all wrong. You were too little to remember."

And I paused on the phone, questioning the truth of all my family ties.

"He was only a neighbor and your aunt was the one who convinced him to go out because she was patient enough, and for some reason he trusted her."

Another pause. But how…?

"She was never engaged to anybody."

But then…?

"He had treatment after that first incident and his family apologized. They were very nice people."

"What was his name?" I asked her, pencil in hand to write down the information and to have that piece of palpable truth.

"I don't remember," my mother said. "He was very young when it happened."

"What about Helena?" I asked, afraid to hear her say that by that time she was not working for my grandmother anymore.

"She was in the kitchen, with us, the women." She completed. "We were preparing dinner."

In the silence of my mother's voice, after hanging up the phone, I walked in my mind through the rooms of my grandmother's house one more time. I saw the piano, where my aunt used to sit and play, her nun's habit reminding us of a wound, of another dimension, another life, of death. It came from there the association I was to make between life and death, of God as something we can only really see if we die – and live again.

I saw my father, my mother, my grandfather, the old phone, the crystal jars glowing against my eyes.

So many things had happened in that house. And I had created so many versions of myself in an attempt to unravel the many mazes that amount to one's life. Now I had found out a mystery in my own lies. I could swear he was a man in love, crazy, in love.

There should be an explanation, and I touched the walls again, trying to find it. She was not the answer, my grandmother, she was the question itself.

From the version of her that was passed on to me by my mother, she was a dedicated housewife who had dreamt of becoming a lawyer. She had been a clever businesswoman who had lived in her husband's shadow, in the shadow of his love for her.

"Once she broke a pile of plates on his head because a woman called him on the phone, at home," my mother loved to tell me, laughing, as if this showed how passionate she was, how much she loved him. I always interpreted it as desperation to decipher her behavior in that famous scene.

So I met her there, holding the phone, and then being told that her daughter had chosen life with God. I met her there in all my versions, always divided, always ready to cook for us, to please us, to surprise us with new recipes. Oh, how I loved her, how I missed her. How I wanted to take her to her future, to my time, and to show her that it was possible to invent, to create new plots, new scenes, new stories for ourselves!

It took me almost forty years to understand why I kept going back to her backyard, to her flowers, to her animals, to her naïve and pure love for nature. It took me so long to understand that I wanted to be like her and to be totally different.

And that man, that man running, screaming, laughing, and finally opening the door. That man taught me something else, in all the faces I imagined for him. The unknown can be scary, but it is the truth of our limited time that has always haunted me. The fact that there are many options, and that in life we have to choose one or two.

I try to put her back in the kitchen, to start from there, but she escapes from me. She has always escaped me. Maybe she needed to close the doors sometimes for migraines were her constant nightmares. Maybe she needed some peace so she could pray for somebody to come and open the door. Maybe she was just resting, happy with her life, happy with her choices.

My grandmother is there, as ancient as myself, she bends, she takes care of her plants. I always knew I was one of them.

Loretta Lewis

I was raised in a small town in New Jersey with the help of eleven older siblings. The house we lived in sat close to the banks of the Passaic River. Its waters were cool and clear and it was our swimming playground in the summer heat and our winter sports palace for ice-skating in the freezing winter cold. The blue-collar population in the town meshed with my brothers' needs for young high school dropouts who would work in a neckwear factory for a minimum wage in order for them to learn a trade.

The year before receiving my high school diploma, I met and married a professional man and was on my way to living the American dream. We had four wonderful children, and when they were fully grown, I went back to school to get my graduate degree in psychology and my M.S.W.

I was nourished and shaped by my work as a private practitioner, a therapist who worked in the field. As an adjunct professor at N.Y.U., as a workshop leader, and as a lecturer, I discovered my own special gifts.

In my saging years, I am now writing my memoirs as I continue to form and develop the contours of my life.

Biloxi, Mississippi, 1942

By Loretta Lewis

I was in the Washington D.C. train terminal, approaching the man giving information about schedules. He looked directly at me with what seemed to be hostility, indicating that he wasn't sure if I was white or black. I looked up at the sign and realized at that moment that I was standing in a line designated for blacks only. Quickly, I moved to the other line as he called after me in a disdainful tone, "Don't you know if you're black or white?"

The man in the "Whites Only" booth stared threateningly and said with a sneer, "Mulattoes belong on the black line."

I was not even familiar with that word, but I knew from the stares and the surprised looks on the faces of the other passengers that they too thought I was trying to pass myself off as a white woman. The white man standing directly in back of me pushed me aside, and I moved towards the exit and up the staircase with my heavy suitcase. In my rage and confusion, choking with tears, I left the station not knowing where to go.

Walking through the busy thoroughfare, I approached a policeman directing traffic. I felt certain that he would help me, and also felt some relief at having escaped from the foreign and frightening world I had just left, where I had been given a strange label.

I moved into the street oblivious of everything around me and as I stood close to the policeman, his hand motioned for me to stand back. It seemed to be a gesture of hostility, and fearfully I moved back onto the sidewalk, and waited.. And waited, and waited. He showed no signs of intention to help me, as I stood there shaking with terror and still enraged at the injustice and humiliation I had just suffered. I don't know what possessed me, but I assumed that he would be able to direct me to the next train to Gulfport, Mississippi, where my new husband who had recently become an army lieutenant was waiting for me. Finally, I called out to him, "I need help. I need help."

When he didn't respond, I walked again to the middle aisle of the intersection, and this time, he heard my pleas.

"What do you want? What's your complaint?" he muttered., and I knew from his sneer that I was not about to get help from him.

By this time, I accepted the fact that I would have to wait until the morning for my train, and gently, I implored the policeman, "Could you tell me where I can find a hotel until I can catch the train to meet my husband?" adding, "He's a soldier in Biloxi," thinking that might help. He carefully scrutinized my dark olive skin, my blue-black curly hair and said caustically, "You ain't gonna get no room in this here town. No hotels here take in mulattoes."

I went back to the train station, still trembling, and there I noticed that the schedule was posted on a bulletin board. I had already missed the 7 PM train to Gulfport. It was now 11:00 PM.

I remembered my family waving a tearful goodbye at the Newark station only 12 hours earlier. Now it seemed as if I had traveled to a foreign country. I had never been beyond the New York, New Jersey area, and had never before encountered discrimination. I was accustomed to stares in my own environment, but there were stares of admiration, especially in my late adolescence. My dark complexion was the envy of all my friends, especially as I added layers of color to it in the summer months when the beach had been my playground.

The hard bench in the terminal made my already exhausted body ache. I held my suitcase close to me, aware that it contained all my possessions, including my money. I tried to comfort myself with visions of Aaron's face and the thought that I would soon be in his arms. At the same time, I was tormented by the knowledge that he would be waiting for the last train, and I had no way to contact him about my delay.

The next morning I boarded the train with a sigh of relief, heading toward my destination, and a heart feeling somewhat lighter with happy anticipation. Eleven hours later, as the train moved towards the platform, I was the first one off, searching eagerly for my soldier husband. But he wasn't there. Alone and frightened and dragging my heavy suitcase, I realized that he had waited for the train I'd missed.

With some trepidation this time, I approached a military policeman asking how I could get a message to my husband. And again, that strange hostile look, "I can't help you." He said briskly.

"Well, could you tell me how to get to the Gulfport Hotel?" I asked, "He's probably waiting for me there. I know he's reserved a room for us there." By now, I should have known what his answer would be, "You ain't gonna get into no Gulfport Hotel, and don't you go tellin' me your husband is waitin' for you there."

I started to push him out of my way with my suitcase, when I saw Aaron standing near the exit. Before I threw my arms around him, I asked him to tell the MP that he was indeed my husband, and we did indeed have a room at the hotel. The Lieutenant bars on Aaron's uniform had the effect of producing a weak apology that came with a nasty smirk. Aaron was oblivious to all that had previously transpired, but as soon as we entered the hotel, the color of my skin, and the tight ringlets framing my face, was a siren call to the registration clerk sitting below the sign that read, "No Blacks Allowed."

"I'll have to call the manager before allowing you to bring this woman into your room," she said testily.

Aaron stood tall in his uniform and said sharply, "I'm a Lieutenant in the U.S. Army, stationed in Biloxi and you'd better give me the key if you don't want any trouble here." And she did.

That night, I wept for hours, telling Aaron, between tears, that I wanted to go home, that I couldn't live in a place where I would be the target of anti black sentiment. He tried to assure me that once I found a place to stay, the problem would go away.

I wanted to believe him, and most of all, I wanted to be near him.

After a long search in local newspapers when I had come to realize how wives of servicemen were being gouged by landlords, I finally found an upstairs room with one twin bed and a large dresser, with torn shades, and wooden floors that creaked, at a monthly rental of $20.00, which was all that we could afford. The bonus was Winona, the landlady and her two adorable kids, two and four years old.

After taking a wrong turn the next morning as I went shopping for food, I realized that I had mistakenly wandered into the black separated area of town, and found myself staring at the shanty houses, and the outside toilets. But what really caught my attention, was the games that the kids were playing. They were tying each other up as though they were a team of horses with a driver, and they were trotting up and down the cobblestone street. I wondered at the inspiration for this kind of entertainment. There was certainly no evidence of toys anywhere in sight. I moved toward the children, and seeing the fear in their faces, I watched them retreat into their homes. As I attempted to cross back to the white section, an MP stopped me saying "At this hour, you are not allowed in the white area."

I pointed to Winona's house, asserting my "whiteness", and realizing that I knew Winona's name, he skeptically allowed me to pass.

Donna and Joey greeted me with their innocent happy smiles, which somewhat soothed the rage that was boiling inside of me.

During the next few weeks, I learned that Winona had taken a job as a waitress at a local restaurant to supplement her husband's inadequate income. They had married when Winona was fifteen and pregnant. She confessed to me that she never would have married Bill once she had gotten to know him. She was trapped in a relationship with a demanding and sometimes violent alcoholic and she worked late hours hoping to save enough to extricate herself from the marriage.

Aaron came "home" every weekend to this one bedroom where all of our social and sexual activities were confined. We would eat quietly in the kitchen, vacating it quickly so as not to intrude on the family. Weekends we would walk on the river paths watching the people fish for their weekly meals. We strolled into town during the humid summer months, a five mile hike that we might not have done had there been any public transportation. There we walked past the bar and grill where Winona worked, a dress shop and a series of different food stores, all separated pushcart style. Everything was outside except the cash register. Of course, we saw the now familiar, "No Blacks Allowed," signs everywhere, and I wondered how the black population survived without places to buy their food. I soon learned that they ate what they grew and bartered with each other, organizing co-ops for mass purchasing wherever they could.

When Winona asked me to accompany her to church one Sunday morning, I told her that I was Jewish. She stared at me blankly, as though she had seen me for the first time, and almost as though to wash away all the intimacy that we had established between us.

"You're a Jew?" she stuttered, "Where are your horns?" I was sure she was joking, and responded, "I don't wear them on Sundays."

The humor went past her as she processed this new turn of events in her life. "I swear," she stammered, "I never seen a Jew before. You sho' nuf a Jew?"

She seemed not to want to believe it. I laughed, hiding my urge to cry, "Well," she said with reluctant acceptance, "I learn something every day. I like you or else I would throw you out of my house."

In a low, pained voice, I offered, "So I may be to you like the niggers you hate because I am different. I guess I learned something about you that I didn't know. I thought YOU were different." This actually brought tears to her eyes, and she asked meekly for forgiveness. I knew that my friendship meant much to her. I'd been the only person she ever trusted enough to reveal her innermost thoughts and feelings. We embraced spontaneously, and I realized that the Winona's of this world felt hate for those who were different because they somehow perceived them to be a threat to their very existence. They only felt safe in their own narrow world.

The next day I was awakened by noises that were unfamiliar to me. I heard the clanging of bells, piercing screams, hysterical voices that seemed to be pleading, and the sound of roaring car engines. The sun was just rising and the darkness parting. I dressed quickly and ran to the street, where I saw that Winona was already there.

"Don't come out," she said to me, "You northerners will pity this man, but I have no pity for him. He'll get what he deserves. He raped a white girl."

Barely listening to her, I ran towards the noises with her voice calling after me, "Don't go there. You'll be sorry." As I got closer to the noises, I felt faint, and saw something that defied comprehension. I had run into the same black area where I had made a wrong turn that first day. There I saw a truck with a rope tied to it on one end and tied to a young black man at the other end, under his arms and around his waist. Sitting on the back of the truck were two large muscular men holding what looked to me like a wheel that firemen have on their hoses to let it slack or pull it taut.

The black man was still standing on his feet as I arrived, but at the very next moment, the rope that was hanging loose on his body was suddenly tightened. I watched his body flail as the truck took off, dragging it across the gravel. This was accompanied by screams of pleasure from the crowd.

I stood fixated, numb, helpless, enraged, and I became lost in my own screams of horror. I watched the body turn from side to side, as blood trailed along the path. Standing next to me, Winona put her arms around me, and held me to her chest, my head on her shoulder as I sobbed convulsively. "They're going to hang him on that tree," she said, amidst the gleeful hurrahs and laughter emanating from a veritable insane asylum, with its population jumping for joy. With Winona holding my hand, I dared to look back one more time, and saw the figure hanging from the rope. To this moment, the vision clings in my mind, the blood dripping from his body, the neck broken and hanging on his chest and the fire that had been lit below him. It was that clear vision that I held in my mind as I marched with Martin Luther King in Alabama years later.

The next day, I packed my things to go back to Newark. Winona's calm, matter of fact voice, telling me that the man deserved what he got, kept ringing in my ears. I had believed in her potential to free herself of past abuse, degradation, humiliation, and the marriage that had been so destructive to her and her children. But she couldn't get past her learned hatred, and I couldn't bear to be in the same house with her.

A Desperate Journey: Learning To Heal

By Loretta Lewis

When my sister Hilda's husband died in the arms of another woman, the tragedy was compounded for this shy retiring housewife and mother of three young children, when the local paper publicized the scandalous details of the sordid affair.

The shame that this prominent business man brought on his family forced Hilda to suppress her rage and grief and to seek expression of these emotions by proving her worth as a woman who could be respected for her prominence in a business that had been dominated exclusively by men.

The lucrative moving and trucking business her husband had successfully built was now her legacy and the challenge to keep it running was a major distraction from her emotional upheaval. But her enslavement to the hunger for power took its toll on her physical and mental health and I witnessed the decline of my sister, in every other facet of her life. This sensitive moral, ethical woman relinquished the values of a lifetime and allowed them to slip away as a shield of armor slowly encapsulated her world.

After five grueling years of frenetic and rigid scheduling, the threat she had long feared was undeniably present. She was in jeopardy of having a complete nervous breakdown if she did not leave her toxic environment

She was grateful for my support and constant presence during her struggle to elude the nightmare possibility of being institutionalized and finally agreed that the threat to her health was real. She decided that the answer to her malady was a retreat which she had heard about from a friend who had suffered from depression and had recently returned with a glowing report of her experience in this healing environment. I supported her decision and promised to visit her if she needed me at any time during the proposed month of her recovery.

Two weeks after her departure, her daughter called me, her voice shaking with emotion. She needed my help to extricate her mother from the *cult*, as she called it. With intermittent sobs, she described her experience when she visited her mother at what turned out to be an ashram led by a guru. Barbara had been asked by her mother to attend a special ritual in which she was to be honored and she wanted her eldest child to share her sacred occasion.

. Barbara described the ceremony as bizarre as she watched her mother's conversion into a cult with a guru doing the rites in which her mother kneeled at his feet, an act painfully contrary to her mother's Orthodox Jewish teachings. The guru then renamed my sister Sadana as he anointed her head with oil

A week later I was standing at the entrance that read *Kripalu.*. The autumn sun was setting and there was a hushed silence in the air except for the chirping of bird songs. I felt an aura of peace and beauty surrounding me as the gentle breezes caressed my face and my eyes met a panoramic view of vegetable gardens ready for harvesting and heavily laden fruit trees gently swaying in the wind in concert with the music of the birds.

When I approached the double doors to the flat-roofed one story frame farm house badly in need of paint, I turned toward the view that had captured my attention and my senses were flooded with feelings of peace and calm. Silent tears filled my mascara-ed eyes, awestruck at the beauty of the flowing hills and the valley surrounding me

Suddenly, I felt a touch on my shoulder followed by a warm embrace, and I found myself staring into the face of my sister who only two weeks earlier seemed haggard and pale. Now her cheeks were flushed with excitement and she looked radiant and glowing with health.

Hilda, dressed in a sari and sandals seemed out of character from the woman who wore designer suits and stiletto heels in her former life. Her natural curly dark hair, formerly straightened into a page boy style, framed her perfectly shaped oval face and her almond brown eyes had a soft tender look. She seemed younger than her fifty years and surely more vibrant than I had known her to be.

I had not anticipated the limited primitive quarters that I would be exposed to on my short "vacation." The sleeping quarters were a small room with four mats on the floor and one shared bathroom. The food, cooked by the female disciples consisted of vegetables picked by male disciples who had been converted from former drug addicts to farmers. The fruits added to the pleasure of this experience, but it was the silence that made me conscious of the appreciation I felt with every bite of the vegetarian diet.

After cleaning up, we gathered together on the floor to do a group meditation. I was asked to get in the middle of the circle, a courtesy they gave to guests. In unison they chanted to the sound of Om. The chatter in my mind faded and I blissfully relaxed into a state of unconsciousness. I was unaware of time and space until my sister sat beside me and hugged me "Barbara will be impressed that you could meditate so easily so soon," she said.

Barbara had placed her faith in my therapeutic skills to rescue her from the grasp of this guru who was getting large sums of money from her mother's business. I agreed to go on the condition that Barbara would be honest with her mother and express her own concern for Hilda's welfare in an environment that Barbara felt may endanger the prospect of her recovery

The next activity was held in the sanctuary. Sadana and I sat with fifty other disciples on benches facing the alter waiting for the ritual to begin. Petals of flowers lined the path where Guru Dev was to walk. He came down the aisle dressed in robes of many colors .He moved regally with his gold leather sandals crushing the petals as his steps moved him towards the alter. Everyone knelt as he ascended the "throne." I was the only one left standing, despite Sandana's respectful request that I kneel to participate in the ritual.

I was struck by this man's extraordinarily handsome face, his chiseled features, dark olive skin long silken black hair and his impressive stature. The instrument that he played was foreign to me but it had the sound of a guitar. The disciples sang to the tune that sounded mystical and mesmerizing to me. The chanting stopped and I found my cheeks moist with tears. An unfamiliar emotional moment had moved me to a feeling of sadness.

Two young very beautiful women moved to the feet of the guru. They removed his sandals and on their knees began to pour oil on his feet and ankles, massaging them in long gentle strokes.

I was offended at this act of subservience and felt a surge of anger at this dominant male figure encouraging young women to take on the role of second class citizens. I was determined at that moment that I would ask for an audience with Guru Dev to express my concern about my sister's indoctrination into this cult like mentality.

Despite Hilda's objections, I followed him after the procession to his private quarters where he lived with his wife and two children His secretary stopped me before I reached the gate. When Guru Dev heard my loud and pleading voice, he nodded to her to allow me to enter.

The room was ornately decorated with Indian artifacts and pictures of his own guru and many poses were posted on the walls, including one of Guru Dev in a ceremonial gown as a young adolescent kneeling at the feet of the teacher.

His secretary asked me respectfully to kneel as I approached the chair facing the guru and when I refused Guru Dev politely waved her away.

I began hesitantly by begging his pardon for the intrusion and then hurriedly went on to explain my mission. "I am here to extricate my sister from the confines of this ashram. I want to bring her back to her children who have great concern about her recovery from her illness."

His voice was gently accented and his words were expressed with compassion.

"You are of another world than your sister, so you don't fully understand her longing to heal her soul. The men of western medicine do not give her a community where she can be with people in a healing environment and can feel free to live a spiritual life in peace. You are welcome," he continued, "to come at any time to learn for yourself our practices of healing for the benefit of yourself and your patients. Man needs to heal not only the mind, but the body and the spirit"

It was these words that I absorbed and digested as we sat in a moment of silence. Then he opened his eyes and smiled, rose from the throne-like chair and retreated.

That night I slept beside my sister. Her body never looked slimmer and more graceful. Her face was never more peaceful and I vowed then to learn the practices of Yoga meditation, Reiki healing and Shiatsu massage. I hungrily explored the offering of this healing environment for myself and for my patients.

Once a month for a period of three years I came to fully indulge myself in the ashram's healing community and as a devotee of Guru Dev.

When Kripalu moved to Lenox, Massachusetts and became a world renown holistic healing center, I found the upscale environment less spiritual than the primitive "home" my sister and I had experienced. The ashram in Sunnytown, Pennsylvania. was a new beginning of a bonding for us that has existed into our healthy "saging" years.

Goddess of Egypt

By Loretta Lewis

We were to be a group of "healers" seeking the relics and signs of the origin of our art in ancient Egypt. We had all immersed ourselves in a variety of the healing models but it was here that we would see the sights and delve further into the mysterious gifts with which we were blessed.

The passengers were boarding the cruise ship The Princess Nile. in Luxor and as I searched the deck for our fellow travelers, my eyes focused in disbelief when I spotted a group surrounding a woman whose face I knew was celebrated all over the world. With a sense of awe, I turned to my friend Martha, asking if that distinguished figure was indeed the famous Jahan Sadat, the widow of the famous Anwar Sadat, hero of the peace process in the Middle East. Without waiting for an answer from Martha, I moved toward the entourage protecting the woman whose book,

A Woman of Egypt, I had just finished reading, The guard standing in front of Mrs. Sadat moved forward to stop me from moving into the circle.

I respectfully requested that I speak with Mrs. Sadat about her book which I had so much treasured. She responded with a warm smile and a direct question: "How indeed did you like the book I wrote?"

My words flowed as the awe and veneration spilled from my mouth. "Your book is now my bible. Your gift to all women who sacrificed for a cause to elevate the status of women everywhere has taken on a ray of hope that radiates in every facet of the Women's Movement. I just want to give you my heartfelt thanks for raising the consciousness about the plight of Middle Eastern women for the American public. You risked your life for a cause that I have struggled to embrace and I need to tell you how much I admire you.."

"Thank you. How very poetic!" She responded, while Martha, standing beside me, tossed her head with approval and cried.

Next morning according to the itinerary, we were to visit the Valley of the Kings to find the source and the origins of the healing arts in Egypt.. Our guide, Lufti, sat at the breakfast table with fourteen of us, consuming exotic Egyptians breads, figs, dates, pomegranates, and their every meal staple – hummus, the eggs and cereals served with ethnic garnishes and plenty of garlic and honey.

Lufti was holding his head in his hands, groaning about a severe migraine headache that was plaguing him at the moment. The group of healers, most of whom had come from California, looked at him with anxiety, fearing that it would be impossible for him to accompany us to this most important site. There was a spontaneous gasp of disappointment when he announced to the group that he would be unable to lead us to the sites planned for our morning excursion. Never one willing to accept "no," my friend Martha addressed Lufti with confident authority, announcing that "Loretta will heal!"

This became a chant of encouragement from the group—many of whom had never met me before. "Loretta will heal! Loretta will heal," rang in my ears as

Martha literally pushed me out of my seat.

As if programmed, I moved toward Lufti,. my hand gently touching his scalp, and in a trancelike state I moved my fingers down his neck through his shoulders, back to his neck and up again to his scalp. Within minutes, his voice almost sounded distant to me. I had lost track of time and space, and only came to awareness when I heard his voice clearly thanking me for healing his headache. His next statement was, "She did it! We're going.."

I was just about getting back to my normal state of being when a gentle hand lightly touched my shoulder, and I heard a voice whisper into my ear, "Mrs. Sadat is respectfully requesting that you help her as you did Lufti. She, too, has a migraine headache."

Without questioning him, I allowed myself to be led by this stranger to the corner of the dining room where Mrs. Sadat seemed to be holding court amongst her entourage of admirers and security people. Wordlessly, I put my hands on her head and then said, "I am privileged that you asked for my healing, but I need to tell you that what I am about to do is simply a Shiatsu massage which is what I did for Lufti." And feeling the need to deflect any expectation she may have had about receiving some sort of magical voodoo, I repeated, "It is nothing more than a massage."

In her gentle, kind voice she expressed her willingness to experience whatever it was I had done for Lufti. I was in a total state of oblivion regarding the hundreds of people in the dining room as well as the people immediately surrounding Mrs. Sadat. I moved my hands to the centers of energy. I don't remember the time I spent. My hands seemed to move without any consciousness. It was only when I heard again what seemed from a distance Mrs. Sadat's voice, her soft words of thanks.: "I appreciate your helping me to relieve the pain that would have kept me from going to places where I too wanted to be." she said with regal dignity. The applause from her table and mine resounded in the dining room.

The trip to the Valley of the Kings was both exhausting and exhilarating and when I got back to our cabin, I just wanted to slide into bed As I entered the room, I noticed that a note addressed to me had been slipped under the door. The simple stationery was distinctly designed with the name of Jahan Sadat.. With excitement and curiosity, I opened the note which read, "I would be most appreciative if you could come to my cabin to help me again to relieve my migraine. If this is an imposition, I will understand."

I could not believe that she would ask me to visit in her suite, and I tried to contain my excitement at being chosen from among such a group of other gifted healers. But Martha's chatty exuberance and obvious awe fueled my sense of pride and humility as she openly, though lovingly, expressed her envy.

Needless to say, I happily attended this goddess whom I had worshipped long before we met. We had several sessions together during that trip, and we had an opportunity to talk as women in an intimate fashion. I learned from her how lonely it can be living on a pedestal away from the normalcy of close relationships. She also talked about the depth of her love for her husband and of the pain of that loss.

I felt like Cinderella when, in gratitude, she sent a limousine to our hotel after the cruise and actually took on the role of hostess in a palace replete with the priceless artifacts of the history of ancient civilizations. Then in a gesture so revealing of her innate need to connect to real people, she and Martha and I sat down for a meal that she had actually cooked herself, while probably 20 or so servants languished behind the dining room doors, allowing us to savor moments of complete privacy. I capture those moments in my head so often, although when it was happening, it felt like an out of body experience.

Even in my most extreme fantasy life, I could never have imagined the kind of relationship that I developed with this most phenomenal yet so humanly vulnerable woman. Such extreme riches comes to so few people.

Sara Mallow

Sara Mallow was born and raised in Brooklyn, New York and married the boy next door, her childhood sweetheart. Together they struggled to become business owners starting with the construction of residential properties in Brooklyn and then establishing a computer business during the "keypunch" era.

Today her children continue to operate the business which sells and maintains personal computers – in New York City. She remains President of the Company and participates in its financial management

As the last living member of her family, in her desire to leave her life history for her progeny, Sara began to write her memoirs. Recently widowed, she hopes to continue to write those stories, from her homes in Boca Raton and New York City.

MMM

Memories Of A Cold Water Flats

By Sara Mallow

What is a cold water flat? Picture a walk-up apartment house about five stories high, maybe six families on a floor where the water runs cold only and there is no heating system. The only means of heating comes from a black cast iron stove that has about six round burner tops and a chimney. These burner tops are lifted with a special holder beneath which the coal is ignited. This becomes the most important part of the house.

Saturday morning was the time for my weekly bath. First the water had to be heated in large pots on the coal stove. After the water boiled, it would be dumped in the bathtub. The boiling water would warm up the cold air and it would become the poor man's sauna. When the water reached the right temperature, into the bathtub I went. First my hair had to be washed with Lifebuoy soap. Shampoos were not known yet. After two washings, my hair was finally rinsed leaving the tub full of suds.

How I loved soaping myself in the warm water which covered me up to my neck. I dreaded to come out and face that cold air again. I'd run to the coal stove which was the center of all our activities. Usually there was a stew or soup cooking on the stove. We had lamb chops grilled on top of the coals when they could afford it. This was the beginning of my love for charcoal broiling.

I looked forward to our Friday night chicken soup. Today they call it "chicken in the pot." My mother shopped in a live chicken market. I couldn't watch the killing when they cut the chicken's neck. She would hand pluck the feathers and they would fly all over the place.

There was no refrigeration for food storage.. We had an ice box which held a block of ice. The food would stay cold until the block melted into a pan underneath the box. If the water wasn't emptied soon enough we were flooded. The block of ice was picked up at the ice dock, usually carried home in an old baby carriage and carried up the flights of stairs. Is this reminiscent of some of the hardships of the recent hurricanes?

Saturday night was "specials and beans" which came from the deli. I can still smell the garlic aroma of the local deli. The smell drifted out of the store almost half way down the block. Unlike the plastic packages of hot dogs we get in the super market, these fat hot dogs were strung together and torn off when they were sold. Plastic was not invented yet.

For entertainment, we'd all get into my older brother's Model T and go to Highland Park or Coney Island. How I loved the swings in the park and the carousel in Coney Island. At night we'd gather around the radio and listen to "Mr. Anthony". People with problems would call in and Mr. Anthony in his very stern baritone voice would give out advice. It would break your heart to hear the wife tell about her husband who abandoned her with three small children for a much younger hussy.

Education was taken very seriously in those days. The teacher was God. I was a very good student in elementary school. I usually got an A in work and always an A in conduct. I never missed a day of school. I remember going to school in a winter blizzard. The school was closed when I got there. I had to trudge back home in thigh high snowdrifts. My mother confronted me, scolding, "I told you the school would be closed. Next time you listen to me." She immediately remedied the situation. My wet clothes were removed and I warmed up at the stove and drank hot chocolate. .

We lived in the Brownsville section of Brooklyn, home of Murder, Inc.We usually moved from one cold water flat to another because the rent was cheaper or we got a free paint job. Each tenement had a front door stoop. The tenants would congregate there where they talked about all the current news and gossip. There was also the roof where the people gathered to either suntan or cool off on hot summer nights. When the heat became unbearable, we'd take our blankets and pillows and join all the other families. Usually nobody slept and it became a continuation of the front door stoops.

What a difference today. We live in individual houses. We press a button or pull a lever and the heat or air comes on. We shower or bathe at least once a day in our individual bathrooms. We have stoves, broilers, outdoor grills and freezers full of meat. We have 140 channels on our individual televisions to choose from. The garage has his and her cars. We drive our children to school or they're picked up by bus.

We have made amazing progress. We have less to struggle for and more time to pursue our dreams. But I still remember those days with fondness. We might have lost some of the camaraderie which was so much a part of the days of the cold water flats.

MMM

The Curse

By Sara Mallow

When a "curse" becomes a reality, it might be interpreted as coincidental by skeptics or it might be judged as destiny by those who believe in mysterious powers .

Such an unusual "curse" took place in the eighteen nineties in the Ukrainian part of Russia. The setting was like the one staged in "Fiddler on the Roof". As was the custom in those days, a matchmaker was called upon to arrange a meeting for two "eligibles"., one of whom happened to be my mother. The preliminary pre-nuptial agreements were settled by both sets of parents with the help of the matchmaker. A meeting was to take place for the prospective bride and bridegroom to meet at the home of the matchmaker.

My mother had not been told that her prospective husband had a deformity of the legs. The meeting was assembled with the father accompanying his daughter and the mother accompanying her son. My mother was so shocked when she saw the young man's condition that she fled from the room in tears.

Her father and the matchmaker implored her to reconsider because the young man had such wonderful qualities and would be a fine husband. But to no avail. The matchmaker tactfully tried to lessen the blow to the young man's mother by trying to convince her that the girl was so young and was afraid of marriage The boy's mother saw through the ruse and in her anguish, confronted my mother blurting out "since you have refused my son because of his crippled legs, your first son will be so afflicted." It was a very painful incident not easily forgotten.

Shortly afterwards my mother married and promptly became pregnant. During her last months of pregnancy, she took a trip to a near-by village riding in a horse and carriage. The icy road conditions caused the carriage to turn over, throwing all the passengers in different directions. Since my mother was strong and healthy, she was merely shaken up but feared for the child inside her.

Soon after, my bother Willie was born. He was a beautiful baby boy with clubbed feet. This was a great sorrow for my mother who believed she was cursed as the mother of the rejected suitor had predicted. The village doctor could not treat his condition but thought there might be hope for correcting the deformity in America. My mother was determined to get to America at all costs.

While my family was saving to go to America, my brother Isadore was born. As was the custom in those days, my father migrated to America, first to find work and housing. When my brothers were two and four years old, my mother joined the hordes of others migrating to America in search of the "golden land." She had some problems getting my brother through Immigration at Ellis Island because of his deformity, but she was a fighter and wouldn't give up.

After the family settled in Brooklyn, my mother searched for a charitable hospital which would accept my brother. She located Bellevue Hospital in Manhattan. In his fifth year he went in and out of the hospital and had many operations. At seven years old his club feet were corrected and he finally walked like a normal child. During these years of hospitalization, my brother developed a kinship with the hospital personnel and became inspired by the good work they were doing. As he grew into manhood, he always talked about becoming a doctor. He finally realized his ambition, supporting himself by working as a waiter, selling magazine subscriptions and giving piano lessons.

Eventually there were three more children born in America. We all looked up to Willie as a celebrity and the whole neighborhood waited outside, no matter what the hour, when he was due to drive home from Iowa Medical School in his Model T Ford. He was our idol and took a great interest in our lives and guided us in our futures. He was the first success in the family and we were aware of his ability to deal with the impossible.

When my parents and the "cursed" child came to America, they had to overcome many obstacles. They had to learn a new language, new customs and had to make do with very few dollars. In spite of these hardships, their struggles paid off. Their courage led the way for the whole family to have a better life.

This was one "curse" that became a blessing.

Z. McGrath

Z. was born in Brooklyn, lived on Long Island for 32 years, and for the past nine years has lived in Boca Raton, Florida. Using her artistic bent, she established Floral Fantasies By Z, a floral design business, decorating store windows, and buildings as well as residences. She has two children, 3 grandchildren, several step-children, and step-grandchildren, nieces and nephews, all of whom remain an integral part of her life.

Z had been a closet writer for years, and only when she began to attend the writing workshop did she feel comfortable about sharing her work with others.

Now she is happy to read her stories and poems to all who will listen.

MMM

Memories Are Ever Young: The Patchwork Quilt

By Z. McGrath

Have you ever noticed how some memories seem untouched by time, that when jarred from its slumber, how the years seem to fall away? And wasn't it just a moment ago that you were ten perhaps eighteen or thirty- two? Whatever the age, it really doesn't matter. You step back into that day, that feeling, as though the memory has just been waiting to be summoned, waiting to be relived.

Unbidden, from its secret place, the patchwork quilt gently settles about me. Memories, released from their confining folds, tug at me, much like competing children, each demanding a share of attention. Shapes and colors vary. Some muted, mellowed by time, some ever bright, seeming to resist fading. Richly textured, dark and light, memory is the invisible thread that continually mends, securing that special moment, the occasional perfect day.

Surprise! A doll's cradle from a Mother generally too practical to trade long hours of hard work behind a bakery counter for toys.

A spring day filled with pale bouquets, the promise of tomorrow, forever. Boundless time spent at play. A bright new pink Spalding, its round perfection, fitting into my cupped hand for stoop ball, or Russian ten. A clothes line, its new incarnation as jump rope for *double dutch*, or *downa Mississippi and the steam goes pushh*. A knobby kneed girl rocking in time to the slap of the rope, waiting her turn. *Jacks*, and *pickup sticks* tumble out in front of me. Roller skates gliding, smooth as silk on flawless cement. A zippered red poplin jacket, dark brown pigtails with red ribbons, and "why" to all the questions that remain unanswered.

Hot lazy summer mornings with the heavy sweet scent of honeysuckle in the air. The sound of water sprayed from a truck whose task is to clean the streets. Sounds of horses hooves, and wagon wheels bringing a cart, double tiered, filled with geraniums. "Choose one," my father says. The perfusion of pink, white, coral, red, flowers are all beautiful. I am unable to decide. I want it the way it looks in the cart. My father laughs, pays thirty cents, and I carry home my prize, three clay pots filled with red flowers. Today, on my front lawn is a cart overflowing with red geraniums. A gift from another loving man as a tribute to a perfect memory

Every evening, on the way home from work, my father would stop at the corner candy store to buy an ice-cream cone for me. He never forgot! A sugar cone, double-dip chocolate with sprinkles. Fridays, payday, an additional treat, a small windup toy hidden in a pocket, just waiting to be discovered.

Bubbah

By Z. c Grath

My Bubbah [Grandmother] spoke Russian and Yiddish with a few distorted words in English thrown in for good measure. Summer or winter, my bubbah wore dark brown lyle stockings, long black dresses, and a fachailitchkeh [kerchief] tied under her chin. To my ongoing embarrassment and to complete her fashion statement she also carried an umbrella, even on sunny days. This too was black. To keep me in line, she would threaten, that if I didn't mind her, "the malchamovis, [devil] would get me."

Fear kept me stuck by her side, all the while wishing her dead, so my Mother would be forced to quit work and have to stay home with me. What must it have been like for her, a Russian immigrant in her seventies wandering Brooklyn, unable to speak English with a resentful eight year old girl in tow as interpreter.

Each Friday she would take me to the fresh chicken market to pick out the Sabbath sacrifice. Nausea bubbled in my throat. Though the entire front of the market was open to the street, it did nothing to ward off the smell of feathers, blood and sawdust which intermingled with the pious unwashed. Fear and fascination peaked at the sight and sounds. So many chickens were running around clucking, shrieking, feathers flying as they frantically attempted to escape the selection.

However my Grandma was not to be put off. She wielded her black umbrella with her right hand clutched me to her left side commanding that I translate her Yiddish discontent over what she considered to be an insult.

The anemic chickens being sold were absolutely not worth the price asked, and if she had to use one of his inferior skinny chickens to make her shabbas [Sabbath] supper, we would starve and that he should 'gey in dread' (go in the earth – be buried!) for trying to fool her. Had he no shame taking advantage of an old woman!

I know this is how I learned diplomacy, never letting on to the man that bubbah cursed him, wishing him dead calling him a gonnif, [thief] accusing him of cheating her. All the while, the chosen chicken was held by its feet, shrieking, wings flapping producing a small shower of feathers, as it made its way to the schoichet [executioner] who would slit it's throat, then drop it to the floor where it would run around, I guessed, saying goodbye to all its friends who were sharing in a similar fate.

With her business concluded, we would leave. What a sight we must have made, Bubbah in her black getup, holding her limp paper-wrapped prize, schlepping [dragging] a knobby-kneed eight-year-old girl. We headed to our next stop, the bakery.

193

A Penny's Worth

By Z. McGrath

A small jar of pennies.

"Mom, isn't it odd that great Grandma Z kept it with her jewelry?"

Treasure, or junk, who's to say? Unrecognizable to others' eyes, its value only a whisper in my ear. Lost unless my voice breathes it to life, blowing away the wrapping of years. One day the jar of pennies will become part of someone else's collection, my story just an echo.

Once upon a time I read fairy tales, and believed in them. I played card games with my grandmother while my mother spent twelve hours a day cheating poverty. Oh how I longed for my mother to stay home with me.

Sitting on the kitchen floor, the linoleum cool on my bare legs, I busily sorted, counted and divided into piles, the pennies I had dumped from a tall tin can where my mother saved them. As I moved the piles, I would recite,

"With these pennies, I can buy you a fur coat, and with all of these," as I added another fistful to a small stack, "a house." "Mommy, if I save enough pennies, I could buy pretty dresses, and food. Then you won't have to work. You could stay home with me."

Daydreaming. So sure of the magic within the stacks of dull and glittering circles that I had counted and recounted. While I was describing all I would do for her, my mother was rushing about the kitchen preparing supper. She was home, singing, smiling at me. I was happy.

Many years later, her world dimmed by blindness, her quick wit slowed by a faulty, stumbling memory, my mother sat on a chair in my kitchen, stuffing an endless supply of pennies into frayed wrappers with which I kept her in constant supply. She was smiling, singing, pleased, to be of imagined help to me, as I rushed about my kitchen. She was happy.

Although my mother is long gone, and both of those kitchens are now occupied by others, I still keep a jar of pennies, occasionally sifting my fingers through them, remembering, and feeling its fallen power.

The Search: Fatal Flaw

By Z. McGrath

Eyes warm, filled with love, just for me.

My Mother's warning rings in my ears.

"Don't think, for one minute, you'll ever find a husband, who is going to love you like your Father." Curse, or premonition? Maybe just an experienced woman's understanding of men, and what we women, spend our lives searching for.

Well, I've certainly tried to prove her wrong. Howie, Joe, Sam, plus an exhausting assortment of nameless ones, all with, "A fatal flaw."

Oh, I looked, but always with an eye on my "ruler," my father, the one that no man could measure up against. Oh God, what a legacy! Yet nothing quite jars me from this yoke of hope.

Desperate, I place an ad in the newspaper, No! Not in the singles column, in the, "room for rent" section. Desperate, that is, for additional income. It had to come from somewhere. Even Swanson TV dinners, cost money.

In 1968, my presence as a single mom, in the affluent north shore Long Island community I called home, was a bone in the throat of complacency, and about as welcome, as pimples on an adolescent face.

My children were the only ones in a school of nine hundred, to have a last name that was different from their mother's. Had I held onto my second marriage, just a few years longer, we would have been able to blend in with the parade of divorced, and disenfranchised, who were soon to follow in the seventies.

This, however, was not to be. My experience with alcohol was a toast at a wedding, or Bris. Waiting for my then, new husband, to get off a train, which he had never boarded, because he was "fatal flaw" drunk, was not exactly my idea, of love and marriage.

Trying to maintain a roof over our heads, kept me desperate. Our home was on the verge of being turned into a kibbutz, which it seemed better to me than a boarding house

Over the phone a deep, pleasant voice asked about the room in the ad.

YES! I was almost there. I described the house, skirting what the privilege of renting was going to cost him. I knew what I needed, I just couldn't tell him, until I had a chance to convince him in person. We agreed to a time.

That Friday in May seemed ordinary enough. Money and children worries, dog drool making a skating rink on the kitchen floor, gourmet TV dinners in the oven, a ringing telephone, a cousin visiting for the weekend in need of entertaining. I could have given new meaning to attention deficit disorder.

I answered the doorbell, and sank into the darkest, saddest eyes I'd ever seen. Paul was literally tall dark and handsome. In an instant, my world headed for a U turn. But while my heart was bonding, reality, by the name of Sam, was uncomfortably, intruding.

Sam was intelligent, curious, compassionate, and generous. He had the desire to taste life with a spoon in each hand. All this, while sitting on the sidelines of real life. Sam was a conscientious observer. He was the kind of person who sits at the edge of the pool, toes splashing in the water, making insightful observations about others who were struggling to keep from drowning. Psychoanalyst by profession and proclivity, he was in perfect balance. Nonetheless, for me, "a fatal flaw".

Then there was messy me, spilling into his space, demanding attention, with no money, a house falling apart, a troubled adolescent daughter, and a young son, uncertain of his position, between two warring females, not to mention a hyperactive Irish setter by the name of Sammy.

Unfortunately the dog's name was now being shared with the man, which created more confusion in a house already in a state of havoc. When we were all in the same room, if I called Sam, both heads turned toward me, each with the same look of anticipation. One with hope of a walk as reward for his attentiveness. The other, wanting to "take a walk.." One wore his leather briefcase as buffer. The other wore a leather collar.

After about four years, Sam, "the briefcase," had arrived at the perfect plan for a suitable family life, in his head, which is where, he lived. "Oops, Fatal flaw."

He would continue total financial involvement, keeping us ensconced in Syosset. He would reside in the city, a safe distance from the confusion of daily life. We would all be together on weekends and holidays, this of course, if his schedule with patients, teaching, lecturing, writing, etc., didn't interfere. However, any night, that I was able to find a replacement to stay with my children, I could join him in his world.

Well, that was not my idea of "together ever after".

Hence, the "room for rent" ad in the paper. My goal! Financial independence.

Enter, Paul, a man without "a fatal flaw."

Mama's New Shoes

By Z. McGrath

Sadness layered innocence.
Rejected, cradled in indifference,
She left to seek a heartier fill

My Mother arrived in the free world, scarred, a beautiful young sapling, slightly bowed from mistreatment, poverty and from hands intent on keeping her down. Her heart filled with longing, coupled with an indomitable spirit, she rose to catch a dream.

Hearing what my Mother's childhood had been like, clouded mine. I was wrapped in her disappointments. The world, *her* world, was unsafe.

They were dirt-poor Jews surrounded by hostility simply because they existed. My mother, Riva Narovlanski, was born on Christmas Day, 1904 in a shtettle [town] on the outskirts of Moscow, Russia, the youngest of eleven living children. Three others had died prior to her arrival.

She was an unwanted burden. My Grandmother was not exactly overcome with joy at yet another mouth to feed. My Grandfather, a religious scholar, spent his days studying the bible. To be married to such a religious man was supposed to be an honor [although a dubious one at that] for Grandpa was above life's details. It was Grandma who was left to scratch out a meager existence, getting up before dawn to sell rolls, [bouletchkes] to travelers at the train station. Bullied and beaten, my mother's childhood was a lesson in survival.

This story in particular, of when my mother was a girl of about ten remains fixed in my memory. It was fall and the Jewish holidays were fast approaching and Riva dreamed of new shoes, her very own shoes and not the worn out hand-me-downs she usually wore. To have a pair of shoes of her own became an obsession. But how was she to get them?.

One day she walked the four miles to the town in the only shoes she had, shoes that had been passed down to her, long after their useful life span was over. There were cracks in the shape of the last wearer's feet, and the soles pulled away, having given up on any connection with the tops. All holes were lined with paper. These make-do shoes were held onto her feet with strips of rags. The clumsy protection the shoes provided was still better than walking barefoot, and so she headed to the shoemaker's shop clutching her dream.

The lie burned red on her face when she told the shoemaker her Mother Chai Russa, whom he knew, sent her to have her feet [mussed] measured for shoes, and that the shoes needed to be ready before the holidays. The shoemaker, not quite convinced that my grandmother had actually sent her, kept questioning my mother but finally relented, saying if she gave him a small deposit of one rubble, he would take her measure.

Desperation and fear beaded her face. To give a deposit of a rubble was as impossible as having her very own dress, or a real doll, not one made from rags. Brazenly she compounded her lie, and with feigned outrage, she asked the shoemaker,

"How dare you question what my Mother wants? My mother doesn't have the time to come in now. She is busy preparing for the holiday. She will be in to pay you in full when the shoes are ready".

Never having encountered anything like this before, he reluctantly agreed to take her measure.

Over the next few weeks my mother would show up at the shoemaker's regularly to check on his progress. Finally, one day the shoemaker said, "Riva, tell your mother to bring the three rubbles she owes me. Your shoes will be ready tomorrow."

As my mother hurried home, her throat tensed in the practiced lie she would soon tell, that the shoemaker had stopped her when he noticed her walking by his shop. "He said he had made a pair of shoes for a girl from another village, but the family must have changed their minds because they never picked them up. He was able to tell by just looking at my feet, that the shoes would fit me, and he could sell them to us for very little money."

My Grandmother told my mother she didn't have money for new shoes. My mother begged, and cried, saying she would do anything to have those shoes. When would a miracle like this ever happen again? It was a bargain! Practically free!

Finally convinced of the wisdom of checking out this potential windfall, they both headed to the town.

When they arrived at the shoemakers', my grandmother asked to see the shoes. The shoemaker produced them from behind the counter, placed them on my mother's feet, beaming, with proud in his work.

My grandmother looked them over, indicating she was unimpressed. She felt them, commented that the shoes were not a perfect fit, however, since he had made them for another girl, and only if they were really a bargain would she would consider helping him out by taking them off his hands. Of course, this would depend on how much he wanted for them.

"What!" The shoemaker shouted, "what do you mean made for another girl? What kind of a devil are you Chaia Russha, sending your daughter to get measured for shoes and then trying to steal them from me. I knew you were up to no good when you didn't come with Riva that first day. You are a [gonnif], a thief trying to cheat me. The shoes are perfect! I measured her feet like you asked. I cut the leather to fit Riva. I made the shoes for your daughter not for another girl."

At that moment my grandmother, arm extended, spun around, but my mother, with an experienced side step, ducked and fled. Heart and feet racing in unison, she ran all the way home in the new shoes. [which by the way fit perfectly.] Trembling in anticipation of the inevitable, she took a very temporary refuge under a bed.

My grandmother did not like being made a fool. She had been forced to pay for the shoes on my Mothers' feet, and that made her hot with anger. Easily finding where my mother was hidden, she reached under the bed grabbing at whatever part was closest. I can assure you it was not her feet, .and my grandma beat my mother without mercy.

As my mother was telling me this, she had a smile on her face. She didn't mind the beating, she said. It was worth every bruise. At last, she had her very own new shoes.

Memories I have of my mother, are as a strong, highly energetic, resourceful woman, courageously reaching out for what she wanted, with a ready laugh and a tender heart available to all.

No matter the blows life dealt her; she never gave up. One of her favorite songs was *Shipmates Stand Together*, I can still hear her deep throaty voice half singing, half speaking,. *"Life's a long, long trip. If you* have to take a licking, carry on and quit your kicking. Don't give up the ship!"

MMM

The Dress

By Z. McGrath

I had exhausted every store within a radius of fifty miles for about five months looking for a dress to make me feel beautiful and confident. I wasn't sure what it would look like. But I was certain I would know it when I saw it.

My son was getting married and I would be walking him down the aisle without Paul. I couldn't bear the whispers, the pity or the questions. What did he die of? Isn't it a shame he was so young. Is she still alone? I heard she had just recently met someone. Is he here? What is he like? Two years and eight months had marched through me day by empty day, and I longed to feel whole again.

Finally, I saw the dress. It was black and had a deeply scooped neckline with a fitted bodice ending in a sheer full angled skirt that was edged in a single line of black sequins. Just what I was looking for. It was elegant but oh, so much more expensive than I could afford.

I was determined to have it, and I refused to let anything as petty as a price tag keep me from my dress. I persuaded the store- manager to either sell the sample or reduce the cost of ordering a new one. But the three hundred dollar savings was still not going to be enough. I then sold off Christmas decorations from my business, picking up an extra thousand dollars, and my favorite, only niece came up with a gift of five hundred dollars. I couldn't believe that the dress would actually be mine. But it was.

Only temporary insanity could have compelled me to pay a small fortune to own a dress that would be worn just once. In fact my Mother paid far less money for a car, and the car gave her years of useful pleasure. So how was I going to make use of or continue to enjoy my dress? Even if my so-called social life required elegant evening wear, being fifteen

200

pounds beyond the one hundred sixteen that I had attained for that evening made wearing my dress again an impossibility. The only future relationship I could expect to have with my extravagant investment, was that I was going to be able to look at it.

Fifteen years have passed and as I sit in my kitchen writing this, the dress is gracing a store mannequin that stands in my bedroom, a permanent beautiful tribute combining past perfect with the pleasure of now. Sometimes when returning to bed after a 2 A.M. trip to the bathroom in the shadowed light, I imagine the dress moving and I can see it dancing with me in it and I smile.

I remember that my mother had a silk taffeta gown in the same shade of blue as her eyes. It was the one she wore to my sister's wedding and it hung in her small closet taking up needed space. No matter how I prodded her to get rid of it; there it remained until the fabric simply disintegrated off the hanger. I never would have urged her to toss her memory if I had understood, but that would take many more years.

MMM

The Naked Bed: The Psychoanalyst's Couch

By Z. McGrath

So why do I dress it? The bed looks perfectly fine as is. I could simply smooth out the sleep lines in the sheet, fluff the pillows and walk away. What am I covering? Or is it that if the bed is undone, there is no place to hide secrets. Does the undressed bed look too vulnerable to me? Is it possible that I'm concealing naked passion behind those ruffled pillows? Well, I'm not certain it's that complicated.

All I know is, each morning I adorn my bed in sunshine and scarlet, grounded on a backdrop of black and white. I love the relief of the crisp white sheet against the black, echoing contrasting emotions. The anarchy of patterns and colors create a controlled riot. The four-poster acts like a vine to the bracks of tumbling wisteria and glass teardrops. Palpable pleasure makes the corners of my mouth curve in a satisfied arc.

Now I do this, fully aware that no one else cares how the bed looks, nor will anyone even see it. No matter! I repeat this ritual daily just as though the bed will be on display in the center of the house. In fact after all my effort, I don't even see it again until the undressing rite takes place before going to sleep. So who cares, or better yet, why do I care?

After I've dressed the bed for the day, I have the additional bonus of a sulking man who feels punished because he has been banned from the comfort of taking a midday nap in it. His campaign starts when he wakes up. At 7:30 AM he announces what a restless night he had and how tired he is. I used to commiserate with him, but now I pretend not to hear him, as this is his Monday thru Sunday litany.

With no response, he continues his attempt to hook me with a graphic description of pain in his back or hands or possibly his ongoing headache. I'm not quite certain this is in reference to me or to a misaligned disk.

None of his complaints, however, prevent him from his workout at the gym, so I heartlessly go on with my obsession. I show no mercy as, God forbid, he should nap in the one thousand dollar recliner I bought for him. He watches as I begin smoothing our comforter and realizes it's quickly becoming hopeless. In a last ditch effort he soulfully asks if I would just not make the bed today.

He always asks this as though today may be different from any other day. When he sees that his begging is falling on deaf ears, he starts his pitch for the following day with, "You can't make the bed tomorrow. I have to be up at six AM for a doctor's appointment, or to bring the car in for an oil change before it gets crowded, or I like to get to Publix before all the seniors get there. I'm thinking, if I kill him now, then he could just stay in the bed for the entire day. Al has quite a repertoire and he does beg well.

Sometimes I think the bed ceremonial is a leftover relic from a time long ago, when polishing my daughter's white shoes each night meant that although I was still in my teens, I was a responsible good mother. I must have reasoned somewhere deep in my subconscious that this is what I needed to do in order to avoid ending up in hell on judgment day for not measuring up. If this is so, it's an awful lot of effort, and for whose review?

The elegant irony! I've spent years creating visual beauty for others. This bed is for me. I lovingly drape the afghan, allowing the fringe to brush the rug. I hurriedly and without so much as a glance in the mirror, pull on a pair of my old jeans. I leave my picture perfect chamber satisfied. Maybe tomorrow I'll deal with my compulsion. Who knows, maybe tomorrow I'll leave the bed unmade.

Clarisse Mello

Clarisse Bandeira de Mello was born in Rio de Janeiro, Brazil, and moved to Florida in 1990. With degrees in the Portuguese and English Languages and Literature, she works as a translator, interpreter and adjunct professor at Florida International University. She has several works on Portuguese translation and teaching in academic publications.

Clarisse writes short stories, having received literary awards both in Brazil and the United States. Reading, cooking and traveling are her favorite hobbies, as well as participating in literary groups for the study of Brazilian and Portuguese literatures. She lives with her husband in Weston, Florida, has two daughters and three grandchildren.

MMM

Yearning

By Clarisse Mello

I am in the theatre, staring at the stage. Tears drop from my eyes when listening to the music. Obsessive, stubborn, the notes insist on dwelling in my memory. A reminiscence of a past long gone, they are a shadow always chasing me, wherever I try to hide.

Once upon a time, there was a little girl…
And her name was Maribel, bel, bel, bel…

****

I go back in time. The theater was crammed on that hot Saturday matinee. My sister's dreams of being a famous actress soon would become reality. Nervous and excited, Aida paced back and forth, whispering her lines before the velvet burgundy curtains were drawn. With shyness locked in an imaginary secret box, she concentrated in her role as Maribel and stepped on center stage. The golden braids tied with deep blue satin laces bounced, while my 14-year-old sister sang, danced, and recited before the delighted audience. At the end, she received a standing ovation. Watching her smile, I believed that Aida had the universe at her feet.

The cotton dress had been made with extreme care to the elaborate details. Aida chose trimmings, buttons, braid laces, and an imported blue madras fabric to contrast with the white, embroidered petticoats. The round-layered skirt would give a glint of the shapely legs at each turn.

"I want to fly on stage like a ballerina", she said, and she laughed at the expression of admiration in my mother's eyes. "Your legs are Aunt Mary's legacy", I told her. Trying on the glossy black shoes, handmade at a very expensive store, Aida wanted everything to be perfect, just as she dreamed.

The week before the premiere, she was at the window waiting for the dressmaker. A broken zipper, some pinpricks, sleeves too tight, and the poor woman would humbly excuse herself.

"I am sorry, so sorry, Miss." Aida had been restless and anxious as she faced the overwhelming task ahead.

The excitement affected our whole family. Well, not all the family. My father had an air of disguised condemnation. In his strict conservative mind, he feared that his daughter might be swept into a disreputable life as an actress. However I think the true reason for his disapproval was fear of losing her. How could he accept her going away, someone so beautiful, young, and full of life. How?

The tickets were sold out. The play, "Pluft, The Little Ghost," was a hit at the time, with short-lived ethereal characters, like cousin Bubble, and other zillion bubbles in rainbow hues. From that day on Aida nurtured her dream of becoming famous. She saw her life as a billboard, lighting up her success for the whole world to see. Even the timing was right for her, as she had just begun to experience passion and tenderness in her relationship with her first boyfriend.

After each performance, we could see how happy she was, although the exhaustion showed on her face when she came home. Then, as time went by, it started to appear more than mere fatigue, an uneasy, mysterious feeling possessed her. If she had fears, she never confided them to me, although we shared the same bedroom. "Tomorrow I will feel better," she tried to convince herself, in the midst of her suspicions. "It is just a minor discomfort, nothing else."

Three weeks passed. One night, feeling sick, Aida dragged herself to the bathroom, her hands leaving stains of blood on the walls. My mother woke up and panicked at the sight of her fragile body, in a long white gown. With a ghostly expression on her face, she lost balance and fainted. After that, everything happened so fast...

Lying down in the back seat of my mother's car, Aida left for the hospital. As the car disappeared down the street, I went to my bedroom and prayed, in the hope that soon we would be sharing our secrets again, that someday we would be playing with our children together - two sisters, in love with each other, laughing at our silly childhood adventures.

The telephone rang a few hours later. My mother's sobbing voice on the other side was barely intelligible. "Acute leukemia," she said. And there I was, alone in the living-room with the phone in my hands, unable to utter a word. A sense of powerlessness and despair took hold of me. Why... why? I asked myself, and the more I repeated the question, fewer answers came to my mind. I sat on the floor, and for the first time, I felt a void in my existence that would never be filled again.

Aida departed after a 2-day stay in the hospital. In the silent house, one could only see the blurred and inert eyes of my mother, hear the desperate lament of my father on the hot summer nights, and sense in my eyes a painful desperation, looking at the bed, empty forever.

Reminders of her presence; the blue and white dress, the shoes, the socks, and the braid laces had been carefully stored in the closet. My father, in his uncontrollable suffering, asked that everything remain as she left it. He wanted her things to accompany him, in his future encounter with her. As the years went by, my mother wept more and more over Aida's absence, living one day at a time, in the hope of seeing her again...

****

Forty years later, as I write my memories, the story starts like that: "Once upon time, there was a little ghost, Pluft, which became human. Maribel became Aida, who became a bubble. She flew higher and higher, towards the infinite, until she disappeared, and her 20-year-old sister wept, impotent, without the courage to pronounce her name. In her remembrance, a frail body in a coffin, in a light pink dress, the black shoes, the face covered with an embroidered handkerchief, the long and delicate fingers crossed on her chest..."

The music continued, stubborn, cruel, with no intention of leaving the stage.

MMM

Wake Up and I'll Be There...

By Clarisse Mello

At 5 o'clock in the morning, he woke up. His eyes, after a bad night's sleep, were red and dull. Lying on the bed beside him, I could feel his heavy sighs, and the restless legs trying to find a better position when nothing seemed comfortable.

He stood up, stretched his arms and went straight to the bathroom. "Do not swallow even a drop of water when brushing your teeth. It will cancel the procedure," the nurse in a green uniform had said, in a poised voice, the day before.

"I must remind myself that I cannot swallow, cannot swallow, cannot..."

The idea of drinking a full glass of orange juice distracted his mind from all the anticipated pain and discomfort playing the tricks of a mean ghost.

Trying to hide our mutual anxiety, we drove towards the hospital, babbling meaningless words to divert our attention. I looked through the side mirror and raindrops blurred my vision of our home, finally disappearing at the first turn of the road.

Sheer nervousness caused Henry to drive fast through the highway, as we counted the minutes to the end of this ordeal. "I want to flee, I want to flee..."

In silence, I laid my eyes on the scenery, being wise enough to be quiet. Any remark might start an argument. My fingers softly squeezed his thigh, letting him know he was not alone.

In the lobby, an elderly man called Henry's name, put a tag around his wrist and uttered in a hoarse, almost unintelligible whisper, "Is this your correct name, date of birth, doctor's name?"

"Yes, I think so." What difference would it make now, when all the poker cards were on the table? His life was in their hands, in the hands of those guys who approach human beings with green gowns, nice faces, half-open smiles, compassionate eyes and butcher's hands to wound their flesh.

Someone took him to the pre-op room, where five or six patients were already waiting. Another 'God knows who' pointed his thick finger to a bed surrounded by tubes, oxygen, gloves, medication, and an annoying stillness. There was an empty chair at the corner, but he was not supposed to occupy it. Maybe it was meant for a visitor, when everything was over.

"Close the curtain, take off everything: clothes, eyeglasses, jewelry, dentures," ordered a black man with a golden watch that would shine miles away.

"I do not have dentures," Henry almost shouted.

"Please, put this gown on with the opening to the back, ask your wife to tie it on your neck," repeated the man twice, looking at Henry's dumbstruck face.

After a few minutes he returned. "Let's check the vital signs, blood pressure, lungs, pulse rate. Open your mouth, stick out your tongue. Good, good. I want to make sure everything is fine. Did you drink water after midnight?"

"Nooooooo!"

What if he had said yes? They would have sent him home. Is that not funny? Now he is completely captive to someone else's intentions.

I know he is thinking, "It is all her fault. She always says she wanted to be a doctor. She was the one who started gaping at my belly button, protruding from a mass of fat. Sometimes, her way of deciding on things irritates me. Most of the time she is right, I know, and that irritates me even more. Some women get away with everything just with the sweetness in their voices."

The sound of an electric razor back and forth on his abdomen made him realize that was not the proper time for rumination. His doctor, 'my master butcher,' Henry had called him, came to say hello, holding not a scalpel, but a pen in his hand.

"What is the point of drawing a smiley face around my navel and then slicing it like a piece of cake? Enough! I want to go home!"

Suddenly, the curtain moved and a gorgeous, fairy-faced woman, with a cap protecting her hair, entered the cubicle where his body had already surrendered to all external impositions. She introduced herself as the anesthesiologist and her smile glowed as in old romantic movies. He felt more relaxed after she pricked his vein with a long needle.

"The itch will last for a few minutes, and then you are going to sleep."

The black man came again. "It's time to go, old guy." And turning to me, "You, madam, get some coffee in the waiting room."

Henry reached for my hand and dragged it towards his face.

"Give me a kiss, one more time."

I kissed his forehead, his cheeks, and tenderly smoothed his hair.

"Not on my cheeks, on my mouth." He held my hand softly while diving into an unconscious state.

"The red lipstick is going to stain your lips," I said with a large smile.

"Please… I lov…"

With his eyelids slowly closing, I gave him a long kiss and felt the undying taste of love caressing my mouth.

Nancy Lee Havens Vaughn Miller

Nancy, because it was the fourth or fifth most popular* name at the time, a good English name, not at all trendy or showy. Lee, for the celebrated general and leader of our side in the recent unpleasantness (which is how we referred to the Civil War should we find it necessary to refer to it at all). Havens, for my father's Scottish family which bet on the wrong prince back in the gone-by. Vaughan, for a brief mistake with one of the two campus heroes at Virginia Commonwealth University where I majored in communications. Miller, for an alliance with the other campus hero, which has not been a mistake for thirty years. Direct descendant of the late, great General Sterling B.Price (also of the recent unpleasantness) and Pocahantas. (Bolling line not Smith.)

Born in Green Bay,Va. (pop. 109) College at 16, then firstjobs, then first marriage, then on to New York City where I was, serially, Executive Vice President, Executive Creative Director of:Wells, Rich & Green, Bates, Ally & Gargano and Lintas. What else is interesting? Hmmm. There's a record somewhere in the UK of a song I wrote, there's an optioned screenplay somewhere in LA that I wrote, but mostly my husband and I try to have very nice mornings, and pleasant lunches and dinners with the best views and the nicest music we can find near our homes in Florida and New Jersey. Twice a week we go to museums or galleries to feed our eyes. And we try to spend as much time with our friends as we can, to feed our souls. That's all.

*Nancy Drew was still the rage.

The Pretty Wars

By Nan Miller

The doctor had said that we should expect the worst. That the family should assemble. And so my sister, Jane, and I had assembled ourselves at St. Francis Hospital in the holy city of Charleston, South Carolina, Jane from her home a few blocks away, me from New York.

Our Mother was, after all, 92 years old and weighed 97 pounds "The family," Doctor Atwater had said "should be prepared." He was a specialist new to the case and therefore not prepared for our mother.

They wheeled her out of the operating room and into recovery. A nurse, wanting to be kind, had sneaked us in to sit quietly by her bed, awaiting the chance for, perhaps, a tender final word. Almost immediately she opened her eyes, looked past me to my sister, and raised her hand in the oldest of feminine gestures. And then she spoke to us.

"Is my hair all right?"

My sister and I exchanged flat, deadpan glances. Lookism was alive and well and everything was normal in the mad way of our family.

Once, while fulfilling a high school essay assignment on genealogy, I had written that our family crest was a tube of circumspect pink lipstick rampant upon a field of clean underwear with the motto *Appearances Are Everything*. I got an A, with a note about my gift of satire. I accepted the A, but the truth is not a gift.

My sister, completely obliging even as an infant, obliged my mother in this one most important way. She was physically beautiful, remarkably so, to the exacting beauty standards of the rural south. Not only that, she was of a disposition sweet enough to withstand our Mother's relentless demands concerning appearance and behavior, and to comply without any outward signs on defiance.

"Isn't Jane beautiful?" we would hear. We would hear it many times a day, every time friends or bored neighbors dropped by. This was in the early fifties, before TV had reached the rural South, and frequent dropping by was the main entertainment. "Isn't Jane beautiful!" We would hear it when we entered the Green Bay Post Office or the general and only store, or Liberty Christian Church. "Isn't Jane beautiful!" It was said with an exclamation in the voice instead of a question mark. There was no question. It would inevitably be followed by a tiny sigh, "Oh, well, Nancy *is* bright." A bit of emphasis on the "is" indicated its ever-so-slight compensatory value. Brightness was not beauty of course, or even close, but better than nothing, one supposed.

Brightness in a female was very small coin indeed in Green Bay, Va., (pop. 109) unless it was attached to beauty as a bonus, as in "and she's smart, too.."

By the age of four I knew that smart alone was chump change, but I also knew it was all I had that could get me anything, and I must have decided then to use it to get me out of there. And so began my life as a soldier, winning and losing skirmishes with my Mother, in The Pretty Wars.

It wasn't looks alone that counted. Perfect deportment had certain redemptive value. But the bar was too high and the field too competitive, as my sister even behaved beautifully.

Then, children were to be seen and not heard, except at recitals and musicales. There they were to be seen as well bred and talented and a credit to their mothers, and they were not to even think about sneaking out of the stage door, while concertizing at the school auditorium, and sliding down the muddy playground slides in their dotted Swiss evening gowns before being introduced to play "The Happy Farmer" on the stage piano.

Publicly scornful of the whole business of prettiness, I secretly yearned for it. But the potential for transformation was limited to one small glass case in the recesses of the general store, as far removed as possible from the work boots and Tennessee tuxedos, the hardware section, the wheels of cheese. I would tiptoe to the case and lower the glass front, then inhale. It was heady with possibilities, this aroma and I would gulp it as if the smell itself could change me. There mingled the fragrances of Cashmere Bouquet, both soap and bath powder in a tin, *Evening in Paris* cologne in a tiny cobalt bottle with matching tassel, Tangee lipsticks and Coty Face Powder. There were even tiny envelopes of face powder samples with pretty-lady pictures on the front and you could take one any time you wanted. Some hair clips, some hair nets, and that was all. The ladies of Green Bay had to create beauty sans foundation, eyeshadow, eye-liner, mascara, false lashes, hair extensions, volumizers, tints, dyes, acrylic nails, laser defoliators, chemical de-wrinkle-izers, surgically plumped up lips or pumped up bosoms.

My sister didn't need any of that. She was perfect. It is very hard to have a sister who was born perfect and had stayed that way for sixteen years, especially when you are between the awkward eights and the knobby nines and have orange hair. Straight.

Determined to understand, if not possess this power of perfection, my cousin Betty and I kept Jane under total surveillance, looking for we weren't sure what. Secrets, perhaps, or tips on how to be her. Or better yet, some indication of weakness in some area. Any area .So one day, when my sister was away visiting relatives, Betty and I decided to go on a perilous mission. We would sneak into my sister's totally off limits room and we would *go through her things..*

The CIA would have been envious of our thoroughness, We turned back the mattress and felt under the bottoms of drawers. We looked behind pictures and mirrors and tried to open her diary with a hairpin. We sniffed her cologne, *Blue Grass,* and lightly touched the creme in a little round red and white pot of Arrid. Then Betty, excavating a dresser drawer with the precision of an Egyptologist on a dig whispered "Look! What is this?" she held aloft a never-worn falsie. Pangs of guilt struck at my heart like flashes of lightening. And lightening fast I grabbed it and cupped it over my shoulder. "Just an old shoulder pad" I said. "But she doesn't even need that.

My sister is perfect." The whole world agreed, even as far away as Farmville, the big town.

"Two eyes walking around with that baby-blue stare. How cute can you get, Jane Havens." That was how the article began, a whole article about how pretty she was, in the Farmville High School paper. Not only that, it happened practically at the beginning of the new school year, when all the important issues were being decided.

Things like status and pecking order and whether the really popular kids would say hello and put your name at the end of it, in the hallways. The most amazing thing about the article, the thing that all of the Green Bay kids discussed endlessly, was that it was the first (and the only) time a Green Bay student was ever singled out by the town kids who ran the school paper. Green Bay, a place without a bay, and not even very much green, did not have enough teens to make up a high school. So at the beginning of eighth grade, any student unwise enough to be born to families that lived in the country were bussed twenty miles each way, to the big town school.

"Hicks from the sticks," the townies called us. And "wood-hooks, shit kickers and local Yokels." They usually didn't say it out loud unless we made them mad in some way, but the words were always out there in the air, waiting. And now, after the article, my sister would never have to worry about that...not have to agonize over Peter Pan collars or circle pin placement, would not have to live in fear that Beca Weinstein, fashion bully, would come up behind her and turn back her sweater so that the label, with its meager cashmere content, would be exposed and read aloud. In magnitude and moment, the article was the Mafia equivalent of being made. In the stroke of a pen wielded by a popular kid from Farmville, my sister had crossed over, passed and been de-yokelized. She was officially special enough that boys would drive twenty miles each way to take her to the skating rink or the movie theater. She could now be in clubs, and on the yearbook staff. She could even be a cheerleader now, some boy would be glad to see that she got back and forth to town long after the school bus had left. I, eight years younger, and severely challenged cutewise, knew that there would be no trickle down effect on my status. And I knew another thing. I would rather be seen dead in a ditch that caught trying to look pretty and failing.

And so began the great Salon Skirmishes. My Mother would return from her weekly shopping excursion in Farmville with a determined look in her eye and a box about eight inches high. We would engage. "*N O!*" I would shout. "*N O!* I do not want a permanent. I hate them. *I HATE THEM. NO CURLS!*" If you have a choice of facing down one of General Patton's tanks or my mother with improvement on her mind, the tank is your move.

Soon I would be hunched in a chair in the Green Bay beauty salon. This was the screened-in porch of Francine Oldisten's little frame house, where she would administer a Toni for two dollars. As a professional touch she would put on a black beautician's smock, over her housedress. To my mind that made her look even more like Vlad the Impaler and other torturers of note.

First there was the tugging, as wisps of my straight orange hair were gift wrapped in small squares of tissue paper and wound far too tightly around little pink plastic wands narrow in the middle and larger on each end. I imagined them the finger, toe and other small bones of previous Toni victims. Then came the real reason for the screen porch location, even in the dead of winter. The curling solution would be opened. Strontium Ninety in a bottle.

A Toni promised curls that lasted for four months, but mine were always shorter in duration. After Francine would admire her work... "Isn't that pretty?" (The curls, not me, being the pretty thing) and my mother had agreed, we would ride home in silence.

Throughout the evening my Dad would send me little secret sympathy smiles and my Mother would watch me even around corners, with her Wonderwoman X-ray vision.

But even superheros have to sleep, and eventually the house would be quiet and dark. And then, by the beam of a flashlight, with my Mother's embroidery scissors, or kitchen shears, or whatever instrument of destruction I could find, I would ceremoniously chop off every curl. I would kick them dismissively into a corner and go back to bed.

No point in now-I-lay-me, even God could not help me come dawn. There were still, at that time in the south, once elegant old mansions whose owners had fallen upon hard times. The smart white paint had long since peeled away, and so the houses stood up naked, their bare walls weathered and grayed. Once I had asked my Daddy why one of our neighbors didn't do something about the way her house looked. "Honey," he said, "Don't you ever look down on her. She is simply too poor to paint and too proud to whitewash." And so, I thought, was I, as far as pretty was concerned.

A Suitable Ending

By Nan Miller

My older sister says she cannot remember either of us ever being hugged by our mother. I can't say for sure, but I do know this--I have seen the homophobic coach of a losing NFL team embrace the winning coach with more physical warmth than was ever displayed in our family.

Still, as tiny Green Bay, Va. (pop. 109) grew even tinier in the rear view mirror, I thought that my Mother might be feeling sad. It was, after all, good-bye. By the mid seventies my parents were reaching an age that required more than Green Bay could supply. They needed to be near a doctor and a druggist and a daughter,

It would have been unfair to transplant my mother, who had lived seventy years in Green Bay, to New York City, unfair to the city. Eight million people would suddenly be expected to have southern manners and to mind those manners. They would need to hold subway doors open for her, to surrender their hard-won cabs in the rain. They would have to offer to carry parcels and to say "Good morning, Mrs. Havens" with a smile, all 8 million of them or they would be subjected to her best look and then taken off her Christmas card list. It would go particularly hard for men with small beards or goatees, as she suspected all of them (Mitch Miller and Skitch Henderson included) of being Communists. No, it was agreed that she would be better off cushioned by the automatic graciousness of Charleston, near my sister.

My brother-in-law called, excited by a house he had scouted. "It's almost a twin of the one they have in Green Bay," he said. "But Mother says she wants a condo," I said.

"Listen," he said, "there is no way on God's green earth that you can please your mother, or make her happy, even for a minute. You know that. But you can please your father. And he needs a yard and a porch and a garage and a tool shed so that he can..." and he paused discreetly.

"Get away," I finished.

My mother had actually seemed to approve of the house, so I had bought it and flown from New York to pack them up. This was only fair. My sister would have her work cut out for her later.

So now the moving van had left and we were following it to Charleston. As the black asphalt of Rt. 360 licked up the last bits of Green Bay, I put an arm around my mother's shoulder and squeezed.

"Don't worry," I said. "You like the house. The location is wonderful, you already know a lot of people there. And you can come back and visit Green Bay anytime you want." She sat up straight and moved slightly away from me.

"I won't miss it, even one little bit,." she said. "I never did care for any of them and I don't care if I never see them again."

"Well, when they were all assembled at that series of farewell parties they had for you, you should have announced that, then." I said, in a lavish waste of irony."

"Oh, no!" she said, and her eyes were wide with horror.

"I couldn't do that. None of them would come to my funeral."

Even considering the source, this so violated my sense of reality that I had a need to confirm it.

" Do you mean that all of this church and missionary meetings and bridge and book clubs, all these years, was so that people you don't care about will come to your funeral when you are dead and don't know it?"

"Of course," she said, "how would it look if they didn't."

But Green Bay people are wise and with wisdom comes kindness. They knew that the first few weeks in a strange place, and an honest-to-God city at that, would have to feel daunting, and empty. So they filled up the big empty spaces with long-distance calls and showers of "Thinking of you" cards. They had the Liberty Christian Church bulletin and the Farmville Herald sent to my parents as a weekly reminded that they were still considered part of things. Often the short *Green Bay News* column in the Herald would report that a Green Bay couple had visited with my parents in Charleston, or vice versa. And I began to examine the notion that my mother had not really meant everything she said as we left Green Bay that day. I started to feel better about it.

And when we returned to Green Bay in long black limousines, to bury my Dad, the Green Bay people cushioned us with kindness. They opened up their arms and their spare bedrooms so that none of us had to be subjected to the meager amenities of the ancient tourist court, eight miles away in Burkeville. Those who were not hosting us, opened up their recipe boxes and filled our temporary havens with delicacies--Smithfied ham biscuits, the richly flavored ham sliced onion-skin thin buttermilk fried chicken. brown sugar pies. And the unimaginable comfort found in a bowl of spoon bread. We knew that it was their love and sympathy they were bringing, and love and sympathy we ate, and nothing else would ever nourish us quite so well again.

The Green Bay people filled the church and the churchyard. The people from Hell's Corner lined the outside of the fence and waited for us, and every one of them had a gift for me...a story about some kindness my Dad had done them, and each one of their stories is written on my grateful heart.

My mother did not mention the stories, but she did tell me then, and countless times over the next fifteen years, the names of the two people from Green Bay who did not attend my Dad's funeral.

For the whole of my Dad's long and heartbreaking illness, he had pretended that it would someday go away.

"When I get better," he would say to everyone sitting around his hospital bed, "I am going to widen the side porch," or "plant fruit trees," or "add another half bath." We gladly went along. But one day, there was just me.

"Honey," he said, "I am not going to be around much longer and there are some things I want to be sure of about your mother."

"Yessir," I said, "You just tell me everything you want to happen, ever. And Jane and I will see that she is taken care of just the way you would, for her whole life." (And we did.)

After he had given me a long and thoughtful list of financial and life style requirements for my mother, and after he had named the possessions and people he thought would comfort her, I had one question.

"Dad," and I hesitated, "has she always been so" I hesitated again and he rushed to complete the sentence with the kindest word possible,

"Peculiar?" he supplied.

"Yes sir."

"Well, honey she has gotten worse as time goes on and I have studied and studied on it. I only came to Green Bay when she was a young woman. But I think it started when she was a little girl. Her father had a little store, and the Post Office at that time. One night it all burnt down and I believe that there may have been some talk that maybe he set it himself for the insurance. Nothing ever came of it, but I believe that she has always worried that the Green Bay people might look down on her a little bit."

"Do you think they did?"

"No, not a bit of it. But your mother has always worried about such things."

That night in bed I cried for my Dad, and myself, and finally for my mother, with all of those years wasted trying to be perfect, and impeccable, and more than she thought that she was.

Of course the Green Bay people came to her funeral. The Green Bay people came with roses and snap dragons and lilies of the valley, and luncheons and dinners. And brown sugar pies. This time, the stories were about me.

"Remember," my cousin said "the time you filled your little purse with white faced bumblebees from the wisteria vine over there, and let them loose in church?"

"Do you remember me?" asked a still-pretty Ellen Bowen. "It was because of that fit you threw that we never got to see the ending of Snow White?"

I had, for the first time in my life, dressed to please my mother. Blameless white suit blouse, simple black suit, skirt carefully below the kneecap, neutral stockings, plain medium heel black pumps, circumspect make-up, perfect page-boy.

My best friend since forever, Phyllis, meeting the car, had inspected me as automatically as though we still met ever day.

"You look like a rich pilgrim," she said. "Or perhaps a nun from an order dressed by Chanel. Your mother would be so proud.

And then Naomi Jenkins engulfed me in a hug, but she was looking intently over my shoulder for someone.

"There's my pretty Jane," she said, spotting my sister. And then, "You know, Nancy, I've never thought it before, but you look just like your mother."

And if she was busy taking attendance, and somehow missed that one remark, I believe that my mother would have considered it a suitable funeral.

Dancing Girl

By Nan Miller

I was found under a cabbage leaf on our farm in Green, Bay, Virginia, (pop. 109). At the end of the 1940's a six year old could still believe such a thing and there were no TV shows or www.porno.com to say differently. The cabbages looked like big roses, only without the beautiful smell. I assumed that my sister, being the pretty one, had been found under the pink rose bush that smelled like magic, and I got left to the cabbage. It was fair.

There would have been none of that stork business I had heard about. My mother would never have allowed it. Dirty thing! Shedding feathers and tracking in dust with its big feet. No, I was sure about the cabbage leaf.

So when Reggie Grand, that jaded perennial first grader, decided to introduce sex education into the first grade curriculum, I knew that he was misinformed. He sidled up on the playground and showed us pictures of grownups doing peculiar things and whispered that our parents did those things too. I hooted in his fat, grinny face. Not a chance! It looked like an activity that would muss your dress, and my Mother would have dismissed it as unsuitable, with one wave of her delicate hand.

I was not an utter fool. I knew, of course, that something went on between some men and some women. My cousin Jean, eleven years older, caused the big boys to sigh dramatically and nudge each other with their elbows just by walking slowly past them.

Jean was dating Sam, the best looking man in town. He was the only divorced person in Green Bay, although it was best not to talk about that.

On Saturday evenings I would sit on Jean's pink chenille bedspread and watch every movement as she got ready for Sam. She had to be beautiful for him, I could see that. I already knew that beauty was the most important thing for girls and that my sister had it in great abundance, but that I did not. I was merely bright, everybody said so. So I watched my cousin transform herself and tried to learn how to be beautiful.

I would read my book while she disappeared into the bath. Her ensemble would be laid out on the bed with the precision of surgical tools in an operating theater peach satin lingerie, so immaculate that each piece looked unworn, wispy nylon stockings, pastel silk blouse, pastel skirt, pencil-slim with matching cardigan and cinch belt. Once on, the cruel belt would squeeze her waist even smaller, which seemed to push out her behind and befront even more. But there was a long way to go between the bath and the belt.

She would emerge from the bath as pink as the bedspread, moving in an aura of lush rose scent. Her legs would be as smooth and hairless as a darning egg. I assumed it was so as not to ruin the fragile stockings.

A large pink towel would be wrapped around her, toga-style, and a smaller one would turban her rollered hair. She would sit beside me on the bed with a look of such concentration that I would hold my breath. As if life itself were at stake, she would begin the excruciatingly slow massage of rose scented lotion on her toes, slowly... feet, slowly...her ankles, slowly, so slowly. She was so serious that I imagined terrible consequences if she should miss a spot .

I had seen this languid sensuousness once before. My parents had taken me on a rare, and precious excursion to Farmville, 20 miles away, to a movie. Normally, a movie would have been an unexpendable luxury of time and money, but this was *The Robe* and it was our Christian duty to see it. In *The Robe,* when Christians were not fighting mean lions, beautiful but virtuous young women would be bathed and perfumed against their will, then dressed up in scarves so see -through they seemed hardly worth the trouble, all to get ready for an audience with Caesar. There, to the best (and to the extent) of my imagination, they would (and here my imagination failed me) dance for him, maybe.

Perhaps my cousin Jean was getting ready to dance for Sam. She would wear a pair of Sunday gloves while she pulled on the nylons. Once again I would hold my breath until her legs were sheathed in runless perfection. I loved it.

Suddenly, one Saturday evening, it was I who was being bathed and powdered and stuffed into Sunday-school clothes, against my will. My mother had decided it was time for a duty call on the elderly Haileys and their son Willis.

The Haileys were a courtesy aunt and uncle, family by generations of close friendships, rather than by blood. The relationships were revealed in the pronunciation. Blood aunts were called "Ahhnt." Long A. Courtesy aunts were designated by a simple short a, and a courtesy cousin was pronounced differently also "We should run down and see A'Mable and Cudd'n Willis". That's the way my mother would have said it.

After the bathing I would have been anointed with Cashmere Bouquet bath powder, then told how to behave: to sit quietly, not to kick my heels or squirm, to speak only when spoken to, and to accept whatever was offered me with a "Thank you," even if what was offered was buttermilk! Or worse, fruit cake with that bitter green citron, "Yes, thank you," was the answer expected, and there had better be a smile at the end of it.

Cudd'n Willis still lived at home with his parents who were quite old, friends of my mother's parents, I believe. In the car, Mother had referred to him as being "a little slow," and ordered me not to comment if he did or said anything unusual. He did move a little more slowly than the others, but as long as the talk stayed close to the weather or other farm concerns, he seemed to fit in.

When the conversation veered toward politics, Uncle Jared suggested that Willis show me the new crop of kittens in the barn. I was happy to get away from sitting so still, and the possibility of fruitcake. And Willis was probably glad to get away from trying so hard to keep up. He reached out his big hand to me, and I took a portion of it in my small one. Off we set into the summer evening, toward the barn.

There was just enough light to make our way across the big back yard. Inside the barn, I could still make out the kittens with their huge eyes and downy ears. As darkness grew around us I could see them less and less but I could still touch their wondrous silkiness.

"You can hold one," Willis said. Oh! I picked one up, as careful as I had ever been in my six-and-a-half years, and lifted its softness to my cheek.

I crooned it a lullaby, so it wouldn't be afraid of being held by a stranger. Willis had sat down on a milking stool and lightly pulled me into his lap. And thus we sat in the soft, summer dark, Willis gently cradling me, me gently cradling the kitten.

Then I felt big work-rough hands touching me where no one had ever touched me before. I was unsure about the polite thing to do. I wanted to get down from those tall knees, and right away, but I didn't know how to do it without hurting the kitten, or Cudd'n Willis' feelings. But the big hands grew probing and hurtful, and I forgot his feelings. My hands still holding the kitten gently, I furiously wriggled my body off his lap and away from those horrible hands. I moved away from him in the darkness. We were both mute as stones. I carefully set the kitten by its mommy and started toward the light of the house, moving quickly. Willis came right behind me. We crossed the yard in silence.

Back in the parlor, my mother ran a quick eye over me for any untidiness. Finding none, she went back to the conversation. I sat perfectly still, as I had been directed.

Finally home, I feigned sleepiness and went to bed. I felt afraid, but I did not know what of. I felt as if I had been a bad girl but I didn't know why. I cried, but quietly, under the covers.

The next day I had a slight fever and funny tummy. My dad made me his famous teakettle eggs on toast, and I stayed in bed with my books and my best teddy bears, and the cat. When dark came I grew fretful, and Dad said that we'd better go to see Doctor York in the morning if I didn't feel better. They tucked me in and said their goodnights by the glow of the night light.

Sometime later, the door opened and light spilled in. My mother followed, on tiptoe. She sat down on the bed beside me, much closer than usual and spoke very softly. "Nancy," she said, "yesterday, when you and Willis went to see the kittens nothing....peculiar happened, did it?"

Her face had an expression I did not understand, almost as if she was asking me for a favor. There was a silence between us as we stared desperately at each other. I knew better than to lie to my mother. It wasn't possible. She always demanded *TRUTH* and knew when she didn't get it. The mother I was used to would stand over me with a pointed finger shaking down at me from an extended arm.

"Truth crushed to earth shall rise again!" she would say. There was always anger in the voice and in her face, at the very idea that I might attempt a fib. But this was a different mother. Her voice was soft, almost pleading. Then I knew I had to say it, but I couldn't look at her. I lowered my eyes and took a breath. "No, Ma'am," I said.

"Good," she said briskly."I didn't think so." She quickly got up and carefully smoothed the sheet, erasing any trace of her presence on the bed.

I was afraid to see Doctor York, or rather, for him to see me. What if there was some sign on my body that only a doctor could see? So the next morning I dressed myself, ate my oatmeal with brown sugar, and headed for the school bus as though nothing had happened.

I had no idea what had happened. I tried to put it together based on the dancing girls in *The Robe*, and my cousin Jean getting ready for Sam, and those stupid pictures Reggie

Grand showed us. It made no sense. I thought of little Anne Benzur. A few weeks before, something bad had happened to her. I did not understand what, but for days, all the grownups shook their heads and whispered about it. I saw the women wiping away tears as they talked. Finally, I overheard one telling another that little Anne had been raked. Raked! How hateful!

I imagined some wicked bad person attacking her with a sharp metal lawn rake leaving big scars. I didn't know why anyone would want to do that. I didn't know why Willis had done whatever he had done. I didn't know why I felt ashamed. But I did know this for sure. Sometimes there is a worse thing you can do than to tell your mother a lie. And that's the truth.

MMM

Mean Robert Gooding

By Nan Miller

Green Bay, Virginia was too picayune to have its own dot on the free Esso maps. But it was large enough to have its own slum.

It was called Hell's Corner and had been so called for so long that it seemed quite official and not at all unusual. No one hesitated to say it out loud, or blushed when they did. Not even the preacher, or those churchy ladies who would have normally expressed such a word as "H-E-double toothpicks" and in a whisper at that. Even we children could say it without fear of a spanking with a Spirea branch."He lives in Hell's Corner," we would say about a person, and that person would be at once placed and dismissed.

There were anywhere from thirty to forty-five folks in Hell's Corner. They all looked so much alike that it was impossible to know whether you were counting separate people, or the same ones twice. They had started out as distinct Goodings or Reillys or Douglases but by now had intermingled alarmingly often. But there was always a new Douglas in the first grade and ten year old Reillys in the second, and Robert Gooding, taller than my father and with five o'clock shadow, in the sixth. He was mute as a box of rocks, although we suspected he could speak, just not to us.

If Green Bay was red-clay rural, Hell's Corner was, we said, so far back in the woods that the monkeys carried the mail. That was silly. Folks in Hell's Corner didn't get any regular mail. Most had neither steady jobs nor bank accounts, neither electric bills or charge accounts or any other business that required the exchange of envelopes.

Occasionally the U.S. Government, not knowing any better, would call one of the older Hell's Corner boys to the draft, although they usually thought better of it once they saw them in person. So a letter would come, addressed to a Reily or Douglas, or Gooding, care of Green Bay Post Office, RFD. Miss Lily, the postmistress, would pass it on to the RFD mail carrier, (my uncle Jake) who was, besides my dad, the only man in the county not afraid to enter the inner depths of Hell's Corner without a police escort. My Dad, in fact, sometimes had to serve as an escort for the police.

My dad had such a profound respect for every living thing, and moved in an aura of such instinctive kindness that no one ever wished him harm. Every once in a while, in Hell's Corner, there would be a Saturday night dispute over a woman or a hunting dog. Being mostly inarticulate, the Hell's Corner boys disputed with knives, and if it got disputatious enough to involve multiple stabbings, the high Sheriff in Farmville would be sent for.

He would arrive with two cars of Farmville policemen, sirens blaring the entire sixteen miles of curvy rural road, with no one to hear them but raccoons and possums, until they hit Green Bay. They would head straight for our house and pick up my dad, who would function as a Tarzan of sorts, keeping both the Bwanas and the Hell's Corner natives safe from injury or injustice.

One day a letter came, addressed to a Gooding. Miss Lily gave it to my uncle who would have sighed a deep sigh as he headed to his vehicle. The car, however, was in no mood to bounce along those winding red dirt roads, and it refused to start. My Uncle was standing, beating at the car with his hat, when my dad and I arrived at the Post Office. He was saying some words I had never heard before. Dad would have said something like, "Don't fret, Jake. Hop in. I'm headed that way directly. I'll give you and the letter a ride. Or I'll drop it off and save you the trip." It was a Saturday, and I, refusing to be parted from my Dad for even five precious minutes, insisted on riding along.

I was not much impressed by Hell's Corner as we wound around the red-clay roadbed. I didn't see any knife fighting or shootings, nor anyone looking drunk or wayward. No one at all, in fact. There were a few unpainted shacks with skeletons of dead cars and box springs rusting in the dirt yards. I was disappointed. I had expected to finally see what lax men and loose women did, and to learn, once and for all, what happened in those Sodom and Gomorra parts of the Bible stories my Sunday School teacher always skipped over. And now there was nothing to see but dilapidated housing and discouraged looking dogs.

The dogs were meaner at the Gooding place, probably worn out by hunger and hard times, just like their persons. The hybrid hounds surrounded our jeep in a flurry of furious baying and baring of yellow fangs.

Dad leaned over the jeep door and said something quiet to them and they all calmed down. Understanding that I would be afraid with nothing but old jeep canvas between me and the dogs, Dad held out his hand, and I took it and went with him across the dirt yard and up a cinder block which functioned as a step, the real step lying in rotten pieces where it had fallen. There was a torn screen door and through it I could see a table and three chairs that did not match, unless you counted being paintless as a decorating theme.

There was no table cloth and no serving bowls. There was just a black iron skillet with patches of red rust, sitting right on the table, and, I had never seen such a thing before, standing in the skillet, a chicken, pecking at whatever was left there.

Mr. Gooding made an unhurried way through the screen door and onto the porch to meet Dad but not before I had seen, sitting at the opposite side of the table from the door, Robert Gooding in the flesh.

He was not wearing any shirt, and his shoulders were covered by a deep crimson blush.

I was at a loss for protocol, but managed a quick flip of a wave and a timid "Hey, Robert." before I turned to join the men. My dad had given Mr. Gooding the letter and was making polite conversation with him about a dog. Mr. Gooding was turning the envelope over and over in his hand. I saw an opportunity to show off the fact that I, at age six, could read grown-ups' words. "Do you want me to read it to you?" I said.

"Hush, Honey, Mr. Gooding doesn't have time to hear you read." Dad said. And I got that feeling in my chest that you get when something is wrong, but you don't know what.

Driving out of the yard, I noticed a clothes line with two shirts, and suddenly I understood everything. That Robert Gooding's daddy did not know how to read, that Robert was, behind that table with the chicken, with his skinny red shoulders sticking out because all his clothes were on the line. It was my first intimation that life was not fair at all and perhaps Jesus did not, in fact, love all the little children of the world equally. My heart snapped.

I started to cry. "Daddy, there was a live chicken on the table." I wailed.

"Honey," he replied, "there's no need to say anything about this to anyone at school or at church. Those people are down on their luck and we don't want to add to their misery by embarrassing them."

"Yessir, I know that." I said. And I did.

Green Bay school, being possessed, in 1949, of neither telephones nor intercoms, used runners. Should Miss Raiford, teacher of third and fourth grades, need to communicate with Miss Thompson, first and second, she would scribble a note, fold it over, and assign a bearer, I was seldom chosen because I had the capability of actually reading such a note--not that I would have. But the morning after my Hell's Corner excursion Miss Raiford needed a note delivered. My heart fell, as her eye fell on me.

In order to deliver the note you had to cross the auditorium when it had no lights on. Without lights the already huge meeting room managed to double and triple in size. And the length to be traversed seemed far indeed for a very small six-year-old. My strategy was to go to the edge of the light that fell from the third grade transom, stand very still and look for ogres and monsters. Seeing none, I would then sprint toward the safety of the circle of light at the first grade door. So far I had always been able to cross that terrifying expanse without being kidnapped or "murderized," pillaged or sacked. That day, I crept to the edge of the light, took a shaky breath, and hurtled myself toward the pool of light across the room.

When I crashed into the bogeyman, impact and fear took all my breath away. My heart was hammering and I could not raise spit or sound. Then the thing spoke, and it was not the bogeyman, but worse. It was Robert Gooding.

He held my shuddering shoulder in one hand and a huge switchblade in the other. He brought it close to my face, catching a faint ray of light from a window, and he rotated his wrist slowly back and forth so that I could clearly understand the knife and all of it's implications. His voice was slow and soft.

"I do believe Im'mo kill you. Yes, Im'mo kill you, little smart-ass bitch. Not right this minute, but Im'mo kill you sometime and you not be knowing when. And if you tell innybody, Im'mo kill you as soon as you do."

I understood. "I won't tell," I whispered. I meant more than just the killing and we both knew it but that somehow made it worse.

That was the longest spring in history. There were countless days of hiding, in my attempt to stall the inevitable. At recess I stayed by the teacher, offering to wash blackboards and pick up papers when she stayed in the classroom, trailing after her if she went outside. I skipped lunches to hide in the girls' bathroom as it never occurred to me that a male, even one bent on murder would ever venture inside. The teaching staff noticed my peculiar behavior and everyone noticed my loss of weight from missing lunch every day.

Almost as bad as the relentless terror was the guilt from all the deceptions necessary to my survival and worse than that was missing my dad and my best friend, Phyllis. I stayed as far away from them as was possible, knowing that one sympathetic word from either of them when no one else was around, and I would tell. And then, I knew, Robert Gooding would kill me, he had said so, and perhaps Phyllis and my Dad. too.

My mother, worried about how I looked, took me on visit after visit to our family doctor in Farmville. He could find nothing, but alarmed by my continuing weight loss combined with our family history of mild diabetes, he had me hospitalized. The hospital was scary, but Robert Gooding was scarier, so I simply lay, grim and mute, through all the testing, until I was released

Mercifully, June arrived and school was out. There was no way Robert Gooding could get me on our farm. There were 800 acres under cultivation and uncounted acres of woods surrounding that. So I veered away from the side that bordered on Hell's Corner and began to forget Robert Gooding. I ventured farther and farther from the house. My appetite came back and I resumed embarrassing my mother by eating unsuitable quantities of fried chicken at church picnics.

But the world is round and it turns. And suddenly there were new dresses and pencil-boxes and school was coming again, and with it, Robert Gooding.. I started having secret nightmares and sneaking my dinner to the dog.

The first day of school I pleaded tummy ache, and when I actually threw up from fear, got to stay home. The next day, however, I trudged to the bus, accepting delivery to my certain doom. By that time, I had a psychic bond with Robert Gooding. I could recognize his bulk in the dark, his shape in a crowd. I could distinguish his footfall before he came into view. But that day, I got no sense of him on the playground. Finally I said, nonchalantly. "I haven't seen Robert Gooding today," but my voice quivered as I said it. Reggie Grand, who always knew everything explained that Robert Gooding, having reached the age of sixteen in the summer, was free to leave school and so, of course, he had.

Deliverance! And I soon returned to myself.

About five years later, when Robert Gooding was old enough to be tried as an adult, he was sent to the penitentiary for cutting a man's throat. I never knew what the victim's transgression against Robert Gooding had been, but by now I understood mine. He had failed five grades. I had skipped two. I had offered to read a letter to his daddy. I had witnessed a chicken pecking in a fry-pan on his table. I had seen Robert shirtless while his few clothes were in the wash. I had seen his face, filled with embarrassment. And worse than that, he had seen mine, filled with pity.

Beating The Bushes For A Flu Shot

By Nan Miller

"What in God's name..." my husband's voice trailed off in amazement. He had opened the bedroom door to find me buttoning a classic grey flannel blazer (thrift shop, $2.50) over an ascot (Hermes equestrian scarf, received on 15th birthday and not out of the box since).

"What does it look like?" I was not being flippant, I seriously needed to know. He stared, squinted, then ducked behind the door before answering, "You look like .." he hesitated, then picked up speed and spit it out. "You look like a Republican."

He waited for an explosion. I am, after all, a yellow-dog Democrat and vocal about it, but when no lamps, or vases, or guns were fired in his direction, he peered around the door, to find me beaming.

"What else?" I asked.

"You look like an old money Republican who has an inexplicable urge to go clog-dancing!" he said, in triumph, like the man who has just guessed a really difficult charade.

"Just what I was going for!"

"If you were thinking of infiltrating party meetings to sabotage them, it's too late." He said, mournfully. "Why didn't you think of this weeks ago?"

"We are going," I said, "to infiltrate Republicanland. Please get your old blazer, and the car."

In the car, in my grey flannel get-up, with an added single strand of small pearls for deep cover, I explained, as we navigated the asphalt jungles of Hoboken and the gasoline alleys leading to the New Jersey turnpike.

"You know" I said, "that I have to have a flu shot."

"I know, honey." He said it gently, as it is an issue of grave concern to us.

"You know that my medication suppresses my immune system, and if I should get the flu I have little means of getting over it."

"I know."

"You know that I have called our doctors in New York, New Jersey and Palm Beach, and all of them say that it is critical that I get it, but no-one has any, or any prospects of any."

"I know, honey."

"This morning I also called the CDC in Atlanta, the Life extension people in New York, eight hospitals, your senior center, and the board of health with the same results."

"I'm so sorry, honey." And I knew how profoundly sympathetic he was. After all, the man had just donned a blazer without a fight.

"Here's what you don't know. I was telling this to Paula, telling her that if I can't find a flu shot I will have to spend the winter like Bubble Boy, unable to be in crowds, ride the subway, go to the Met or BAM, or classes, won't be able to campaign. And the campaigning made us think of Republicans and that inspired her.

"Do you think that Stephen Forbes and Christy Todd Whitman have any trouble getting a flu shot?" Paula asked. There was steel in her voice.

"I doubt it." I said. "I bet when Stephen Forbes or Christy Todd Whitman or any of their nearest and dearest want a flu shot they just call the family doctor and say "I want your very best quality flu shot, with a chaser of anti-pneumonia, right away, in your sharpest needle, and make it a double."

"Are you impersonating Christy Todd Whitman? I don't think I ever saw her wear that shade of lipstick. Or shade of hair." my husband said, looking dubious.

"Of course not! Do you think Christy Todd Whitman wants her cook or housekeeper down with flu? Do you think Stephen Forbes wants his secretaries interrupting one of his brain waves on policy reform with a bunch of snuffling and whufflling and blowing? Suppose he were to come up with something else as astounding as the flat tax and there was no-one to write it down because his staff was out with chills and fever. Paula says there are clinics for that sort of thing. So I looked in the yellow pages and made a list of emergency walk-in places all around Bedminster and PeaPack and environs. And I called.

'Hi.' I said, "are you giving flu shots?" and after three long days of nothing but "no," apologies, hollow laughter and deep signs, this woman said 'Are you a priority patient?'

I told her about my Rheumatoid Arthritis and she said, 'I will give you an appointment for four p.m. but you might have to wait.' Then I asked for an appointment for you, as you are sixty-five, *and I got it!*"

"Cool, Babe. That explains everything, except those shoes."

"Trying to look horsey. A lot of people in equestrian areas wear them because they're built up high and keep the feet up out of mud and stable muck. I got these for hiking, as they are enormously comfortable. In fact, I wish I had them in every color."

Even the foliage looked richer as we approached the target area, luxuriously leaved in moneyed shades of bronze, green and gold. My husband had started to worry.

"What if they require proof?"

"Letter from my Palm Beach doctor, and a three thousand dollar bill for last week's meds." I waved it at him.

"What if the shots are just for residents? I read where some townships are having lotteries."

" Fake address."

"What if the fake address doesn't match my Medicare address?"

"Most of those people live in at least three places. We'll blend.

"Look entitled,." I said, and we sailed into the clinic.

The staff was kind. Unctuous, even. The shots were right on time. I had to remove my blazer disguise, and once removed, did not put it on again. The antibodies were now irretrievably in my plebian body.

"Turn here", I said, at a saddlery sign.

"We're not buying a horse, are we? I mean, we *got* the shots."

"No, I just want to see what rich people pay for clogs."

They pay less. Much, much less. So much less that I got some in every color.

At bedtime, my husband said "Are you watching TV or shall I turn it off?"

"Not just yet. There were promos for stories about criminals and senators getting flu shots when other people could not."

"Same story." he said. "Go to sleep, babe."

And so we did, two ancient but unrepentant hippies, to dream, even now, of peace and plenty for everyone.

A Matter of Taste

By Nan Miller

Setting aside my Aunt-by-marriage-Bett, who was the sort of woman who would put mustard in the potato salad, the women of Green Bay were excellent cooks. Except for three. All three worked in the kitchen at Green Bay Elementary school.

At the sound of the lunch bell we would reluctantly line up and reluctantly shuffle past the pass-through window. The lineup order was youngest children first. Having just-turned-six and not looking even that, I was first, the canary in a gustatorial mine of tuna wiggle, macaroni and something, stewed tomatoes with sweet and soggy bread crumbs, and macaroni and something else. Once a week there was a square the size and texture of a small kitchen sponge, only brown, with a suspicious liquid poured over its center and puddled around it. Meat loaf and gravy, perhaps, or gingerbread with hard sauce, no one could say.

But, worse than the tuna wiggle, worse than the creamed turnips which masqueraded themselves as applesauce, the better to be spooned into innocent mouths, worst of all was the peas and carrots combo.The peas were the size of marbles, and they were gray. All green, all flavor, and certainly all nutrients had been cooked away. What remained was an awful furry feeling on the tongue. The "carrot coins" had been devalued on the steam table into soft, pale yellow rounds. I could wrestle them into my mouth, but my throat would simply close, and refuse to swallow these peas and carrots. An atavistic survival reflex no doubt. Children know more, now. Today a savvy first grader would simply call the EPA on his Mickey Mouse cell phone and report them for toxic waste. But in Green Bay, Virginia, pop. 109, in 1949, there was no EPA. And I was, alas, not savvy.

At around 10:45, on a P&C day, the Eau de Pois would boil over the pots and escape in a foreboding steam that would sneak out of the kitchen door and billow across the back of the auditorium, straight into the first grade class room. If you have seen The Phantom of the Opera, there is such a menacing fog in the "Music of the Night" scene. They used dry ice. But Green Bay school peas work just as well.

On P&C days I would follow my protesting nose to the pass-through window. I was so short that I would have to place both hands above me onto the outer edges of the sill and do chin-ups in order to communicate with the server.

"Please," I would say in a piteous plea, "please could I not have..."gravity would interrupt, then another chin-up .."..not have any peas, please?" My sweaty little hands would manage one last fast and desperate chin-up." Please?"

It never worked. I had learned the hard way not to say they made me sick, and food allergies had not yet been invented. A thick, off-white crockery plate with dividers too shallow to protect other possibly edible food from the P&C liquid would be handed down and I would bear it away to the table farthest from where the teachers sat.

If there is anything at all good to be said about being short, it is that your viewpoint is different, and you see things others do not, such as a hole in the hollow metal table leg where a large bolt had fallen out. What size hole? Just about the size of a large green pea.

But this day Reggie Grande had taken my seat. And I had no option but to push the peas and carrots around and around and wait for something to happen. I had already tried the pocket trick. Ag Billup, the laundress, told my mother. I had tried bribing the Douglas twins, who would eat anything. They refused to eat more P and C. My dog was not allowed back into the lunch room. I was stumped.

The meanest woman in the whole wide world lived in Prince Edward County. She was also the ugliest. I thought that her heart was so full of ugliness that the overflow had found its way to her face. My Dad, who had never been heard to say anything unkind about anyone except Hitler and Joe McCarthy, made an exception in her case.

"What on earth," he asked my mother after a sighting of the woman in question, "would possess Muriel Scott Mann to put that hat over that hair, over that face?"

"Henry," said my shocked mother, "she can't help how she looks."

"No," my Dad said, shaking his head in wonder at the memory, "but she could stay home."

Miss Mann hated all men, disdained all women and despised all children. So she was made Superintendent of the county schools, a choice that allowed her to reduce male principals, female teachers, and children of all persuasions to tears with each visit to a school.

Pearl Harbor! A surprise Mann visit on a P & C day! I was conducting a battle of my own. Peas were cowboys and carrots were Indians, when a silence came over the lunch room. Even the Douglas twins stopped chewing and sat, paralyzed, their cheeks pooched out with green slurry. Everyone avoided Miss Mann's glance.

I felt safe, as I was so short that the top of my head barely showed above the table edge. Emboldened by my invisibility I whispered to my best friend, Phyllis,

"Look. There's Miss Mann. She's so mean she steps on baby chickens."

The sudden gargling sound and the chocolate milk running out of Phyllis' nose attracted Miss Mann's attention and suddenly she was upon us. She pointed a bony finger at me. "This child has not eaten her peas and carrots."

"Please, Miss Mann" I whispered, "I can't eat them, I try and try and I just can't."

"Nonsense," she said loud enough for everyone to hear, "This child will sit here until l she eats every bite of those peas and carrots. She should be grateful for them!"

Children are logical creatures, constructing their theories from available information. I pondered the options open to me. I did not know how long a body could stay in one place. Quite a long time, hopefully. I strategized. Perhaps I could have naps on the bench at night. Perhaps Phyllis could sneak me a cookie or a Nehi grape drink occasionally. What I did know for sure was that I could not eat those peas and carrots. So I sat.

Eventually the other kids finished their lunches and straggled out to recess. Nobody noticed me in the lunch room. (Too short to be seen above the table edge.) Nobody missed me on the playground. (Too short to be required for any game).

So I sat. Finally I put the offending plate on the floor, curled up on the hard bench and told myself my favorite bedtime stories.

Just after three our housekeeper noticed that I had not gotten off the school bus, and told my mother, who drove the three miles to school, and with the janitor, found me. She was furious, though not, for once, with me. In my memory she even hugged me in her relief, but my older sister says that could not have been. My mother was enraged with Miss Mann for causing her such fright and loss of composure, and so the very next day she put on her most severe suit and drove to Farmville to tell Miss Mann that she was never to speak to, or about me again. It was the first, and was to be the only, time in my life that my mother ever took my side on an issue and I kept that memory high in my heart and told it to myself over and over.

I also took it as license to see just how long a body can go without eating a vegetable, and it is a very long time.Years and years.

So years and years later I found myself in China. Miss Muriel Mann was not there to watch me but 13 million Shanghaiese were. It was early days for outside visitors, and so they gathered in throngs to trap me in doorways and up against store windows. There they would crowd so close that I could feel their breath as they touched my skin or gently rubbed strands of my hair between their fingers. "You must understand," said Emily, my translator, "they have only seen hair like yours on a lion at the zoo."

"And skin so pale on nobody.," said Lily, my other translator. So I told myself to behave myself, to try and act as an unofficial ambassador of good will for America.

On my first full day out of the hotel, we raced from appointment to appointment, only slowing down whenever groups demanded to touch my hair, or take a picture with me, or walk hand in hand with me down the streets. When it was time for lunch, Emily and Lily herded me along the Bundt to the street of grand hotels where the fabled British merchant kings once lived in splendor with their families. Emily and Lily were dressed in their best, as this might be their only opportunity to dine in a "number one" restaurant.

. The hotels were not so grand now, their splendor gone with the merchant kings. Their ballrooms had been stripped of all signs of Western decadence and filled with hundreds of wooden tables for four. No-nonsense tables with clean but dingy tablecloths that barely covered the surface, leaving their long, awkward legs exposed like those of gawky adolescents. All of this I could see through the large ballroom doors across the anteroom. But first I had to run the gauntlet. The anteroom was dim, its only light coming from the aquariums, four walls of aquariums girdling the room. I stared, blinked, stared again. Dear God. At first I thought "It's snakes doing an exotic Asian form of synchronized swimming!" as each aquarium occupant undulated in the same direction. Emily and Lily attempted to pull me closer and indicated the snakes with a flourish. "Choose your eel" they said in unison, pleased with the bounty they were able to provide.

Now the self-styled ambassador of goodwill was put to a real test. Could I, in the spirit of hands across the sea and all that, possibly bond with one of those eels doing the hula and then nod approvingly as it was brought to me, and then *eat* it?

Well, no. *Oh Hell*, no! Forget saving face. Have ill will. Have a war, for all I care, but zero eel will pass my lips.

"Let's just wait until we see the entire menu," I said, airily. We entered the room watched by hundreds of Chinese businessmen, and dozens of eels. The waiter handed us menus. There were short, rather abrupt English translations under each entry.

"Sea slugs and fish lips "read the first item.

" Sea slugs and crispy fish tails" read the next. A waiter passed, bearing a bowl of soup on a tray, The bowl was plain thick crockery, but of a graceful shape. Very wide, with shallow sides, the better for me to see the clear broth, and the chicken feet that floated in it, claws pointing skyward.

The waiter stood, pencil poised. "Listen," I whispered to Emily and Lily, "Please don't let them bring me anything with eyes. Enough people are staring. And another thing, don't let them bring me anything that looks as though it might recover, given a chance." Lily giggled and pointed discreetly to the lower menu.

"Broccoli," I read, and "sautéed spinach, green beans with mushrooms."

It is a long way from Green Bay, Virginia, (pop. l09) to Shanghai, China. But it was there, 3,000 miles and forty years later, that I learned to eat my vegetables.

And to be grateful for them.

Bernard Perron

Born in France in 1933, Bernard the oldest child and only boy, quickly followed by five sisters, was raised in a financially challenged but warm family atmosphere.

Growing up during the war years under German occupation, although difficult, was not without humorous situations, and living in a frugal atmosphere where work was expected at a young age, proved to be a very good start in life.

Terminating his formal education at fourteen, Bernard started his apprenticeship as a Pastry cook and graduated with honors two years later. He then started what was then called his "Culinary tour de France" which meant spending times in different parts of that country and learning their specialties.

Three years later aiming to broaden his scope, he decided to discover the New World and at age 19, he immigrated to Canada where he spent two and a half years.

From there, seeking a sunnier climate, he moved to the Bahamas where he met Cathy, who had been raised in Western Canada. They have been married forty-eight years.

In 1975, in an effort to stabilize their lives and to have access to more sophisticated schools for their four children, they moved to Boca Raton, Florida where they still live.

That same year, they opened their first restaurant in Boynton Beach, which is a thriving Catering place, now called *Benvenuto.*.

In 1981 they added another landmark in this area, *Brooks Restaurant.* Both places are now under the management of their son Marc, daughters Anne and Lisa and their respective husbands, Jean-Philippe and Jon, two superb Chefs in their own right.

Attending games, plays or school functions involving their four grandchildren keep Bernard and Cathy on the go and enjoying every minute of their lives.

Rural Life In France- 1943

By Bernard Perron

A long, sharp slicing knife in his right hand, the left one holding a two pronged fork firmly planted in a huge leg of veal, its crusty darkly roasted skin contrasting with the whiteness of the inside meat, Mr. Trouillez, the farm owner, even in this dimly lit great room manages to cut a majestic figure.

Sitting on benches around two long tables of 10 to 12 persons, the Trouillez family, the helping neighbors and paid hired hands were enjoying a well-deserved evening meal after a long day in the fields.

The harvest has been plentiful. Rain fell early after the sowing. A dry end of summer had given to the shaft of wheat a chance to mature slowly and now the grains have been separated and have produced one of the best crop in years.

With combines today, separating the wheat from the shaft is an easy thing to do, but in 1943, without this modern technology and the additional shortage of diesel fuel, we were depending on an old wood fired steam tractor with a system of pulleys and belts attached to a "batteuse" or thrasher.

This twenty year old black tractor, its steel wheels brightly painted red, the large brass boiler with its multitude of pipes surrounding it, was a true piece of art;

Once the fire was lit and the water reached the boiling point, steam oozed very impressively from everywhere and its whistle alone gave the unmistakable sign that something big was happening.

As children, neighbors and friends of Mr.Trouillez our jobs were limited but still important. We were in charge of feeding the fire and keeping enough water in the boiler. Another of our functions was to keep the huge flat belt connecting the tractor to the thrasher like a big embryonic cord in perfect shape which in this case meant that we had to keep it heavily waxed in order for it to maintain its traction and stay cool and supple.

The thrasher was a big wooden contraption, now in a faded green. While in operation a cloud of dust surrounded it, making it most difficult for anyone working on it. The clicking and banging, deafening as it was, always gave the impression that some part was ready to come lose and fly away.

Almost as a miracle, the wheat loaded on the very top, with the help of three men below who were armed with long farm forks and two men on top receiving it. The wheat shafts would very rapidly be converted into golden grains falling regularly into three Crocker bags below and the straw being ejected ended up in neat bundles that would be piled in mounds up to twenty feet high.

The whole operation took ten to twelve men as some had to carry the 150 pounds. bags on a steep ladder to an attic, a difficult and back breaking job. Some men would rest at all times as the heat and dust would affect even the most diligent workers.

At this moment everyone is resting, our usually laconic farmers now enjoying the feeling of a job well done are in a jovial mood. The wine has been flowing; the first three courses were excellent and they now are ready for the piece de resistance, veal, which is always a favorite.

Having served the ladies first, Mr. Trouillez, a smile on his face looking towards Pierre a farm hand who is profoundly deaf and pointing to the roast veal very innocently asks him.

"Pierre would you like to kiss my ass?" And Pierre answers innocently, "Yes, and with a little gravy on top."

The laughs in the room let him know that once more he has been caught, but with a smile on his face and without rancor he would just say. "You son of a bitch you got me again."

Being part of the farming community in those war days was very much the envy of city dwellers, as farmers controlled the food production and the city people depended on food stamps.

Farmers were a very homogenous group, dependant upon one another for the harvesting of their wheat, grapes and sometimes potato crops. Feeding one another was not only a tradition, but it had become a form of competition, an effort to produce the best meals.

By contrast today a communal combine does the same thing in a much more efficient way. Operated by one man, it will harvest and process the wheat. The only closeness the farmer whose field is being cut will have is by driving his truck next to the other machine to collect the grains.

The camaraderie, the feeling of friendly competition, the family-like atmosphere, no longer exists. But this is what is called progress.

Memories Of My Youth: The Town Crier

By Bernard Perron

RATATATA,RATATTA,RATATATA OYEZ…OYEZ,…OOOYEZ.

Those sounds, now forgotten, were familiar over sixty years ago, when I was a child living in my small old French village.

The peeling of bells from our Romanesque Church signaled. Weddings, fires, funerals etc. but nothing could equal the human touch that our Town Crier brought us.

Today, except in Renaissance Fairs or in restored historical cities such as Williamsburg in Virginia, the Town Crier is as obsolete as the dinosaur.

Modern means of communication have eliminated them, but I can remember how dependent we were on our Crier, and how important he was in our lives.

In my hometown of Lencloitre, a veteran of the First World -War, who had lost a leg during the battle of Verdun, filled that position. For us children he was a hero, and as a matter of fact our only one. His battery of colorful medals always polished and proudly displayed on his chest during all holidays or other formal occasions, was all the proof we needed.

As being a town crier is not a full time job, Monsieur Gagnon also doubled as "Garde Champetre" or keeper of the fields.

Understanding the governmental logic in staffing such a position with someone who was physically handicapped is rather puzzling. How could he run after poachers, jump over ditches or as he also is responsible for the proper flowing of our river, climb riverbanks? Nobody has ever explained it and I got to admit that he did a very commendable job and replacing him for someone more agile was unthinkable.

My recollection of Monsieur Gagnon is one of a man of fifty, fifty-five years of age wearing an oversized gray-blue smock. Always jovial, a kind word for everyone and a ready smile in his voice.

I can still see him riding his bicycle with a snare drum hooked up on its handlebar, his wooden left peg leg resting on a stationary pedal and his good one, the right leg churning furiously, trying to move his rather portly figure at a painfully slow speed.

He would stop every couple hundred yards, announcing his presence with a long roll of his drum, his booming baritone voice bouncing from house to house, then he would blare any new law or government information, and usually to every listener's joy, he would give his own commentary on the subject, depending on which street he was "working"

As children we would follow him and invariably, he would involve one of us in his announcement, such as:

"By decree of Bernard Perron, Sunday July the twenty fifth will be National Election Day. Polls at City Hall will be open from 7:00 am till 7:00 pm. anyone who wishes to object should consult the secretary general Mr. Jack Gaudin." (my best friend)

Having received our two minutes of fame, we would return home and in the next street it would be the turn of different kids to star in his announcement and then they would feel as fortunate as we,

Market day, the first Monday of every month was his most glorious. He and he alone had the responsibility to collect the merchant's occupational fees and at eight o'clock, when all eyes were on him, with a roll of his drum he would declare the market open.

Having successfully achieved that important function, he would take a semi-break and in order not to offend anyone, with his usual grace, and in a gesture of goodwill, he would visit the eight bistros surrounding the field.

By 10:00 am having enjoyed his coffee and a few brandies, he could easily be coaxed into doing his "tour de force" his big number.

Balancing on his peg leg, trembling, hesitantly, he would hold his balance with the tip of his right rubber boot barely touching the ground.

Concentrating, he expelled few grunts and his rubicund face turned a shade or two darker than usual. His military style cap was precariously perched on a nest of curly gray hair, and hesitantly at first he would start swinging his right leg. After two or three slow but well measured or timed efforts, and with a quick jerk, he would spin on his wooden leg and do a 360 degree turn.

Graceful he was not. Nevertheless it was quite a sight. With his ballooning smock he was more like a Dervish dancer than Nureyev and always some impressed onlookers were willing to reward such an acrobatic feat with a well deserved one or two glasses of wine.

Around noon and by now exhausted, he would retire to his apartment at City Hall, where he was also its guardian, and get a well-deserved rest.

It may be true that today, CNN and its 24/7 news competitors have taken over Monsieur Gagnon's main job, the dispensing of news, but there is no way they can replace the human warmth, quick wit, and personal relationships that Town Criers of bygone days provided for local townspeople.

MMM

The War Years

By Bernard Perron

184, 185, 186. Together counting softly, my closest friend Jacques Gaudin and I are oblivious for a moment, that it is 2:15 am. It is May 1944 and we have forgotten, even, the haunting; two long blasts of our Town Hall siren, which awakened us twenty minutes earlier, announcing another air raid.

187, 188, 189. Now we are laying down head to foot in a shallow ditch, in Mr. Lejeau's asparagus field, nervously awaiting the outcome of this new scare. But nonetheless, we continue to count.

White asparagus, Lencloitre's pride and specialty, like Belgian endives, need to grow in the dark. To achieve this farmers bury the plants, and right now we are lying between rows of earth mounds about a foot and a half high, hiding those precious vegetables, which hopefully are protecting us from flying bullets, shrapnel or any other objects that might come our way.

190, 191, 192. There is nothing cozy about this place. There is dew on everything and the sandy soil cakes our bare knees, elbows, and hands with earth. It is a cool moonless night. The tops of the pine trees, which surround the field, sway gently in the light wind. A few dogs let us know that they are still furious at the wailing of the siren and there we are almost motionless, trying to identify any foreign or strange sound.

193, 194, "Slow down, not so fast, let's start again. 193, 194, 195. There he goes. I won, I knew it."

I won the bet, two marbles. Jacques and I had taken, the opposite position about whether, if we counted up to two hundred, Grand Pere

Foucteau could, control his bladder. I knew that he couldn't hold out till we counted to 200. Jacques thought he could.

Grand-Pere Foucteau is very old, at least seventy years of age and from experience we know his routine, but till tonight, we have never timed him.

Now the show is starting. Breaking the stillness of the night, grunting like a stuck old boar, he raises on all four. His head slowly appears, covered with his usual black beret ensconced almost to his highbrows, his gold rimmed glasses reflecting whatever faint light there is. We watch him wrestling with an uncooperative cane sinking in the soft ground, cursing the night, the Germans, the pilots, the Mayor, God or whoever he can think of.

Eventually all of his five foot two inches are almost stretched out, and he hesitantly starts to walk away, when his wife, dutifully tries to bring him to his senses or at least make him realize the gravity of his recklessness.

" Ernest! You cannot get up like this, they are going to see you, and you are going to get us all killed."

"They," are the American or Canadian pilots twelve thousand feet up in the air. They can also be, more closely, the German soldiers using our secondary roads while evacuating the western part of France, or even members of the French underground who have the reputation of being rather trigger-happy.

Bending down, Grand-Pere makes himself even smaller than he is, trying to step over the asparagus beds, apologizing to the people he does step on, still cantankerously muttering, "When you got to go, you got to go and the all the f--- German Armies can't stop me."

About three weeks ago, he had been in a hurry to relieve himself and he came a bit too close to a family in hiding. "You are a pervert." whispered the Father. But Grand- Pere couldn't stop himself and he asked them to close their eyes, a very wise solution, to a delicate situation. Who says that country people do not have class?

This type of distraction signals every child under six that he too has to go, and suddenly the field comes alive. By now, in these pre-radar days, flares held by little white parachutes are used to illuminate targets. Thrown from advance planes at fourteen thousand feet, they are followed about five to ten minutes later by bombers flying at about four to six thousand feet in the hope of being able to see their target.

Tonight it seems that the goal of this raid is to destroy the railroad tracks, linking Bordeaux to Paris line presently used by our occupiers to retrench as rapidly as possible. As it is about fifteen miles away from us, we can now relax and admire the descending lights piercing through the clouds. Sporadic waves of planes can be heard in the distance and from time to time the muffled sound of a string of bombs hitting the ground.

At about three o'clock the drone of the planes' engines having disappeared, our siren once more tells us that it is safe to return to our homes but still too excited, sleep will be elusive tonight.

We hate the Germans, the occupation, and the senselessness of the war. We hate the destruction and the uncertainty. Four months ago in the middle of the night we were awaken by armed helmeted German soldiers, going from room to room in our house piercing all our beds with their bayonets, looking for French underground soldiers who had attacked their convoy. Not finding what they wanted they took my father and all the men in the village and lined them against a wall in our town square, machine guns trained on them.

Stunned, under a curfew, communicating with anyone else outside, has become impossible. We are prisoners in our own home. Too anxious to sleep, we stay up. Daybreak will be in a couple hours. Ignoring the damage to our beds, not even wanting to look at them, my mother, my four sisters and I are in our kitchen –cum dining room. Each a bowl of café au lait in front of us, but none of us can drink. Incidentally coffee is unavailable these days, so we use a mix of, deeply roasted barley and dried chicory root.

We are like zombies, walking aimlessly, doing some meaningless jobs, except for my Mother who, I guess, in order to mentally escape, has started to knit a wool scarf, a craft that she usually reserves for late afternoons. For the fifth or sixth time, she asks us if we noticed if our Father had taken a sweater with him as it is a chilly morning. We had not.

Having been told to get busy, my sister Nicole, a year and a half my junior, and I have to feed our animals, and as it is almost easier to be outside than in, volunteer to clean the rabbit cages, a task that I usually hate to do. The mood in our courtyard at ten a.m., except for the lack of noise is almost normal.

Then, the shouts, the noises of diesel engines asthmatically starting, the rumbling of tanks destroying our streets, indicate that something is afoot. Still not daring to go out we wait another ten minutes, until we start to hear laughter and loud talk outside, and there they are at the end of our street, my Dad, Mr. Lejeau, Mr Bourdois, and the rest of our neighbors, strolling slowly as if going to a picnic. It is noon, and for some unknown reason they are free. As on queue, all the wives and children are in tears. It has been a very long and painful eight hours.

A few weeks later, on June 10th to be exact at "Oradour Sur Glanes," the people in another small village roughly forty miles from ours, under similar circumstances and in broad day light, were corralled by members of the Gestapo. Everyone in the village, men, women and children, and in a matter of two or three hours were locked up in the local church. The Gestapo soldiers then set it on fire, killing all 642 people. A few farmers working in their fields were the only survivors and sadly lost everyone dear to them. Today this village has been kept as it was found and used as a reminder of the atrocities committed under the orders of a deranged leader.

As children we tend to push such atrocities out of our conscious minds, as we turn our attention to play, and try to hold on to the routines of our lives.

Under those stressful times everyone helps one another. The community becomes more homogeneous. It seems that we have an unwritten agreement and bartering becomes de rigueur. Food is not a major problem since we produce it. Our large courtyard is teeming with chickens, ducks and geese for eggs and meat. Twenty or so rabbits fill up the cages against the back wall and in the small shade from October on two pigs invariably called Mussolini and Adolph Hitler are raised.

My parents have figured out that with such names, my sisters and I cannot get too attached to them and will not shed many tears when the time comes to slaughter them. Incidentally, the mailman is also the village butcher. So when a pig has to be killed, the mail must wait one more day to be delivered.

As news is censored our only unauthorized contact to the world, is the BBC in London. Listening to it is a rather dangerous affair; being forbidden by our invaders to do so, if you get caught, the death penalty is the price you pay. Now at eleven years of age and considered grownup enough I can enjoy the privilege of listening to it as my parents defy their orders.

At 8:00 pm. all windows close and we make a circle around the handsomely decorated cabinet of our old Thompson radio. We hear only crackling noises and screeching sounds, until my Father painstakingly finds the proper setting on the short band waves and, there it comes. Tic-

tic-tic. Tic-tic. Tic-tic-tic, a Morse code signal tells us that the program so anxiously awaited is finally here.

In French we hear, "From London, this is free France." Great news. After a fierce forty eight hours battle, the Allied forces are now controlling the city of Monte Cassino in Italy defeating the Fifth German tank division now almost completely out of contention. We are sorry to tell you there were heavy casualties on both sides but we are victorious. London has not been bombed for the last seven nights which means that the Fuhrer's Air Force is now inoperative. From North Africa; Casablanca we learn.."and the voice continues for fifteen minutes.

The program always finishes with coded personal messages. These messages are for the young guys in the underground, a way to let their families at home know that they have reach England safe and sound or that they are moving to Switzerland or that a parachute drop will happen tomorrow in someone's neighborhood. These messages sounded strange until we understood that they were codes.

"Twins were born to the Milkmaid last night, Mother and children are well"

"In Normandie, apple trees are in full bloom. Expect a great crop."

'Traveling pigeons never miss their goal.'"…etc… And at the end of the program, the Marseillaise, our National Anthem is played. With tears in our eyes the radio is quickly turned off and very often my Father pulls out, a well worn out map of Europe and our Allies' progresses are dutifully noted.

Now in Lencloitre, there is hope. The Germans are definitely retreating. The lonely one responsible for our village has left us two weeks earlier. The Russians are now in Poland. In North Africa, general Rommel is on the run. We can feel a change in everyone's attitude. We now walk a little straighter, and even begin to make plans for when our freedom will be returned.

Job Hunting Immigrants in Canada

By Bernard Perron

Imagine pieces of a broken windowpane placed into a bag and rattled constantly.That is the sound of a freezing river when its edges begin to solidify. But eventually under the strength of the current, it breaks away, and four to six inch long pieces separate and collide against one another. This irritating, persisting sound had the power to make me believe that small chards of glass were penetrating my body at all times.

It is 4 am. on this first day of November and John Bertranou and I are on the edge of the Fraser River, presently in a culver under the railroad tracks about a mile East of Prince George, the "Lumber Capital of the World" in British Columbia, Canada. How did we get here?

For the present, we are partially protected from the blowing, piercing wind by scraps of cardboard, abandoned by some homeless person. Wrapped up in our only belongings, we succeeded in collecting enough dry leaves to form a cushion isolating us from direct contact with the cold concrete of our new home as we try to rest and keep away the cold. We are half dazed looking forward to the opening of the railway station at 6:30 in a couple hours. We are dreaming of warmth and a chance to groom ourselves, and hoping this new day will bring us the steady jobs we have been searching for, during the last six weeks.

At the end of our summer season at the Manoir Richelieu, a luxury hotel in the eastern province of Quebec, and our first experience as cooks in Canada, we had been ready for a change. One evening, analyzing what we had learned as new emigrants about the customs, foods, work habits, etc, we finally realized that, the better paying jobs, were held by English speaking employees.

That was a revelation and since John and I were anxious to earn good money, we decided that learning English should be prime on our agenda. What could be better than a complete immersion?

Since French was spoken throughout the province of Quebec, we would have very little incentive to learn English. Toronto in Ontario was a possibility, but we were also here to see the country, and jobs were plentiful everywhere, so we decided to go west to see the Pacific, and Vancouver was our destination of choice.

Speaking to other cooks in our hotel, everyone was of the opinion that our decision was a sound one. From a cooking point of view, the West was ripe for employment. Everyone had a friend or some acquaintance there, earning five times as much, as we had been earning in Quebec. I am certain that there must be a law of probabilities, regarding chances of succeeding. It seems the farther the distance, the greater the financial rewards.

Three days after leaving the security of our summer jobs, as the night was falling, we were on board a wagon of the Canadian National Railway for a five day trip across Canada. Now we are ready to educate and save Vancouver from culinary failure.

We had found a place to store our suitcases and duffel bags and through an oiled, smeared window we are looking at the horizon and the disappearing lights of Montreal.

To save money we had not taken a sleeper car but gambled that two or more seats would be available to us, so that we could stretch ourselves and sleep comfortably. Fortuitously we found a comfortable stretching space.

Lulled by the onomatopoeia of the wheels on the steel rails, we slept soundly and were awaken the next morning by the screeching sound of the train coming to a stop in Sault Ste. Marie. With twenty minutes to spare, we had enough time to purchase a few Danishes and two cups of coffee, enough to hold us till noon.

The landscape was mostly composed of lakes sandwiched between forests and a few clearings. As we were far from civilization we were expecting to see a bear or a moose appear at any moment, but no such luck.

On our second day, after leaving Winnipeg, we entered the prairies and from there until Edmonton saw one unbounded field after another, sparsely dotted with short stubby trees. At that time of the year the fields were denuded of the wheat that had grown there earlier. Once in a while a herd of cattle would appear but no humans. From time to time we would stop in the middle of nowhere at a railroad station near a silo with no other sign of life. In contrast with Europe, where you are constantly in sight of a house or a building, here you can travel two hours without seeing a man-made structure or sign of civilization. As we experienced the vastness of that country, we began to reconsider the sanity of our move.

Our visual reward came on the fourth day when we began to discover the true nature of the west. In Edmonton at the railroad station we saw men with white cow- boy hats and honest to goodness decorated boots. Three hours later, we were penetrating the magnificent Jasper National Park with its sharp mountaintops covered with permanent snow, deep blue lakes, and exhilarating vistas of forest and glaciers. There, I saw my first totem pole and had my picture taken in front of it.

Now we saw an abundance of wild life, mountain sheep, like snowflakes on the flank of a mountain, an occasional moose leisurely grazing, and wild horses challenging us to a race. From Edmonton to Vancouver it was a feast for the eyes. Everything was still lush and green.

After two days in Vancouver, having been rejected by every major hotel and high class restaurant, we realized that something had to be done and rather quickly as our funds were melting away at an alarming rate.

The kitchens in hotels are always multilingual and easy for us to adapt to. Small restaurants, diners etc, are not, and between our difficulty to communicate and our lack of experience with local cooking habits we were in deep trouble.

Almost as our last dollars were being spent, we were hired, by the British Columbia Reforestation Service, to plant pine trees on the flank of mountains, around Newgate, near Cranbook. Every morning we were dropped at the foot of a mountain, along with a group of ten other guys. There were four thousand small pine trees and we had a pick axe each. We would climb two or three hundred feet, and where motorized planters could not go to, for the next eight hours, we would be planting trees, each of them a foot apart. Not very exciting, but we had two great meals a day and free lodging in trailers. I also had my first English lesson. A bible-reading gentleman in our group took the time to explain to me that although widely used in our camp the word "fucking" did not necessarily have to precede the words "pancake, water, knife, bread or others." You actually could be understood, by just saying. "Please pass me the butter, or whatever." In fifteen minutes time I had lost fifty per cent of my spoken vocabulary.

Around the tenth of October, just when we were beginning to fall into complacency in our newfound rural life, frost at high altitude became a problem, and it was impossible to dig and plant. Our group was dismissed, so back to job hunting we went.

We were certain that jobs were available in Montreal, but we did not have the money for the return trip. Our failure in Vancouver was painful, and we decided that since we were not in a position to choose. Prince George with all its lumber mills would give us the best opportunity either as cooks or as laborers.

Arriving there, we found a city crawling with lumberjacks. It was the "break up" period, during which the dirt roads are too soft to allow heavy equipment to circulate on them and therefore all sawmills are shut down.

We spent our first week in a cheap hotel and started on a daily diet of two marmalade and peanut butter sandwiches. They were cheap and nutritious. Once in a while we would cook soft-boiled eggs in our room by simply putting them in an empty marmalade jar, attached with a string to a faucet and letting the hot water run on them for twenty minutes or more. The safest time to do this was around 4:00 pm, when nobody was taking a shower.

Everyday we would walk the streets looking for job opportunities, reading the classified ads. Somehow hundreds of other guys were doing the same thing, and without much English, we found that communicating was a problem. At that time we also realized that our wardrobe, which may have been adequate in Paris, New York or Montreal, was going to be very flimsy in this area.

To stretch the last few dollars we had, we transferred to an old decrepit, boarding house near the railroad station. We had a room on the second floor as the first floor was rented to prostitutes, which meant that from 10:00 pm. until 4:00 am, there was constant banging of doors, shouting, and once in a while a visit from the Royal Canadian Mounted Police.

On October the 30th, without food or money, and blaming one another for our situation, John and I had a fight, and I threw him through a French door.

The noisily breaking glass and our loud mutual accusations and curses almost immediately woke up the owner who within minutes appeared armed with a baseball bat, his wife in tow, curlers and all. Even their squeaky thirteen-year-old daughter had her own opinion on this matter. All yelling at the same time, I can guess that some unflattering remarks were hurled at us, which thankfully we could not understand.

As we were already one week in arrears in our room payments, we were under the amused look of other guests who by that time had been awakened by the commotion. We were promptly asked to leave the premises and our luggage was confiscated. As the railroad station was closed, we started to look for a place to get away from the cold and finally about a mile away we found our culver, our hole in the ground.

Yesterday a bum did share his tea with us. I guess he understood without our having to speak English, that although we were well dressed, we were in dire need of nourishment. We all drank from the same smoky Campbell soup can. It was hot, and we were very grateful for that.

And now, on November first, the mood started to change. All of a sudden the ground was frozen solid. Sawmills were reopening everywhere. At 3:00 pm, passing in front of a taxi station, we saw a sign advertising for a cook and a lumberjack helper.

In anticipation of actually being able to earn some money, we settled on the only fair way to approach the job situation,

" Okay," I said to John, "let's flip to see who goes for the cook job." He was hesitant, but went along with the suggestion.

"Right! Yeah," he said prophetically, "lumberjacking is not so bad.."

Later that evening, having retrieved my cookbooks, knives and working clothes, I was driven in a taxicab to Shaede Sawmill at Pinchi Lake.

We arrived there around 8:00 pm, darkness having blanketed the area. After presenting myself to the foreman, I was taken to a cabin where a fire was brightly burning. For the first time in three days I had a bed, a brand new sleeping bag, and a pillow with a clean pillowcase. I was then introduced to the kitchen, which would be mine for the next eighteen months. I was given carte blanche to eat whatever I wanted, but the only thing I could swallow that evening was a very sweet cup of tea.

In my warm bed that night, basking in so much luxury, I knew that to survive and fit into this environment, learning English had to be one of my priorities. As the only non- English speaker in the camp this was the complete immersion I needed.

Two months after arriving in the camp, I registered at the University of British Columbia, in Victoria and by correspondence took English one and two.

The University advised me that in addition, I should read comics and Life magazine, as the drawings or photographs very graphically explained the texts. Eventually I graduated to the Reader's Digest, and two years later, I met my English speaking wife who certainly was the most attractive teacher I ever had, and my real incentive for learning English.

Edited by: Emily Rosen

My First Day In New York City

By Bernard Perron

I left the French liner "Liberty" on the East river, not far from the Staten Island terminal and therefore severed the embryonic cord to my old country. I enjoyed my first ever taxi ride, ensconced in a Checker cab. Eyes wide open, I started my bouncyride up Broadway towards mid-Manhattan.

On this brilliant spring day, I was awed by the cascade of colors, tumbling through the streets. Red Coca-Cola trucks majestically driving by, yellow cabs darting like busy bees, green buses nonchalantly ferrying their passengers, and…automobiles! Desoto, Buick, Cadillac, Studebaker, Pontiac, all with so many different colors, from white to pale blue, to apple green, to reddish brown and with gleaming chrome everywhere.

Coming from France where our choice of cars was limited to Renault, Peugeot or Citroen in colors of black, deep blue or gray, it was a revelation to find that such diversity.

Having dropped my luggage at a friend's apartment, and eager to start my sightseeing tour, I chose the nearby Grand Central station as my first destination.

Although imposing from the outside with its colonnade façade, it did not prepare me for the sheer size of the cavernous Main Hall, its majestic Grand Staircase or, in the center, supervising the constant traffic, the four faced clock. Having seen it many times in movies, it was a familiar face, a friend greeting me, in an otherwise rather forbidding environment.

Continuing West on 42nd Street, I quickly arrived at Fifth Avenue. Looking north, having never seen a building over six floors, I discovered the awesome sky scrappers, rising thirty, forty stories or more, above this magnificent street. A gentle breeze was waving the colorful flags of Saks and Rockefeller center and at the end of the avenue I could see the inviting green splash of Central Park. What a memorable vista!

As it was close to noon, it seemed that every office worker had decided to enjoy this first day of sun, to stroll on the busy sidewalks. Carried by a human wave, all speaking something that I was unable to understand, I found myself isolated, having lost my identity. I could have been deaf and mute and it would not have made any difference.

My Berlitz English had not prepared me for that and I felt very inadequate. It is at this moment that to compensate for my ignorance I started to observe body language and tried to interpret people and conversations around me. It can be most entertaining as you are in full control and can come to any conclusion. On a more realistic note, it takes a couple years in a foreign country to master enough vocabulary and understand the different tonalities, but with that acquired experience I can always tell during a conversation if the person I am trying to communicate with is inclined to be nice to me or not.

Now having wandered on Broadway and starved, I had lunch at Jack Dempsey's tavern where, I was served the biggest ham and Swiss cheese on rye I had ever seen. To my surprise customers drank coffee all through their meal, something that until now I had always seen reserved for the end of it. As I was exploring the culinary choices of my new world, I finished lunch with a piece of New York cheesecake with cherries on top. It may be junky but to this day remains one of my favorite desserts.

Needing to burn a few calories, and as it was a must see on my list, I aimed towards 34th.street, and the Empire State building. With a swishing noise and a speed that I had never experienced before in an elevator or anything else for that matter, I was transported from the lobby to the 86th. floor in what seemed less than a minute, and then in a second slower elevator, to the 102nd.floor. At the outside deck, I experienced my first bird's eye view of the city.

What a sight! Even in my dreams I had never expected anything like this. At that height, buffeted by the winds, my eyes watering from the cold, I could see the Hudson River on my right, with its barges and ferryboats, the East river on the left still holding on its quay my boat, my ex- home, and that little shiny dot far, far away, the statue of Liberty.

The people were ant like, dotting the sidewalks. Barely audible, I viewed the colorful serpentine traffic on the streets below. On the north side, majestic Central Park, its lakes and water ponds bouncing lights like the facets of a giant cut emerald stone decorating the finger look alike that is Manhattan. I was told to expect a concrete jungle but instead, I saw a city with tree lined streets and parks everywhere.

I stayed there maybe half an hour, soaking in the view, wanting to memorize every nuance, every detail, even the almost maritime smell of that journey.

My hosts for the next two days were, Pierre and Jacqueline Evieux. Pierre was the brother of my boss in Paris and here the owner of a small restaurant. Together they decided that they were going to introduce me to the American way of life.

Our first stop was at the longest soda fountain in the world. To my surprise it was in a department store cum pharmacy. With glee they ordered for me, and I discovered, complete with maraschino cherries, the imposing "banana split." I thought for a moment that it was for the three of us, until…. two more desserts appeared.

Window- shopping and chit chatting, we walked leisurely up Fifth Avenue and made a quick visit to St.Patrick's Cathedral, where we admired its Rose Window, its great organ, and its famous and beautiful marble Pieta.

As darkness was approaching, we followed our church visit with a carriage ride in the softly lit Central Park, enjoying the scenic hills, and lush meadows, the lace looking bridges, and the seductive walking paths protected by huge canopied trees. Serenely gliding through the night, the only sounds we could hear were distant muffled horn blasts and the much closer rhythm of our horse' shoes striking the ground. It was for me the beginning of a long love affair with New York.

That evening, exhausted, we ended up in Harlem at the Cotton Club. The low lights, the sweet smoke of American tobacco floating up in the air, the exciting music of an all black band, throaty females singing the blues, all made me feel that I was in the "sacro -sanctum" of jazz. That had been my dream for many years or to be exact, ever since I heard Sidney Bechet in Paris.

I was completely dazzled by the sheer size of everything: the imposing sky scrapers, St. Patrick, seating 2400 guests, Central Park with its 840 acres, the generous portions of food, and now, this heavenly music. I could sense that this country would offer me a lot of opportunities.

Also very apparent was the energy and seeming contentment and happiness of the people. I knew that I was in a very different world, that it might be difficult at times, but I wanted to join, to belong, and to this day have never regretted it. I am very proud to be part of the American dream.

Nassau, Bahamas 1956: A Love Story

By Bernard Perron

I am lying under the shade of a grape tree. A refreshing soft breeze carries the intoxicating, spicy smell of the Island. A cloudless, blue sky blends seamlessly with a turquoise sea. It is March, 1956 and I have come here to write a letter to my parents, telling them that I have found the most wonderful girl in the world and yes, that I am in love !

Twenty-four months earlier I was knee deep in snow in my Canadian lumber camp, but .now I am working as Chef Garde-manger at the Emerald Beach Hotel in Nassau. A Garde-manger is the person in a hotel or large restaurant in charge of all the cold items: appetizers, salads, cold soups, buffets, and decorative centerpieces such as ice carvings or tallow sculptures.

The slowly invading swishing sound of the incoming tide harmonizes with the chiming of the aluminum mast and riggings of our rocking fiberglass Sailfishes, creating a musical background. From time to time the beat is accentuated by the thump, thump, thump of a small motorboat, leaping from wave to wave.

On the hibiscus bush on my left, a colorful hummingbird bounces from bloom to bloom as if hanging from a bungee strap, its wings fluttering almost invisibly, hovering in front of these delicate pink flowers, its long beak foraging, seeking some nutrition in the yellow pollen that cover their hearts.

Having left the logging camp in the spring, I returned to work for the summer season at the Manoir Richelieu, in the Province of Quebec. Basking in civilization again I enjoyed being with people my age, dating, going to movies, and not having to carry a compass whenever I decided to go for a walk.

With the season over and the hotel closing, our executive chef asked me if I would be interested in working with him at the Mount Stevens club, a rather swanky, upscale place in Montreal. I agreed to do it, despite the fact that I just about had it with the cold weather.

Now almost below my chaise lounge, a hermit crab looks tentatively from the opening of its burrow. With one claw up in the air as if testing the wind, he tries to decide whether or not he should go on a stroll. Having finally made up his mind, he hurriedly runs away and disappears under some saw grass and dried leaves.

Except for the weather there is nothing wrong with Montreal. It is a charming and lively city, but the gray skies and constant cold rain were getting to me. In early November a chance to escape occurred when I received an invitation to join the kitchen staff of the Fort Montague Beach Hotel, in Nassau Bahamas, for the 1954-1955, winter season. This was my chance to escape from a gloomy Montreal winter.

Two weeks later, on my way to the islands, I experienced my first airplane ride, aboard a DC.4 owned by Colonial Airlines.

Now, months later, in this sub tropical island, on this pristine, fine, white sandy beach, with eyes closed, I am savoring this enchanted moment.

My life had turned around in January, when during a break in a busy evening in the hotel kitchen, I noticed that we had a new food checker. She was the cutest girl I had seen in a long time, with a delicate face and fair complexion, framed by jet –black hair.

Unsure of my English, I was nonetheless determined to start a conversation with her. Her name was Cathy Walker, and she was from Calgary Alberta, and had just taken a three weeks cruise, from Los Angeles to Nassau with a girl friend.

The lure of the Island had influenced them to plan to spend the next six months in the sun, rather than returning to snowy Canada in the peak of winter, which I thought was very reasonable.

Cathy's sparkling brown eyes were enhanced by the small wisp of bang almost hiding them. She was conservatively dressed, and her warm smile illuminated the rather dreary elevated food-checking desk that was her office.

As I approached her, I noticed that she was knitting and later learned that they were to be booties for a nephew born a few weeks earlier in Toronto. I found that fascinating as I had always thought that knitting was reserved for more mature ladies.

Kitchens are usually very noisy. With the banging of pots and pans, shouting of waiters, excitement flowing everywhere but here at her desk she was an island of tranquility, and speaking softly, I could feel my heart racing and my knees weakening.

It did not take me long to ask her for a date, and she kindly agreed. After a week of going out together I knew that she was *it*, the person with whom I wanted to share the rest of my life.

One evening, not wanting to rush anything, but nevertheless anxious to make her aware of my feelings as casually as possible, I told her that someday I was going to marry her.

To the best of my recollection I believe that she told me that I was completely nuts, pointing out that she was English Canadian and I was French. She was Protestant, I was Catholic, and as final blow she was three years my senior and I, just a baby. It was her opinion that we really should cool it.

Girls always worry about details, and being my usual optimistic self, I believed that without knowing it, she had almost said yes, and that there was a strong possibility that we could make it work.

It was true that we did not have many things in common so far. But we did both wear glasses and we both came from families with six children, so we are accustomed to sharing …. That's a start in the right direction, I figured.

Perseverance paid off. Six months later, both having transferred to another Bahamian hotel, the Emerald Beach, we started to go out steadily.

Communicating was rather interesting. Sometimes, as she speaks rather quickly, she would start telling me a story. Smitten by her charm, I was under the spell of her voice. I did not understand a word she was saying, but I would look at her animated face, cute little nose, and intense facial expression and, restraining myself from the magnetic attraction I was feeling, congratulated myself on the fact that being in her company made me the luckiest guy alive.

Interrupting her speech, breaking my dream, she would then asked me "What do you think?" and I had to admit that I had not understood a single word of what she had said. Then she would start all over again, and this time I was really concentrating and she was speaking more slowly.

I am preparing the words I will write to my parents, and the image of Cathy flashes before me. She is not stunning, just simply elegant, five foot six, slim, always stylishly dressed. The most simple outfit, through her choice of colors, and a silk scarf smartly knotted, makes her look like a picture out of a designer's sketch book.

My reverie continues as I become more aware of the things I want to tell them about her. It is not necessary for her to wear much make-up, as she is naturally gorgeous. I love the way she talks, the way she walks, her gentleness. Never have I looked or felt for a girl this way in the past. Never have I known the same excitement of being with someone, the joy of belonging and at the same time the peace and calm that stability brings. I was a gypsy who had found a safe heaven.

The staff quarters where twenty-five to thirty of us employees live is next to the hotel, on the beach. Men are on the right, ladies on the left, and a lounge in the center. As we work odd hours being in the service industry most of our evenings begin at midnight.

On a typical evening, we walk to the hotel pier and there, sitting on a bench, the music of our hotel orchestra under the direction of Beecham Coakley and his Calypsonians floating by us, a gentle warm breeze making the palm fronds in the back ground do a slow dance, in this idyllic condition close together, very close together, in one another's arms, as all lovers do, we talk for hours.

Once or twice a week, in my other pride and joy, a two and a half liter "Riley," an English Grand touring four-seater convertible, we go for a spin and invariably end up at a night club, *The Silver Slipper* over the hill, where the native Bahamians live. There, we meet other people in our industry and it has almost become our social club

The Silver Slipper is a rather primitive affair. A fairly large courtyard in Nassau Street sandwiched between brightly painted wood clapboard houses, elevated on concrete blocks. A bandstand and thatched bar raised a few feet are the center of attention. White wooden tables and chairs protected by umbrellas, advertise Myers' rum, Heinecken beers or Booth gin and are surrounded by a tiled dance floor that, once upon a time had displayed a very elaborate decorative design. But today, after years of wear and tear and the replacement of broken tiles by some who only had size in common with the originals, the floor looks more like a poorly balanced quilt.

The entertainment is very predictable as it is a family affair. The band playing there is formed of brothers, half brothers or cousins of Freddy Munnings, a very affable Bahamian singer with a great voice. The show consists mostly of Miss Peaches the fire dancer, who certainly is taking this art form seriously. However, she looks more like someone trying to escape from being singed by the flames below her, rather than the gyrating lady dancing voluptuously to the beat of the band. She is cute and tries hard, and everybody likes her, and anyway she is Freddy's current girlfriend.

Sweet Richard, the limbo king who is also Miss Peaches' brother, performs the closing act. Always with sunglasses or shades as they are called here, summer and winter with an eight foot white scarf wrapped around his neck, which he uses as a prop, dressed in the fashion of an escaped clown from Barnum and Bailey circus, he manages with the simple act of sliding under a bar leaning backwards to entertain the crowds for half an hour.

Other than his great vocal cords, Freddy is reputed to have, as of last week, fathered thirty-six children. An outstanding feat even by Bahamian standards and especially since the guy is only in his late forties. Someday he may have his monument on Market Square.

Around two in the morning, Cathy and I usually leave and pay a visit to a secluded local bar on Wolf road called *The Coconut Palm Bar*, where the owner, Big Bob (about three hundred pounds) makes the most delicious conch fritters, our favorite.

Here again there is entertainment. Professor Willy the piano man has developed a rather unusual way to play that instrument. His style is unorthodox as he manages to sit between two pianos in a V formation with one hand on each keyboard as he hammers the ivories. Mozart Piano Concerto In D minor he does not play, as his style is more reminiscent of Jerry Lee Lewis and his most popular song "Great Balls Of Fire "

Around three or three thirty, after having danced to the beat of more meringue and Calypso music, it is time to be reasonable, go home and catch a little sleep before going to work in a few hours.

What about the letter to my parents? Well, it is almost four P.M.. As she is working the day shift, Cathy should be free in a few minutes. I have not seen her for eight long hours, an eternity, as I miss her from the moment we separate. I am definitely, wonderfully in love with her. The letter can wait for the time being. Tomorrow for sure I will write it.

Zachary Plesser

I am a seventy plus senior, but when I shave each morning, I am always surprised by the strange face in the mirror. Inside, I don't feel as old as I really am. The zest for living is still within me. I have an insatiable curiosity about everything and an untiring desire to add to my life experiences. Those experiences are the fuel I feed into my writings.

My past business life and my family are unremarkable. What counts most, is what I do today and tomorrow, especially when it comes to writing.

MMM

A Mother's Unconditional Love

By Zachary Plesser

Tante Chanah was my grandmother's sister, my great aunt. She was tiny, as compared to my grandmother who was a stout, Hungarian peasant, but she was equally religious, orthodox to the extreme.

Tante had four children: Helen, Rosalind, Aaron and Samuel. The first three were clones of their parents: devout, observant, hard working, law abiding good citizens.

But Samuel--aah, Samuel was a different story. He was the aberrant child, an orthodox Jew who strayed from the fold, and became a felon, an armed robber.

By some quirk of fate, Samuel decided that hard work was not for him. There was a better, much easier way to get rich quick. That way was called "a stick up."

In due course, Samuel was caught by the police, tried, convicted and jailed. The first time, the sentence was 1 year in jail, the second such felony brought 5 years and, finally, his third conviction earned him a life sentence in accordance with New York State Law which demanded he be incarcerated for the rest of his life, as a "three time loser". He served his sentence at Sing Sing Prison in Ossining, New York.

My Tante Chanah, never discussed his guilt or innocence or whether she felt that the sentence was too harsh. All she knew was that he was her son.

So, every Sunday morning, she would take the BMT subway from Borough Park in Brooklyn, to Manhattan, then change subway trains, and arrived at Grand Central Station, where she boarded a New York Central railroad train to Ossining and Sing Sing.. She always brought home-cooked bread and cake and fresh fruit for her Samuel.

I once asked my mother how long Tante Chanah had been making that trip. Her reply was, "As long as I can remember. certainly, for more than 10 years. She never misses the trip unless a religious holiday falls on a Sunday."

That's how I learned what unconditional love really means.

Sibling Rivalry

By Zachary Plesser

Yes, all is well with sibling rivalry. It has always been around and it was never more so than some 30 years ago---between my brother and me.

My brother had an IQ of 188. I know that to be true because I saw his test report. I saw mine, too, only 157. He was designated a genius, and I, only of markedly superior intelligence. This knowledge of inferiority rankled me, and made me very susceptible to seeking vengeance, or actually, "one upsmanship" might better describe my goal.

My chance for retribution came many years after seeing those test scores, when I read an article in the New York Post describing a belly dancer named *Little Egypt* who had been admitted to *Mensa*, an association whose sole claim to fame lay in the fact that its members all had dramatically high IQ's.

The article provided a *Mensa* phone number for those interested in joining and I, of course, was curious enough to call.

For my $ 3.00 fee, I received a self monitored intelligence test, which I completed, returned and passed, making me eligible to take a 3 hour formal, supervised test at a downtown Manhattan location, the fee for which was $10.00.

I had come this far, and there was no stopping now. So, on a very hot day in July, I traveled to New York City to take the test.

" What kind of fool would be taking a *Mensa* entrance exam on day like this ?" I wondered, "There will be no one there, but me. Anyone smart enough to be concerned about a *Mensa* score, that is, anyone with any sense at all, would surely be at the beach."

Not! Upon entering the large meeting room, I mingled among 75 other "fools," all with the same desire to join Mensa.

The test was long and tough but I completed all the questions. I had always been a good test taker, but this time I was not really sure if I had "aced" the exam.

Two weeks passed with no word, and finally, the mail came with a letter that read: "Congratulations.You are eligible to join *Mensa*. Please send us your $15.00 membership fee."

By now, I had figured out that those in charge of *Mensa* were the real intelligent ones. They had already collected $13.00 and now another $15.00.for a total of $28.00 per person, times who knows how many applicants. And that was probably just the beginning.

My entrance into *Mensa* presented me with the opportunity to score a triumph over my brother. I made a careful plan for his upcoming birthday. My birthday card to him was accompanied by my gift, an application to take the *Mensa* tests, all the fees pre-paid by me. My card read, "You should become a *Mensa* member. You belong in such a group."

Of course, I did not mention that I had already passed and was a member but that secret was not long lived.

The next day, he called, and I could hear the laughter in his voice ."You've laid a trap for me," he said, "I know you. You must have passed the test already. There is no way I will take that test now that you have passed. Can you imagine how I would feel if I failed ? I can't take the risk. The consequences would be unbearable."

One of my great chances to "get even" had vanished, and I finally recognized that he was indeed, smarter than I.

The True Believer

By Zachary Plesser

My grandmother was a devout, Orthodox Jewess. She was part of a sea of my religious relatives: grandfather, uncles, aunts and cousins, most of whom frightened me when I was very young. Their harsh, intolerant comments and looks scared me

On the other hand, "Bobbie", as she was called, was soft spoken and kind. Moreover, I was fascinated by the fact that she wore a wig. In Yiddish, it was called a "sheitel." Orthodox women, to avoid distracting their husbands from studying the *Torah* shaved their own hair and wore less attractive wigs.

Once, I actually saw Bobbie's head, with her wig off, in all her baldness, and, WOW, was I ever astonished!

The prevailing opinion held by all my relatives was that we were the Chosen people, the "We" being not all Jews, just the ultra Orthodox.

Non-religious Jews and Gentiles were lumped into a group called worthless. This attitude disturbed me then, and still does to this day.

So, you can imagine my surprise and delight when I heard my grandmother say---"there is room in heaven for everyone." That phrase is within me, even to this day, Her gentle tolerance set her apart.

Ever since I heard her say that, I have cherished my grandmother as a person who actually lived her religion, a true believer, and I loved her for it.

Sonia Ravech

Sonia Ravech is married, the mother of four and grandmother of seven. She and her husband, Richard, reside during the summer in North Falmouth, Massachusetts on Cape Cod,

They spend winters in Boca Raton, Florida. In addition to writing, Sonia enjoys traveling, gardening, and entertaining her large family and many friends.

MMM

Dreams Can Come True

By Sonia E. Ravech

For years I wanted to travel...to visit far off, exotic places I had read about in books. I clipped articles from the travel sections of newspapers. I browsed through brochures and magazines. I even invited friends to share their travel photos and experiences with me. However, being a full time homemaker and mother of four active children, I was forced to put those dreams on hold. "After the kids are grown and out on their own, then it will be my turn," I would say to myself.

Time passed, the children grew, went off to college and three of the four married. It was finally time to share my fantasies with my husband, to transform them into a reality. But, to my disappointment, he was not enthusiastic. He didn't have the same passion for seeing the world as I. This surprised me. In the past, he had spent hours watching National Geographic, Animal Kingdom and the Discovery Channel. I couldn't understand his negative attitude towards having an opportunity to see in person those places he had visualized on television.

Being a creature of habit who enjoyed the comforts of his home and sleeping in his bed every night, he had no desire to sit on a plane for hours, live out of a suitcase for weeks at a time and tolerate all the unexpected inconveniences that travel often involves. I was confident I could change his mind. I tried to convince him that travel was fun, interesting and educational. I bought books and videos to entice him, but to no avail.

When I celebrated my 60th birthday, I accepted the reality that my husband wasn't interested. I picked up the phone, called a travel agent and several weeks later left on an exciting tour of Africa. My adventure was everything I always fantasized it would be. I felt more confident than ever that I had made the right decision to go it alone. My only regret, I waited so long.

Since then I have traveled to China, Israel, Egypt, Australia and New Zealand. I've visited Alaska and toured most of the National Parks within the United States. Along the way, I've met numerous friendly, interesting people.

Recently, I began to travel with my sister, as well as with my daughters when they can get away from their family responsibilities. In June I plan to take four of my grandchildren, ages thirteen to twenty-one, on a two week trip to Europe. I am anxiously looking forward to this unique bonding experience.

The moral of this story: If you really want to do something, and have the means, just do it. Follow your own dreams. You won't be disappointed. If you wait for someone else to help you make them come true, it may never happen.

MMM

Morrey

By Sonia Ravech

Morrey was a mentally challenged man in his mid forties who lived across the street from me when I was a child. Regardless of the weather, Morrey always wore a long, tweed overcoat and a brown wool cap. Born nearly ten years after his older brother, his immigrant parents were unsure how to raise a child with special needs. They loved him; made sure he was fed and clothed, but in their ignorance, made no effort to secure the services for Morrey that would have helped him lead a productive life.

When Morrey's mother died, his father was at a loss as to what to do for Morrey. Every morning when his father left for his job as a locksmith, he gave Morrey $2.00, locked his front door and told Morrey he should return home when he saw the porch light lit.

Morrey passed the hours by riding the trolley on Blue Hill Avenue. He rode north to Egleston Square, the end of the line, and then reversed his direction riding south to Mattapan Square. He repeated the trip again and again until he tired of this activity. Then he returned home and sat on the stoop waiting for the kids to come home from school.

He liked to watch the boys play kickball in the street, and sometimes begged to join them. As kids so often do, they mocked and teased him calling him "retard" and "dummy." Morrey was wounded by their mean response.

When Mama became aware of this situation, she scolded the boys for their insensitivity, and invited Morrey to come to our house to play with my siblings and me. We had a lazy mutt of a dog, and Morrey took to him instantly. He grinned and laughed when Wolfie licked his hand or nestled his wet nose under his chin. And so our family's relationship with Morrey was born.

Morrey and Mama developed a special bond, perhaps because she was kind to him, and he missed his own mother. He called Mama Mrs. "Y" because he couldn't remember Yassen. Morrey tried to show his appreciation to Mama by bringing her little gifts, dandelions from the backyard or a shiny stone from the sidewalk.

When the cold weather approached, Morrey shared tomato soup or hot chocolate with us when we returned from school. Although he was content in our home, he kept returning to the window to see if the porch light was lit.

He didn't understand the concept of moving the clock back an hour in October and wondered why his father didn't come home when it got dark, the way he had done in the past.

Mama reassured him that his father would return. When the porch light finally glowed, Morrey put on his cap saying, "I gotta go, gotta go," and shuffled back across the street.

Late one night, there was a loud pounding on the front door. Mama jumped from her bed to see who was there. It was Morrey, barefoot and pajama clad, babbling incoherently with fear in his eyes.

Once Mama calmed him down, she realized something had happened to his father. Morrey kept repeating, "I can't wake him up. He won't wake up." Mama rushed across the street, and as soon as she saw Mr. Weiner's crumpled body on the floor, she knew he was dead.

She went to the phone and called for an ambulance. Above the phone, tapcd to the wall, was a card that read, "In emergency, call David, 555-6764. David was Morrey's older brother who lived in New York. Mama dialed the number and relayed the sad news to David. She told him not to worry about Morrey. He could spend the night with our family.

David and his wife arrived early the next morning, and Morrey returned home. David packed Morrey's belongings, along with several other items and loaded the car and then, he and Morrey came to say "goodbye."

David thanked Mama for her kindness and returned to his waiting wife. Morrey hugged Mama and patted Wolfie on the head. "Gotta go, gotta go," he said as he waved goodbye and crossed the street.

Seconds after he left, Mama found his cap on the table and rushed to the door to return it. David's car was rounding the corner, and Mama chased after it shouting, "Your cap, Morrey. You forgot your cap." Morrey stuck his head out the rear window, waved and shouted back, "I'll get it tomorrow, Mrs."Y"

MMM

The Blue Hat

By Sonia Ravech

"That's her, Mama, that's Jane." My daughter Marcie shouted excitedly as she jumped up from the rear seat of the car. I looked in the direction she was pointing and saw three girls walking side by side.

"Which one is Jane?" I asked.

"The one in the blue hat," she responded. I smiled since I was finally getting to meet Jane, albeit from a distance.

Having recently moved to a new house, Marcie had been understandably apprehensive about attending a new school and making new friends. Within weeks, however, she began to chat constantly about Jane, a classmate who befriended her. I learned that Jane's father was a judge and her mother a social worker. They lived in the large Victorian house on the corner. Jane had no siblings, but she did have two cats.

I was surprised to see that the girl in the blue hat was African American. With all the information Marcie had shared with me about Jane, it never occurred to her to mention her race.

I learned an important lesson that day from a nine year old child. It is more significant to acknowledge a sweet smile, a friendly wave or the color of one's hat than to notice the color of one's skin.

MMM

The Conversation

By Sonia E. Ravech

Two men sat on a bench at the front of a woman's clothing store. They were both waiting for their wives to finish shopping. They commentated on the weather, how sunny, cool and dry it was. One complained to the other about being stuck in a store on such a beautiful day when he could be on the links playing golf.

"What are you going to do?" he said. "My wife doesn't drive anymore. Seven days a week I'm tied down to this woman. If it's not one thing it's another. On Monday I drop her off and pick her up from her bridge club. On Tuesday she goes to the library. On Thursday it's the supermarket. Friday she has her nails done. Saturday she goes to the beauty parlor. It seems I'm always schlepping her one place or another. I never get a break."

"I know what you mean," said the other. "I'm tied down by my wife, too. She has kidney disease. Three times a week I take her to the hospital for dialysis. Twice a week she has to go to physical therapy for a chronic back problem. In between she needs to visit the doctor for a variety of ailments. It's really rough. When I'm not at a medical appointment, I'm doing other errands or chores around the house. She's too sick most of the time to do much of anything herself. Today is one of her better days, so I suggested she buy some new clothes. Most of her old ones are too big. She's lost so much weight lately. It's not easy but what choice do I have?"

The other man shook his head in agreement and shrugged his shoulders. "I know, I know. What are you going to do?"

A Love Story

By Sonia E. Ravech

An elderly couple sat across from me in a restaurant. The woman had apparently suffered a debilitating stroke and was in a wheelchair. When their food arrived, the gentleman tied a bib around the woman's neck. He cut her chicken into small pieces and proceeded to feed her.

Her head hung slack and saliva filled the corners of her mouth. Occasionally, he wiped her mouth and chin with a napkin He raised a glass so she could sip a drink from a straw. His own meal grew cold as he concentrated on helping her.

He spoke to her tenderly and patted her hand reassuringly. When their meal was finished, he got up from his chair and helped her into her sweater. He brushed the hair from her face and kissed the top of her head. She lifted her eyes towards his and tried to smile, to express her appreciation for his devotion,

I suppose.

As he looked into her face, I wondered what he saw. Was it the face of the sick, helpless invalid that was seen by others in the restaurant, or that of the beautiful bride he wed so many years before? From the love that radiated from his eyes, I'm sure it was the latter.

Joyce Altman Rosenberg

Joyce Altman Rosenberg was born in Brooklyn and went to Brooklyn College. She also received a degree in interior design from the New York School of Design. Joyce was married for 48 years to a wonderful man who passed away too soon from a brain tumor. She has three children and two entertaining granddaughters. Joyce has been writing poetry, stories and life reviews her whole life. She is also an artist and sculptor. For fun, she plays golf, cards and loves to travel.

ΛΛΛΛ

Wills

By Joyce Rosenberg

Who gets possession of our memories, the forty-seven years we spent together?

What person will care enough to go through our lives, our dreams, our joys, our realities, the funny ways we spent our early dating days?

Years of building our todays, living through our tomorrows, yesterday's news -- will it matter again?

The music we loved, places we lived, people around us.

The jokes we shared, the talking without saying a word.

The look that said, "Let's get out of here"

How you become one being, but still independent sharing each other's happiness and sadness.

Sounds like everyone else's life. But no! Ours was different----- special

People said I made you happy, I pushed and you followed, But they didn't know the truth. Maybe in the beginning I would push but then you'd take over, and fly. You were a magnificent pilot

Our lives were better because you found the extra special things to make it right. You laughed when I'd cry at Bette Midler singing, "Wind Beneath My Wings."

How apt that song was for us. The tears come so easily. Funny, how everything can be a memory.

Who else but me will remember all the nuances --tall, blonde, blue eyes--washed out light blue denim jeans and Eisenhower jacket, white socks and brown loafers, my smoking car at Heshie's pharmacy, Ellie and me running out thinking it will explode, seeing you for the first time— laughing.

Not enough time. So alone! I'm not good alone

And yet …now --

New memories starting to happen…..

Phyllis Rothman

Phyllis Rothman has had a varied career in advertising, public relations, education, retailing, importing, free lance writing, volunteer work, as well as being a wife, mother, and grandmother. She has traveled extensively in the United States and Canada, South America, Europe, Asia and the Caribbean Islands.

She was born in Brooklyn, New York, and moved with her parents to Queens, New York at age six. This move was her first cultural shock because her Brooklyn in the 1930's consisted of redbrick apartment houses, a few trees, gray pavements, and mostly ethnic European first and second generation neighbors.

When her father opened a meat market in Queens, the family moved to this newly developing borough, which was home to more second generation Americans than she had previously known. It was also, at that time, mainly a community of one and two-family homes with acres of trees and grass. And it was here that she grew up and stayed until she and her husband purchased a one-family home in fast-growing Nassau county on Long Island in 1965.

In 1988, with their children grown and starting in promising careers, the Rothmans opted for retirement and moved to Florida, where they have resided ever since. Although they love the warm winters, they still maintain a small residence in the New York City area, where two of their children live with their spouses and four grandchildren.

They also make frequent visits to Atlanta, Georgia, where their youngest daughter lives with her husband and two children. One of the high points of Phyllis' retirement years has been writing and listening to the stories written by her fellow workshop writers.

Aunt Yettie, the Queen of Clean

By Phyllis Rothman

Aunt Yettie was the "Queen of Clean," the "balabusta" (outstanding housekeeper) of the family. She could make a rusted metal garbage pail sparkle like a mirror. In a family of dedicated entrepreneurial businesswomen, Aunt Yettie's skills were often dismissed, if not ridiculed, but she ignored those who laughed at her and kept on cleaning. Perhaps that preoccupation often helped her maintain her sanity, which, as my mother had explained to me, left her from time to time

She cleaned windows, washed floors, dusted every day, did laundry by hand, ironed even underwear, among all the domestic chores that she performed. No crumb ever lingered on her floors, because Aunt Yettie's sharp eyes could spot one from across the largest room. She was a volume of information on soaps and detergents, strong and weak, and all the sisters came to her for advice on cleaning. No one could refute her expertise since her home stood as a "shining" example of her professionalism.

Aunt Yettie and Uncle Morris, were always poor. The most prosperous period of their lives was when they were eligible to collect social security, and later on, could count on Medicare to pay their medical bills.

In the 1950's, they were able to move to a middle income City of New York housing project, which at that time was a very safe, clean place to live. It was the first time they had lived in a building with an elevator, and with an incinerator to dispose of garbage. This apartment also offered them their first electric refrigerator.

However, I always associate Aunt Yettie with "walk-up" apartments and "ice boxes" to keep their food chilled. Hers was the only home I can remember without an electric refrigerator.

While Aunt Yettie could have succumbed to squalor, she never did. Among her domestic skills, she also excelled at exterminating roaches. She never moved into an apartment that did not have them, and she never left an apartment that did have them.

Indeed, remembering how my aunt rid her apartments of unwanted pests, when I moved to Florida, I resorted to her time tested remedy, boric acid, and I can report that Aunt Yettie knew her business, when it came to bugs. I even amaze my exterminator with what I learned from my aunt. Besides being the enemy of roaches, she was also adept at exterminating bedbugs, which was a common problem among those who could afford only used furniture.

The only down side of Aunt Yettie's housekeeping was her cooking, which was bland and tasteless. With the advent of television, however, in the late 1940's, she started to watch the cooking programs, and suddenly she became a very accomplished chef, thus rounding out her domestic talents.

Aunt Yettie must have loved her housework because I always remember her as the smiling aunt. As I think of my mother's sisters, the only happy face that comes to mind is that of Aunt Yettie. I wish I knew how she, who had so little, could have left me with such a lovely memory.

MMM

The Visit to Aunt Rae

By Phyllis Rothman

About once every three or four months, my mother would announce, "I think we'll take a trip to Aunt Rae this Sunday. We haven't been there in a while. She let me know yesterday, when I spoke to her on the phone, that no one ever comes to see her."

This was true, I knew. Not only was it a long journey for us by underground subway and Third Avenue El (elevated train), but when we finally arrived there, we would be entertained in her grocery store, which was literally her "living room," the place where she spent all her days from 6 A. M. until Midnight, on many days.

If we were lucky, she would sell out all the milk by dinner time, and then she would close the store. If there was even one bottle of milk remaining, however, she would hang a sign on the door, "Will reopen at 8 P. M.," and then we would all trudge up the two flights of steps from her stale smelling lobby to the second floor, where the odors improved as we passed the apartments sending forth fresh fragrances of pot roast, chicken soup, fried onions, "gribbenes" (frying chicken fat), baking ruggelach, apple strudel, and assorted other Eastern European favorites.

Entering Aunt Rae's apartment, I would always wonder how she and my mother could have been sisters. Mom's motto was, "Cleanliness is next to godliness," and she lived by those words. Aunt Rae, on the other hand, seemed totally unfamiliar with that proverb.

The first odor that assaulted me each time I walked into that apartment was the smell of her unwashed toilet, which was located right off the entry foyer. It was as if she and her children, Norman and Shirley, seemed unable to make it in time for their urine to fall inside the toilet bowl. There were times when my parents and I would spend as many as six hours visiting Aunt Rae, but I would rather burst a kidney than enter that foul- smelling room.

On the rare occasions when I could no longer hold it in, I learned to hold my breath in that bathroom so long that I thought my lungs would explode. Indeed I may have set some breath holding records there. The only comparable experience that I can remember in my lifetime was the stop at the public toilet at the bottom of the Great Wall in China, where I almost fainted from its noxious odor that was slightly worse than Aunt Rae's toilet.

Although my mother was not bashful about offering advice, she long ago seemed to have given up on trying to improve the cleanliness in Aunt Rae's apartment.

My aunt's strongest housekeeping virtue was her cooking, which was about as "Old World" as you could get. My mother had told me many stories about what it was like to live in her grandmother's backroom kitchen behind her bakery in a Polish shtetl. And whenever we had dinner at Aunt Rae's, I felt transported to that setting. Mom never came close to duplicating the flavors and aromas of a dinner at Aunt Rae's home. Her "dozen egg" sponge cake was her Passover and Rosh Hashonah specialty, and each year we would make the pilgrimage to the Bronx to bring one home. Laden down from that dozen-egg dough, it was a load for my father to carry on the long journey from the Bronx to Queens.

Among her other cooking virtues, Aunt Rae excelled at making gefilte fish (a hand chopped fish made into patties, and stewed for hours in a spicy liquid). Nowadays, it is usually purchased in jars at the supermarket. Which modern American woman has the time to make this delicacy "from scratch"? My aunt's pot roast "melted in your mouth" my mother would say, but what I loved most was her mashed potatoes with chicken fat, something my mother never made.

Mom, who had certainly never studied nutrition, was way ahead of her generation in understanding that chicken fat "was poison" as she would say.

When dinner was over, my cousin Norman, who was five years older than I, would permit me to read his latest "Big Little Book," a series of cowboy stories that measured about three inches by three inches and was about one inch thick. Being a good reader, I could usually finish reading one before we left for home. These stories were a novelty to me because I was an only child, and had no brothers to help me expand my female world.

Because my parents felt unsafe leaving Aunt Rae's neighborhood in darkness, we visited her more during the Daylight Saving Time season than in the winter. On the two block walk from Aunt Rae's store and apartment, we had to pass a bar and grill on the corner of East 171st Street and Third Avenue, where we were always assaulted by the blaring sounds of jazz and swing, and could peek through the opening and closing swinging doors, as they exposed the gyrating men and women, laughing and shouting, dancing wildly.

If one of them spotted us, he would point in our direction, and we would nervously speed up the pace, and heave a sigh of relief, after we climbed up the steep flight of steps to the El and arrived at the train platform, where there was an attendant in the change booth. Once inside the train, we could relax, and think about how lucky we were to be returning to Queens with its trees, grass, and neatly tended gardens. And it was somewhat of a relief to realize that we had paid our "Aunt Rae" dues. We were off the hook for another few months.

$$\bowtie\bowtie\bowtie$$

It's The People You Meet

By Phyllis Rothman

"Venice! Why you go to that stinken sewer Venice?" I heard the man with the heavy Italian accent ask of my husband. He was sitting in a wheelchair, cheerfully expounding on the joys of his hometown.

276

Meanwhile, his booming voice kept interrupting my concentration on "The New York Times."

"Forget Venice, you come with me to Misano on the Adriatico. It's bewteeful, clean, you and your wife, you stay with my wife and me in my mother's house. I show you the real Italy...not those tourist traps you going to."

I looked at my husband and read his mind. Not on your life, I said to myself. Planning this trip has been a labor of love for me. This stranger in an airport is not going to sabotage my carefully made plans.

Stan looked at me pleadingly.

"We're meeting Kay and Sid in Venice in two days," I said, in my "case closed" voice.

"Whatsa you wife's name, Stanley?" Salvatore asked.

"Phyllis," I replied. "It's very kind of you to invite us, but we're on our own for just the first night. Then we go to Venice to meet our friends". This ought to quiet him, I thought.

I soon discovered. that nothing can quiet this man,

"You phone your friends and tell 'em to meet you in Misano on the Adriatico," I heard Salvatore say. "You want to relax and have fun. Misano is the real Italy, not those overpriced filthy tourist traps. You following my brother Armando and me from the airport, and you see scenery in the Tuscan hills like you never seen before. Trust me. Do I look like a guy who would fool you? Not me. Not Salvatore."

At the mention of "scenery like you never seen before," I became less skeptical. "Tell me about the Tuscan hills. What'll we see? Where'll we go? How long is the drive?"

"Paradise. You see hills and trees and farms. Soooo green. Like you never believe. We eat lunch outside in a grape arbor near Orvieto, like no place you ever ate before. I show you my Italy, not the phony one the travel agents sell you."

Salvatore's enthusiasm was boundless and he was getting to me. It sounded great, but who was this man? We can't let ourselves get carried away by such a character. What kind of person invites complete strangers to stay in his house? That's crazy.

From out of no where a woman appeared and spoke to Salvatore in perfect English, a Norman Rockwell portrait, who personified his rendition of the American dream grandmother.

"Meet my wife Helen," Salvatore introduced her.

She looks so normal. Maybe we should consider his offer, I told myself.

"Helen, tell them about Tuscany and Misano. I want to show them the Italian Italy, not where the travel agents send Americans. They going to Misano with us. Eh, my friend?" Salvatore assumed that interest meant consent.

"We need to know more about Misano. I really don't want to impose on you, Salvatore. Can we stay at a hotel?" I tried to slow down this whirlwind of a man, but he was unstoppable. I gave my husband a look, meant to decelerate him, but he was caught up in our enticer's web.

After what seemed like an hour or so, we heard the boarding announcement for our plane. It had actually been a four hour wait, but being in Salvatore's company and listening to his stories about Misano and the little town where he lived in upstate New York, had transformed a usually monotonous experience into an adventure.

As the boarding passengers gathered their hand luggage, Salvatore suddenly sprang out of his wheelchair.

"Sal, I thought you couldn't walk," Stan said.

"Sure I can walk. I get the wheelchair so they put me up front. Then I get a good seats for Helen and me. My mother, she has a smart son, ha ha," Salvatore chortled. "Hey don't tell anyone. You a nice guy. I know I can trust you."

This is who Stan wants to travel with? I must be crazy for thinking that I would go along on this mystery ride. When we get on the plane, I'll finish this very quickly. I don't know a thing about this man. His wife looks all right, but he's a loose cannon.

Thanks to Salvatore the flight to Rome passed quickly. When we disembarked at Ciampino Airport, he had everything worked out for our auto caravan across the Tuscan Hills. "My brother Armando, he's a meeting us at the airport with his new Mercedes. You go get your rental car and then you follow Sal and me to Misano."

When Stan pulled up in our rented Fiat, Salvatore announced, "I drive until we pass Rome. You get lost here if you drive. Phyllis, you sit in the back." The man was a sorcerer. Gone was my resolve to get away from him.

Once on the bypass around Rome, we realized how fortunate we were to have Salvatore taking over on this leg of our journey. Despite all the research I had done, I was totally unprepared for the unlimited speed limits on Italian highways. Sixty five and seventy five miles an hour was a crawl in that country. While we did learn to speed up eventually, we certainly appreciated our self-appointed "guide." A few miles past Rome we rendezvoused with Armando and Helen, and Stan took over the wheel, while Salvatore returned to his brother's Mercedes.

As our stomachs growled that lunchtime was approaching, we began to see signs for Orvieto. Finally, we followed Salvatore off the road into a clearing. The minute we pulled into the parking area, the momma and poppa owners of this easy-to-miss eating establishment came running over to Sal and Helen, kissing, hugging, throwing their arms around each other.

"I bring my friends from America," Sal proudly announced."You bring out the grappa, Mario. You ever drink grappa?" he asked, as he turned to me. "You drink grappa and you never be the same again."

After experiencing the grappa, we tried to stand up. Wobbling, we both wondered about our sanity. Nonetheless, I took the wheel despite the fact that I had a hard time keeping my eyes open. Stan fell asleep in the passenger seat almost immediately. Armando, in the lead car, seemed impervious to the grappa, but I dared not stop or I would lose our leaders.

As we drove through the Tuscan hills, the grappa began to wear off, and my apprehension subsided every time a new pastoral scene appeared after each bend in the road. There was no way that we would have found this by ourselves. No matter what awaited us in Misano, I knew that we had made a smart move by following Salvatore and his brother.

Heading toward our seaside destination, we entered Misano through a street that seemed like a reincarnation of Miami's South Beach.

To this day, I don't know which came first, the two and three story art deco buildings in Misano or Miami Beach. It was late afternoon and suddenly Armando, in the lead car, turned into an alley, bordered by similar buildings on each side. Directly in front of us, we were startled by a double line of waving people, ranging in age from toddlers to elderly, black-frocked, gray-haired grandmothers. When they saw Armando's car, shouts of joy went up. While we could not understand what they were saying, the body language said it all. Salvatore and Armando waved excitedly to the cheering crowd of 20 or so people, and signaled us to stop. It was as if we were extras on the set of an Italian movie, and Salvatore was the director.

"I bring my American friends," he shouted out the window, in English and Italian, inviting us to join him in greeting his relatives.

"You wait here," he said to us. Two minutes later Salvatore returned with Mama. "She don't talk English, but I tell her all about you. But Stanley, I have bad news. All the bedrooms are full. My family from Bologna is here. But I don't want you to worry. Across the street is a very nice hotel, very clean and cheap like you not gonna believe. I go now to talk to the owner."

Much as I had not wanted to stay in Salvatore's house originally, I found myself disappointed after meeting his warm, Italian relatives. Before I had time to voice my disappointment, however, he reappeared.

"I have good news. I talk to the hotel owner and they have a good room for you, immaculate, with three meals. Guess how much? How much you pay in Venice for your hotel room?"

The year was 1982. "$150 a night," Stan reported with some embarrassment.

"Oh," Salvatore gloated, "when you hear what you pay here, you cancel your reservation in Venice." He paused, "$14 a day with three meals! How you like that for a deal, Stanley?"

"But Sal," I protested, "We're only here for two meals, dinner tonight and breakfast tomorrow. Then we leave for Venice."

"Wait," he responded as he raced back to the hotel.

Two minutes later he returned. "Because lunch is the big meal here, the owner he take off $3.00 a day. Now you only pay $11.00 with dinner and breakfast."

Salvatore had us hooked, but only for the night, I made my husband promise. We sat for hours after dinner in Mama's backyard singing Italian folk songs, drinking home made wine and grappa, eating Mama's delicate cookies, while Salvatore's brother accompanied us on the accordion. We knew we were in the real Italy.

Were we crazy to follow this stranger? Probably. But ask us about Italy, and this is our best memory.

Laundry

By Phyllis Rothman

Laundry is my salvation, my escape, my excuse to myself. It's also a useful chore with an end result that makes life more pleasant for my family. What a strange task for a women's libber to enjoy. I suppose it's one of those holdovers from my mother, who took great pride in producing a sparkling white wash.

When I was a little girl, in the pre-washing machine days, I remember the laundry sink with white wash pre-soaking in a mixture of soap and bleach. If I didn't see it when I walked through the front door, I could always smell the bleach. No matter how tired my mother was, the white wash had to go through every step: the washing, the scrubbing, the bleaching, the bluing, the rinses, and finally the starching. The stiffer the blouse was after ironing, the bigger the smile on my mother's face.

Her proudest laundry moment occurred when I was in high school. Although I was always an indifferent physical education student, one day, Miss Capodifero, my sophomore gym teacher, found something important about me to compliment. "Miss Brownstein," she announced from the lectern, "please come to the front of the room."

. For sure, I imagined, I had made some terrible misstep when we were doing calisthenics. Overcome with embarrassment, I marched without expression to the front of the gym and faced the class, feeling the red heat of a gigantic blush covering my face.

"I want everyone here to see what a gym shirt should look like when you wear it to class. See how starched and white it is. This is what I expect from everyone. Thank you, Miss Brownstein," and with those words, Miss Capodifero earned my everlasting love and gratitude. For the balance of that semester, I actually found myself enjoying gym class.

When I told my parents the story that night, my mother's pride was so great, that she called each of her five sisters immediately to relate how my shirt had been singled out from those of 200 girls in our gym class. Never did I forget Miss Capodifero's kindness to a girl who, until then, had used every excuse imaginable to avoid "phys-ed."

I, too, take pride, as Mom did, in the finished product. I know that sometimes I use laundry as an excuse to get away from writers' block, and other mental activities that are stressful. There's something rejuvenating for me in the change of pace. The mindlessness of it gives my brain the rest it needs.

Sometimes, when I'm folding the laundered clothes, I remind myself that there can be self-esteem in work that does not bring national recognition or millions of dollars.

Rhoda Rubenstein

Writing always gives me a sense of fulfillment. When I was six years old I collected poetry in a black and white notebook which I still have among my fading memorabilia. These days I get great pleasure out of creating memoir pieces.

Dividing my time between NY and Florida and traveling whenever and wherever the mood strikes, has given me a broad canvas on which to express my thoughts and feelings. The smallest incident will provide the material for a story. The future holds great promise.

***

Grandma Chana

By Rhoda Rubenstein

Last night I thought of Grandma Chana. I can see her in her flowered house-dress and long blue apron, standing at our black and white enamel stove. Whenever I came home from school, the aroma of Grandma's cooking floated down the stairs and greeted me like a hug. A glass of chocolate milk and a freshly baked treat were always waiting for me; apple cake, rugelach or a thin slice of zwibach filled with raisins and nuts.

If I were lucky, Grandma would be cooking chocolate pudding. Then I would rush in impatiently, stand on tip toe and try to peek into the pot as the wonderful mixture turned magically from white milk and brown powder into rich, thick sweet smelling ambrosia right before my eyes. When it was done Grandma poured the pudding into glass 'dessert' dishes, one from grape jelly, one from baby food or peanut butter. It didn't matter that the dishes didn't match. The only important thing was that Grandma let me scrape the pot and lick the spoon. Ah, heaven!

Some afternoons I sat on Grandma Chana's lap while she told me wonderful stories of her childhood in Poland, stories so realistic that the people she talked about became my friends: Rachel, the girl on the next farm, Levi the baker, who always had about him the aromatic smell of fresh baked bread and Tante Helen with her beautiful clothes and sophisticated city ways. These were the characters who peopled Grandma's faraway life, like the players in the soap operas she listened to every afternoon as she worked in the kitchen. The melodious voices of Stella Dallas, Lorenzo Jones, Our Gal Sunday drifted in from the big domed radio that had a place of honor in the corner of the living room.

Grandma was tiny and wore her salt and pepper hair in a bun that she held in place with big tortoise shell hair-pins. She favored round steel rimmed spectacles way before they became a fashion statement and spoke in a soft sweet voice, never losing the Polish accent she brought with her so many years before. By the time I was 10 or 11, I had grown taller than she and Grandma would look up and laugh, saying soon I would have to lift her up to hug her. Each day, after school Grandma Chana sent me to the grocery on the corner to pick up the items she needed to cook dinner. Mr. Walfish, the proprietor, was always dressed in a white apron, tied around his waist with the bow in the front. It covered him from chest to knees and I don't remember ever seeing him without it.

I can visualize the dairy case filled with tins of fresh cottage cheese, farmer cheese and pot cheese. Grandma used her own blend of these in the airy and delicious blintzes she prepared and served, golden brown, right from the frying pan. Sometimes they never even reached the table before we grabbed and ate them with sighs of pleasure. I don't seem to be able to replicate their unique taste no matter how I try.

Those times are only memories now, tucked away with the innocence of childhood. I miss my Grandma Chana, with her quaint, beloved European ways. I miss the boundless love she gave me, love that required nothing from me in return. But sometimes, just sometimes for a happy moment I can feel my Grandma's soft arms around me as the sweet smell of cinnamon and apples floats gently through the bakery's open door

Green Wool Coat

By Rhoda Rubenstein

My grandfather was a silent man. I don't remember ever having a conversation with him. I didn't know his dreams. I didn't know him. He was just there, part of my world. I never knew whether his silence resulted from a lack of fluency in an unfamiliar language or a reticence born of reluctance to become part of a world where everything was unfamiliar.

He came with those immigrants seeking freedom to practice their faith and relief from the pogroms that shattered their existence. He found the freedom he sought, but the life he knew, all that comforted and sustained him was left behind when he boarded the ship

Grandpa worked as a tailor in the garment district, leaving in the morning in the silence of a sleepy household and arriving home in time for his evening prayers and dinner.

When I was five years old he made me a green wool coat. It had a velvet collar and cuffs and tight velvet leggings that hugged my skinny legs and kept them warm no matter what the weather. My coat had a satin lining that gleamed and glistened and felt as soft as mother's caress when it rested against my bare skin. It had a matching velvet bonnet with one pert feather in the band that swayed jauntily with every step I took. How I loved that hat and coat. When I walked with my mother, I could see my reflection in the windows of the stores we passed. I felt like a princess.

I wore my green wool coat and leggings until my arms and legs protruded like popsicle sticks, but still I wouldn't let my mother give it away. Somehow, it comforted me to see it hanging there, squeezed among the more appropriately sized skirts and dresses.

I cried and fussed whenever my mother threatened to include it in the bags of clothing for the poor children and she would reluctantly put it back in the closet to hang and wait until the following season.

One day, I opened my closet and the green wool coat was gone. I ran to my mother for an explanation. She told me she had given the coat away many weeks before. Someone came to collect the old clothes. I was at school. I hadn't noticed.

My grandpa didn't talk much. I don't remember ever having a conversation with him. But that green wool coat spoke to me of love and whenever I think of my grandpa, that is what I remember.

The Green Car

By Rhoda Rubenstein

When I was eight years old, my father bought a new car. It was a pale green Chrysler with brilliant, chrome grillwork and doors that took all of my strength to push open or shut. This model was the epitome of modern technology with fluid drive transmission instead of the standard shift, and an am/fm radio. It had the remarkable smell of newness, heady, pervasive and unmistakable.

My father loved this car. He waited a long time for it while he drove our disreputable black Dodge with the worn-to-no-color fraying upholstery. From 1940-1945 the purchase of a new vehicle was put on hold while all available steel production went to the war effort.

It didn't matter that Moe ordered it before the war began. He still had to wait. My Uncles Milton, Joe and Bernie laughed at his patience, claiming that, "face it Moey, your request is probably at the bottom of a pile of orders marked 'get lost'". But my father never gave up hope and three months after the war was over he drove down fifty-third street in Borough Park, Brooklyn in his long awaited brand new car, to almost everybody else's surprise and to his great delight. My father didn't know then that this would be the last new car he would ever own.

We had that Chrysler for all of my growing up years. Woven through the fabric of many happy days is the memory of the car. It was a member of the family.

When I was eighteen, I learned how to drive in that pale green baby and had my first accident the day after I got my driver's license, just a fender bender, one block from my house, while I was busy waving frantically to my friend Ada Dellin and trying to inspire her envy.

One evening shortly after that, on my way home from college, smoke started pouring from the engine and I thought surely it was the final death rattle of the old girl. I slammed on my brakes and jumped out before the expected explosion, leaving the car in the middle of the street with the door wide open. I called my dad to give him the bad news and he rushed to my rescue taking two buses in the process.

Moe never uttered a word of reproach even after he released the emergency brake. "Next time, Rhoda, don't forget to do that *before* you start driving," was all he said.

On humid summer nights at a time when air conditioners were not de rigueur, my dad would pile us into our waiting chariot. With the windows opened wide and the warm breeze blowing talkative me into silence, he would drive to Canarsie Pier where, for a blissful hour, we could bask in the cool salty air and dream the dreams of the innocent. On the last day of my girlhood, dressed in a filmy white gown and flowing lace veil, my father and mother drove me in that same pale green Chrysler, now his "old" car, to the first chapter in my new life

MMM

The Unforgettable Jonathan Logan

By Rhoda Rubenstein

`Whenever the seasons changed, instead of looking forward to pale, tender buds, or brilliantly colored leaves I watched, unhappily, for the hand-me downs that inevitably came my way.

The daughters of my mother's friends went through their closets in spring and fall and I received their 'discards' If they didn't fit, but were still in good shape my grandmother would 'fix' them for me.

I hated those hand-me-downs. I wanted to be the one giving away last year's clothes to make room for a new wardrobe, not getting someone else's old things, but that's the way things were.

After my father lost his business, I guess we were poor. I just didn't know it then. We always had enough food to eat, fifty cents for the movies on Saturday afternoons, but not a lot of stylish clothes.

When it was absolutely necessary to buy something new, my mother didn't shop in the better department stores in Brooklyn, like A&S or Martin's. It was always Mays, where you could get a bargain. If we went to Manhattan, it was Kleins on the Square. I couldn't afford the baby blue cashmere cardigans or the pink angora sweater sets Carole Leonard wore, which I envied so much. I usually got something sturdy and practical that was a little too big so that I could 'grow into it'. I was out of my house and married before I realized that I could buy clothes that fit. I wasn't going to grow any taller.

But one dress that I owned during my childhood, was different. It was pale green taffeta, as soft and as smooth as a baby's dimpled hand.

"Try it on, sweetheart," my mother said as she handed it to me reverently. The watered silk of the dress fell softly over my shoulders and the fitted bodice clung snuggly to my budding breasts and tiny waist

. "Look," my mother said. "It's a Jonathan Logan." I went to the mirror to see myself. It was as if the dress had been made to order for me. The misty, sea green color matched the green of my eyes and the cap sleeves showed my slender, young arms off to perfection. The rounded neckline curved innocently around to tiny mother of pearl buttons in the back and the flared skirt drifted like gossamer, falling just below my knees. I was transformed in my new dress.

I wanted to wear it forever. "Rhoda darling, you look wonderful. This will be perfect for Sarah's wedding. Come, take it off so I can hang it up. You don't want to soil it, do you?"

Reluctantly, I slipped the shimmering vision over my head. "And see, it's a Jonathan Logan," my mother repeated as she pointed to the label.."You have a Jonathan Logan."

The night of my cousin's wedding I walked into the reception like Cinderella at the ball. Jonathan Logan and I were a perfect couple. My aunts and uncles looked with raised eyebrows and surprised smiles. When had I become so grown-up? My boy cousins couldn't wait to ask me to dance and as I fox-trotted off in my first pair of black suede high heels, my green silk taffeta dress flowing smoothly around my nylon clad legs, I forgot about hand-me-downs. I felt beautiful and I knew I was.

Alan J. Shalleck

Alan J. Shalleck is a pioneer in translating children's stories into audio and video format. He has produced, written, and directed 104 Curious George video episodes which were seen on the Disney channel. Twenty eight of those episodes have been published by Houghton Mifflin directly from the film. He has produced and directed other video titles for Troll Associates and child play books which include fairy tales, read-along and classic stories. Alan lives in Boynton Beach Florida

Mom

By Alan J. Shalleck

Mom lived many different lives. I know her as a most unhappy lady. The youngest of three boys, I can still remember the moment when I was ten and about to leave for school. Mom was still in bed, and I went to say goodbye to her. Her eyes were open seemingly staring at nothing. Her eyebrows were down and her mouth was drawn. I went over to the bed and whispered "good bye" and placed my two index fingers at each end of her mouth, and gently lifted her lips..

"Smile," I said, "You look prettier that way." It was the best thing I could do for a lady whose dreams were wearing out.

My middle brother was six years older. As he was growing up, his mother was a busy housewife, who socialized with friends, kept her household together and lived what seemed like a nice middle-class lifestyle.

My oldest brother by thirteen years, knew a young, vivacious woman, dressed in the stylish fashions of the late twenties. I have a picture of that woman wearing a long skirted suit, topped off with a narrow b rimmed hat and an egret feather. Her white gloved hands were delicately poised and her face was filled with assurance.

After Mom and Dad died, I invited my brothers to a very special meeting. I wanted to find out what Mom was like when they were young. It was then that I knew we each had a different Mom.

I came late in her life, and unexpected at that. If she had to have another child, she desperately wanted a girl, which is how I became an over-protected, fussed-over boy. I was a mystery to my Mom, not like either of her other kids. She had expanded dreams for me. I would be a lawyer, or a doctor, or a successful business man, and I was forever trying to please her, to get her approval, to assure her that I would have a good life. And I always tried to make her smile.

During the last days of her lingering illness, I wanted to give her a final gift, something to comfort her. I bought a ribbon for her hair. She had always loved to try new hairstyles. The morphine was doing its job and through the slur and mindlessness of the drug, she suddenly seemed years younger, joking and laughing in her delirium. She was that other Mom. The pieces of her life were coming together.

She was smiling again.

MMM

My Heart Talks

By Alan J. Shalleck

Men don't get hot flashes, or so I thought til I started to wake up dizzy in sweat-soaked pajamas. My body was out of kilter, and I resented it.

A stress test cut short by the anxious doctor proved my heart was indeed a-flutter, a warning signal that I could not ignore. Pills will work their medical wonder of dilating my old arteries that have probably pumped enough blood around to fill a small lake, but I had to confront myself.

Who am I? What do I want out of life? I'm finally free of career pressure when idiot bosses made my blood boil. And now my grown kids battle their own demons. I hope they survive.

To want little, is to be rich, so I am the richest man alive. Sure, I want socks without hole and a few pair of underwear. My closet is packed with slacks and shirts and shoes to outlast my tired heart if it were to beat for three lifetimes. I even feel guilty at this closet wealth when so many are less fortunate.

I will, however, keep the Fiesta Ware that I just bought, since it is lovely, and a metaphor for more spiritual values. My heart tells me not to cancel my planned trip to Santa Fe where I shall revel in the beauty of the mountain colors and their serenity.

My heart tells me I am not immortal, and it's time to think deeply of those I love, and set out a will leaving them my sparse but hard earned holdings. Lingering, festering family misunderstandings must be wiped clean with a hug and a kiss and apologies given or accepted.

My heart also tells me to do what I still must do in my work with children. I must teach parents and clinicians and teachers to see the uniqueness in each child, and to see the world with the wondrous eye of the young. My heart knows that while each child must be seen holistically, the one constant in this fast changing world, is the need for love, hugs and words of encouragement.

My heart tells me this, and since I have been listening to it these so many years, I know it has spoken the truth.

MMM

A Spiritual Spa and Me

By Alan J. Shalleck

Once you arrive at *Ten Thousand Waves,* a Spiritual Spa set on a knoll in the desert, just twenty minutes from the heart of Santa Fe, you know you're in Shangri-La, an eternity away from ---everything.

This Japanese Spa combines grandeur and simplicity in its raw wood structure which melts into the landscape. New age music creates a sense of calm that stays with you during any of the chosen treatments - a hot stone massage, an East Indian cleansing treatment, and aromatherapy massage, an herbal wrap, salt glow or complete massage.

I chose the latter, and Brooke, my massage therapist ushered me into a private redwood room on a private lower level flanked by pines and juniper.

In his mid thirties, Brooke is a Buddhist. He's never been married, and has two children from two different women. One son had just entered college. The other is three years old.

Buddhists are not concerned with Christian morality, according to Brooke's interpretation of the teachings. And sensuality has a distinct place in the living process. A sense of inner calm and peace is the pre-requisite for a happy, productive and successful life.

As I listened to him I was experiencing his acupressure, and I began to melt away. His trained hands continued to pressure my body, and he seemed to be molding the stress outwards. The pleasure pain absolved me of any convoluted thought processes, as the real world slipped ever farther away from my consciousness. I was becoming immersed in Brooke's inner calm.

"If you love yourself first, you will love others more completely," he said.

I thought about that.

Was I living a moral lie? Does Brooke have all the answers within his Buddhist instincts? I had never taken the time to meditate on a daily basis. His touch had me wondering.

No, I am not rushing off to Nepal, to its highest mountain. I am not going to meditate in any prescribed fashion. And yet, I just might create my own version of Brooke's beliefs, because right now, I don't know what I believe in. I do know that I am numbed by this experience, these sounds, these feelings.

I do know that I never was able to blindly accept a tangible Deity. I cannot accept, just for the sake of accepting. My personal God is more like a cloud, a symbol of all that is good. I have adopted my own Heaven and Hell with no plates to pass around, no tickets to purchase for the holidays, no obligatory stipend. Unlike Brooke, who follows a prescribed path, mine is a home study faith.

But if my faith is focused within, who can I share it with? Is this my new direction? Wasn't I supposed to have a sense of responsibility to my parents, and then my wife, children, work, friends, neighbors? Did I lose myself in the process?

The hour is up. I go into the hot tub. I towel off. I pay the bill. I'm like jelly. Pretty heavy stuff.

Will I think about all this tomorrow?

Elaine Sharfe

Elaine Sharfe is a free lance writer and the author of a children's book, *There's A Dinosaur In My Room*. She and her husband live in Saskatoon Saskatchewan, Canada in the summer, and Boca Raton Florida, in the winter. They have four children and eleven grandchildren

My Brother's Suitcase

By Elaine Sharfe

My brother was the only person in our family of four to own his own suitcase. It was reddish-brown with a black handle and opened and closed with two silver clips that snapped with a zing. Garry liked to travel with that suitcase and he moved often, from his bedroom to my parents' room, then to the living room and sometimes to the rumpus room in the basement. Most of the time he traveled light, with only his favorite blue "blankey" tucked inside.

Every summer our family would motor ten hours to the southern part of our province to see my mothers' parents. Garry would be the first one packed. Of course he didn't have to go into the storage room to find his suitcase, as it was always tucked under his bed, sticking out ever so slightly so that he could touch the handle in the middle of the night if he needed to.

Garry would begin to pack about a week before our trip. His thin blue flannel "blankey" with chewed satin edges went into the suitcase first. Then he'd add whatever pieces of left over sweets he had hidden under the bed or in the corners of his drawers--a square of chocolate from Halloween, a half eaten yellow Easter egg, a green lollipop with its crumpled cellophane wrapper still intact.

After that it didn't matter what else went in, pajamas or a sweater, a bathing suit (even though there was no place to swim at my grandparents' home), or the cream pants with last night's supper splattered over the front pockets.

Sometimes our mother would get involved with the packing. Then she'd order Garry to throw out the dirty pants or the sweater that was missing a top button. One time she opened the suitcase after it had been sitting closed for several days. It was the middle of July and the last few days the temperature had been plus 90. Those were the days before air conditioning, when the inside of the house could be hotter than the outside, and when the night breeze only cooled you off if you slept directly underneath the open window.

Mother was in Garry's room, making his bed. There were chocolate stains on the pillow case and the bottom sheet. Garry's suitcase was resting suspiciously beside the pillow. One of the metal slats was open. Mother lifted the other. Inside she found three empty crumpled chocolate bar wrappers and the melted remains of a fourth bar oozing onto a pair of striped pajamas. The chocolate had also leaked onto the lining of the suitcase, and was still sticky.

When Garry came home from school, mother presented him with the suitcase. Opening it, she showed him where she had washed the lining with Downy and lots of water. The inside was still very wet. According to mother, the suitcase was now in quarantine and would not be traveling with us to Grandma and Grandpa's house.

One afternoon I came home from school to find Mother helping Garry pack his bag. They weren't putting chocolates into it. Mother was sitting on the floor of Garry's bedroom underneath his dresser drawer folding real clothes into the suitcase. Garry was sitting across from her, leaning on the wall with his arms hugging his legs, looking down at his feet.

When the bag was full, mother stood up and held out the bag. Without looking up, Garry stood up, reached for the bag then stalked out of the room. I heard him walk down the hallway and then I heard the front door open and close with a bang.

A few minutes later the phone rang. The call was from my aunt who lived across the street from us. She wanted to tell us that Garry had just appeared on her doorstep with his suitcase. He was running away from home.

"Yes, I know," mother replied. "I helped him pack."

Garry's suitcase lived with him until he went off to university. Over the years it moved out from under the bed, into his closet, and then down into the basement where it slept with all the other traveling bags. When my parents sold their house and moved to a condominium, I was given the suitcase for safe keeping. Garry had outgrown it and I was married with children who were its right size. My daughter stored her Barbies in it and when she was finished with it, my son packed it with his miniature cars and trucks. A few years ago I found the suitcase sitting under another bag in our luggage compartment. Its spine was bent, the reddish brown color was more brown than reddish. One of the metal clasps didn't close. I phoned my brother and asked him if he wanted it.

'So you've got my suitcase," he said. "I've always wondered where it went."

I found a box that could hold the suitcase. I found a small piece of blue flannel and stuffed it into the back pocket. I threw in a small chocolate bar. Then I mailed it to my brother. He told me that he keeps it under his bed.

MMM

A Jerusalem Diary

By Elaine Sharfe

Here we are again, waiting on Air Canada, Flight 086 to depart for Israel. I can't count the number of times my husband and I have done this. So many that I almost forget I don't like to fly.

We're off to see our children and grandchildren, and to do some site seeing. I haven't wandered through the city since the beginning of the second Intifada.

Surprise! I didn't know there was a new airport at Ben Gurion. One thing hasn't changed--we wait almost forty-five minutes for our luggage, and when it floats down the carousel, our Priority tagged bags come last.

We rent a car and drive up to Jerusalem. It's almost Shabbat and parts of the city are already at rest. We always stay at the same hotel. I recognize the guards at the door and they smile as though we're old friends. As soon as we get into our room I change into my religious gear-- long skirt, long sleeve- high collared blouse and a hat that covers most of my hair. Now I am comfortable in this religious neighborhood and ready for my children.

After Shabbat we drive to the Jerusalem Mall. There's a long, slow line to get into the parking lot. Two young soldiers, who don't look old enough to be carrying guns, check the trunks of every car. We park and walk to the Mall entrance. Another soldier stands at the door and looks into my purse. I'm cleared. When the Mall was built several years ago, a cousin said to me:

"Israelis don't do Malls."

Was she wrong! The place is teaming with families, carriages and strollers. I see lovers holding hands, body-pierced teen agers, modestly dressed Haradim (religious people), Arab women shopping in groups of two, some seniors and lots of soldiers.

I head for the jewelry store called Michel Negrin to look at the multicolored beaded earrings, flowered bracelets and lacy necklaces that are so popular in North America. My husband leans against a rail outside the store while I struggle through the room full of people. I wait in line to pay, because one women from Boca Raton, Florida is buying a sample of everything- rings, necklaces, bracelets, earrings, four pins, and a dozen packets of gift cards.

I begin each morning in the hotel gym. Today I'm stretching on a mat when a strange man walks over to me, leans down into my face, and puts out his hand to touch the silver necklace I'm wearing.

"Yaffe" (beautiful) he says, then retreats. I smile to myself: "Only in Israel."

I want to go to the Shia Agnon House, home to the 1966 Nobel Prize Winner in Literature. I carry the *Jerusalem City Guide,* into the taxi. After determining that the driver can read and speak English, I point to the name of the house and its address. I tell him that it's in Talpiot. He argues with me.

I open the car door and ask for directions from my buddy the security guard. He looks at the *Guide* I've handed him, then rattles off something in Hebrew. More confusion. Another taxi driver comes by and offers his opinion. Soon a fifth voice joins in. Suddenly my driver throws up his hands and smiles:

"Beseder." (Okay)

We're off. The driver is making up for lost time, whipping over the Begin Express Way at high speed and winding around the Talpiot neighborhood a little faster than I like. The roads are busy and I wonder if I'm going to live to see my destination.

Today I'm walking to the ultra religious neighborhood of Mea Sharim with my husband and our son. I've avoided this place since I was accosted ten years ago while shopping with my daughter-in-law.

We were sauntering slowly down the street when someone bumped into me. I felt a hand groping for my bum cheek, then a pinch. I turned and a man slithered past with a disapproving shake of his head Later my daughter-in-law told me that he might have been making a statement about the long gauze skirt I was wearing. Unknown to me, it was see-through in the bright sunlight. Even so!

Today no one looks at me. It's winter, and I blend in with my covered hair, long skirt and tightly buttoned jacket. We go into a restaurant for lunch. It has six tables in a room that should only hold four. We all order chicken, rice, soup, salad and soda. The bill is $10.00 US. My husband protests.

"That can't be the right"

"Too much?" the man asks?"

"No. Too little."

"Ah," he says. "You're American. Most of my clients are poor."

We leave a big tip.

It's Thursday. One more shopping day till Shabbat. I'm looking for kippot (skull caps) The Kippa Man is on Jaffa Road in a tiny shop that can only accommodate two customers at a time. He has hats for babies, children and adults, big heads and bald ones. They come in solid colors: red, white, purple, brown, gray, green, black, or combinations of those colors with swirls, squares or lines. They also come with the Kippa Man's blessing: "Mazel and good health." With his help, I can now live to one hundred.

We have one more Shabbat in the Renaissance Hotel and invite our children to move in. Breakfast is included with the room, but Friday night's dinner and Sunday Lunch are extra--$39.00 for adults, and $29.00 per child. It seems expensive.

The hotel is teaming with other three generational families and there's also a group doing a Sheva Bracha (the compulsory after wedding party in honor of a bride and groom). They have a special room for tonight's dinner and another one that has been set aside for them as a synagogue. The women are fashionably dressed in textured pastel suits with skirts that fall just below their knees, wide brimmed feather hats to match, and three inch stilettos---in sharp contrast to the local women who choose long dark skirts, loose fitting tops and head-hugging hats or sheitles. (wigs)

"They're from France," my ten year old granddaughter tells me, in a whisper that is either derisive or hushed in awe.

"How do you know?"

"I just do."

She's right/ They're speaking French.

It's 5:30 and the hotel is quiet. The shops are closed, and there's a screen in front of the reception counter that conceals the possibility of any money transaction.

The men rush off to the synagogue in the hotel or one in the neighborhood. The women stay behind. If they're not grandparents, they are either pregnant, pushing a stroller or walking with several children. Some are doing all three.

I follow them down to the lower lobby. A large round table is glowing with over one hundred candles. A steady parade of women move reverently to the table. Each one lights at least two candles, closes her eye, covers her face with her hands, and slowly sways her body while silently moving her lips in prayer. I'm moved to do the same.

The men return and we go into the large dining room.We are assigned a family table, and make our own kiddush. (sanctification over wine). We walk to the buffet table and with one glance I now understand why the meal is so expensive. We have a choice of duck, chicken, turkey or meatballs, and over thirty different salads. Second helpings are free.

The children try everything and leave almost everything, except for the dessert. They bring us green Jell-O, raspberry and lemon pudding, parve ice cream, honey cake, sponge cake and eight different cookies. Before leaving, I see other families packing up napkins full of food, and we do the same--"just in case".

By 4:30 Saturday afternoon, all the children, including ours, are moving around just a little faster than necessary. My grandson tells me that only old people use the Shabbat elevator that has been programed to stop at every floor, which is why all the kids are running up and down the stairs. (I use the elevator.) Most of the boys look a little bedraggled now, their white shirts stained with wine and orange juice and flapping loosely over and down the sides of their pants. The girls have shed their demure body language and shoes to squat on the lobby chairs. I think the hotel staff should be paid double to clean up the pudgy finger prints on the windows and the cake crumbs on and under the sofa cushions.

Today is my last day in Jerusalem and I need a Kotel (Western Wall) fix. A taxi takes me to the Jewish Quarter and I walk around before going to the Wall. The place is alive with young soldiers. Occasionally a "black hat" floats above or between them. Just before I reach the stairs that will take me to the Kotel, I pass three people who are holding out an offering of red strings, the latest rage in mystical armor. They want money; protection costs!.

I see the Kotel. The stones are dazzling white in the bright sun. A charge of electricity hits me, and I have to still myself on the edge of the railing before I can go any further. I step down and through the security zone then walk to the women's section. I squeeze between two women in order to touch the Wall. Walking backwards, I search for a space to pray. I find an empty chair beside a young woman who's holding a book of psalms in her hands. Silent but steady tears are wetting her cheeks. She doesn't look up to see me and that's good because I need to cry as well. I cry just from the emotion of touching the Wall. I'm overwhelmed by the two thousand years of Jewish history written into these stones. I cry for this country that has seen so much pain, and I cry for my parents who are dead. I cry tears of gratitude and thanksgiving for my husband, our children and grandchildren. I cry because I'm leaving Israel tomorrow.

We go to the airport and walk through seven check points before getting into the secured area. The first thing I do is go to the Money Exchange counter to collect the 17% that's due from the VAT on our purchases. Most of my purchases are with our checked luggage.

"Show me what you bought," the stern young man behind the glass wall asks me. Without making eye contact. I show him three items I have in my carryon, the necklace around my neck and the bracelet on my right arm.

"Your receipts show me that there's more. I need to see everything."

"What is going on here?" I ask, fighting to keep my voice level.

"I've done this for almost thirty years and no one has ever asked to see my purchases."

"That's the rule. We're in a new airport now and we follow the rules."

He hands me a few dollars.

Fortunately I don't have time to be angry because our flight is called and we board quickly. I plug into my seat and we take off. The plane flies over the lights of Tel Aviv, then onto the Mediterranean and into the dark sky. I close my eyes and remember Jerusalem, our children, shopping, Shabbat in the hotel, the Kotel. Suddenly a flight attendant interrupts my reverie.

"Would you like the National Post or the Globe and Mail?"

I pull back with one last thought: "I'll be here again in July."

Margaret A. Sorensen

My parents met and married in their senior year of high school and divorced after 6 years of marriage. My father remained in the family home in Platteville, Wisconsin. My mother went to Chicago to attend business college, and my sister and I went to live with our maternal grandmother in a tiny Iowa town, called Delaware. Five years later, we joined our mother in Chicago.

I met my husband Bill when I was 17, and we were married eight months later. In the next eleven years we welcomed our five children; son Jeffrey, and daughters, Dawn, Margaret, Joy and Diana.

I was a home-maker for 20 years and at age 38 I attended college, where I realized that I really enjoyed writing. Years later, I made each of my children a scrapbook and wrote stories telling about their childhood experiences.

I had three careers in my adult life: Motherhood, as a Fitness specialist for the YMCA and as a retail manager of two thrift shops in Florida.

Along the way we had weddings and ten grandchildren. My husband worked for IBM for 33 years before retiring.

We enjoy traveling, reading, friends and family, and I like Emily's classes because she gives constructive comments and suggestions.

I look forward to writing more stories. I have many memories and a long life to draw upon.

Dead Man's Suit

By Margaret Sorensen

"I've got the job" had sounded so good when Bill came home from his final interview with *IBM*. "I start working in three weeks," he said.

There was only one problem. At the interview he had been told that IBM required their employees to wear a suit, white shirt and conservative tie. Also, black shoes and socks.

Bill had one suit, and he didn't like it and never wore it. He said he was saving it for his funeral. He liked casual clothes like jeans and flannel shirts. Nothing dressy.

The next day we went shopping for some suits. We only had about $100 and even the cheap suits cost more than that, and they were ugly.

My mother came up with a possible solution. Her friend's husband, a man about 50 years old, had recently died of a heart attack and her friend was trying to sell the man's suits to help pay for the funeral. The dead man had been about the same size as Bill except he had a pot belly and longer legs.

We went to try on the suits and we noticed that the quality of material was much nicer than anything we had seen in the store. The suits were beautifully tailored and they fit Bill. The sleeves were good and the jackets needed only minor adjustments. We would need a good tailor to take in the waistband and shorten the legs. The colors were perfect, dark blue, dark gray, dark brown and black.

The widow brought out a pair of black shoes and when Bill tried them on, they fit. She gave us a basket of socks and about 10 neck ties to go with the suits. We gave her $100 and she was happy. Bill and I were delighted.

The big day finally arrived. Bill was up at 5:00 am to get ready for his first day at work. He put on his favorite newly tailored dead man's suit and calmly said, "I look just like an undertaker," and away he went.

Working for IBM required a few adjustments to our existing lifestyle. Every day I would iron a long-sleeved white shirt, and every day Bill would cuss a little while putting on a tie.

Three months later, Bill had his first job evaluation. His boss told him he had done well on his job assignments and he praised him for having a good appearance.

Bill never told anyone where his new wardrobe had come from, but he and I knew we had made a very good investment when we purchased the dead man's suits.

Summertime

By Margaret Sorensen

Hot summer days remind me of Chicago, Lake Michigan, sandy beaches, icy water, sunburns and mosquito's. When I was in high school my social life revolved around going to the beach. That was where we met our friends. We spent the day sun-bathing, telling stories about anyone and everyone, swimming and eating. Occasionally, the boys in the group would grab one of the girls and swing her back and forth between them and then release her so she would fly into the cold water. Other days the girls would double up and push one of the guys off the edge of the rocks.

We weren't sissies and for sure we didn't need life guards. We ignored the 'No Swimming' signs posted along the shore of the lake. We knew how to swim and we wanted to be in deep water instead of on the beach where the guards whistled you in if you went past your knees into the water.

My group of friends settled on an area called "The Rocks." It was about a block and a half north of the public beach. The rocks were part of a conservation plan to hold the water at bay. Large flat boulders had been installed and then leveled out to a flat surface. The rocks covered an area about a mile long and about 40 feet across. The water here was very deep with occasional pilings topping out above the water. We were able to swim far out into the lake and then rest on top of one of the pilings.

One day, my friend Marian and I had been out swimming for a long time. We climbed onto a piling and stretched out on our stomachs for a much needed rest. The hot sun on our bodies felt good. It was a beautiful day to be at the beach.

Marian and I had been friends for a long time. We shared many interests. One of them was our love of swimming. Another thing we had in common was our eyes.

We were both extremely near-sighted. Without our glasses, we couldn't see the big E on the eye chart. .

Marian saw something bobbing out in the water. She pointed it out to me but it was far away and I thought it was probably a paper plate or piece of paper floating on the surface of the water. We continued our conversation which was more than likely about boys, another interest we shared.

I fell asleep and I think Marian did also. When we woke up we noticed quite unexpectedly that the bobbing object we had seen in the water was now right in front of us, no more than two feet away, and it was the top of a man's bald head.

"Oh, my god," I shouted. "That's a man out there. Let's get out of here." We jumped into the water and swam as fast as we could to shore. We knew we had to get help, or do something. We didn't know what.

When we reached shore we got out of the water and told our friends what had happened. The boys quickly jumped into the water to swim out to see the man. The girls watched. Marian and I ran the distance to the public beach and found a phone.

Neither of us had remembered to bring money. I picked up the phone and dialed the operator. Thank God a real body was on the other end instead of an irritating recording telling us what to do. I told the operator where we were and all about the bobbing man in the lake. She connected me to the police and I repeated the story. The officer said they would arrive shortly.

Marian and I returned to the rocks to wait for the police. When we saw their car approaching, we waved to them.

The beach patrols had arrived before us, and were trying to retrieve the man from the lake. The police arrived and told everyone to get out of the water. An ambulance arrived. Also a reporter from the Sun-Times newspaper.

A crowd had gathered to see what was going on. I won't say the Beach Patrol pulled the guy in like a fish on the end of a pole, but it was similar. They dragged the body in close to the shore and covered him with a plastic sheet and lifted him out of the water onto a stretcher.

The body was completely dressed. Brown shoes were on both feet, and he wore a plaid necktie. In his suit coat pocket was a wallet with his identification and money. One of the officers surmised that the body had been in the water for about three days. He thought that possibly the man had fallen off of a cruise ship and had not been rescued. The dead man was placed in an ambulance and was quickly driven away.

Within minutes the swimmers jumped back into the water, the card games picked up again, and the boys flipped another girl into the lake. The police left, the photographer snapped a few more pictures and tried to get more information. The crowd that had gathered went back to sun-bathing and listening to their portable radios.

Marian and I were still upset. We were hungry and tired and we wanted to go home. We folded up our blanket and grabbed our towels and started to leave. We had a long bike ride ahead of us.

"Let's hurry," said Marian. "I can't wait to tell Mom about this day."

"I wouldn't do that if I were you. She'll never let you out again." I said.

"Oh yes she will. But she will kill me if my picture is in the paper tomorrow."

"We probably won't see this place for a long time." I said. "I will be grounded for not staying on the public beach."

"We might be in a bit of trouble," said Marian, "but we sure have a lot to remember."

"Let's peddle fast," I called out. "Maybe we can see ourselves on the evening news."

MMM

The Football Game

By Margaret Sorensen

Autumn reminds me of football, and football reminds me of one deadly game. Our high school was the only one in Chicago where Greek was taught, and any student of Greek origin was permitted to attend regardless of where he or she lived in the city. It was located in a community of Swedish immigrants, sprinkled with other nationalities.

It was common at our school to witness many ethnic-based fights between the Swedish and Greek kids. For no apparent reason – was it merely being different? they seemed to hate each other.

One fall Saturday afternoon, our school team played against another Chicago high school on our turf. Many other high schools in the area had only benches and a field for their games, but our school had a stadium large enough to seat 5,000 people.

With my little clique of girlfriends, we would choose seats as high up in the stadium as possible so that we could see a large panorama of people assembling long before the game began. This was a major social event and we never missed a game or the post-game dance that was the highlight of the day.

During the third quarter we noticed a few disturbances in the stands. Kids were throwing hats up into the high seats and drink cartons were being tossed about, activities that were not uncommon on such occasions. This time, however, two boys were deep into argument, with high pitched shouts, swearing language and ugly hand gestures. Although my friends and I were seriously into the game on the field, we were distracted by the activity in the stands.

Suddenly we forgot about the football field as we watched one of the boys pick up an empty coke bottle and hit another boy in the face with it. And then everything happened very quickly. The boy who had been hit, lifted the other boy off the ground, seething in vengeful anger, and thrust him over his head as if he were made of straw. He moved with his captive the few steps to the three-storied wall surrounding the stadium and with one bold movement, he threw the boy over the wall!

Astonished, we rushed to the wall, and looking over it, we saw the victim lying on the ground far below. We started for the stairs, and pushed and shoved with hundreds of others all the way down the stairwell to the outside of the stadium.

The game, of course, had been stopped, and adults in the crowd were trying to keep 4500 young people under control. But it was not possible.

When the ambulance arrived, the paramedics began their examination, and within moments, pronounced the boy dead. His head had hit the concrete.

The crowd was stunned, confused, sad and angry, a profusion of emotions. The loud speaker announcement asked that everyone go home immediately, and that the remainder of the game had been called off. The paramedics placed the dead boy on a stretcher, put him in the ambulance and left.

On Monday morning, our home room teacher reported that the dead boy was Charley Olson, and that Christopher Pappos had thrown him over the wall, and that Christopher was facing criminal charges.

For me and my friends, it was a blown-up version of the old story: hatred between the Greeks and the Swedes.

Our school was in mourning, but beneath those feelings of sadness there festered intense anger. The Swedish kids were bent on revenge and the Greeks growled back at them in defiance. And none of us felt safe in that environment.

Soon the principal summoned an assembly in our large auditorium where we all stood for the Pledge of Allegiance and the singing of the Star Spangled Banner.

The student president announced that the Board of Education had mandated that all remaining football games of that season would be played without spectators, and the stadium would be locked for the remainder of the season. Any further disturbances, we were warned, would result in expulsion.

What I learned from this senseless tragedy has remained with me throughout my life. Human beings come in many packages. It is important to open the package and see what's inside before you judge its contents. Character is what is important, and not ethnic background..

Prejudice and ignorance killed a 16 year old boy just as surely as a gun would have done..

MMM

The Wedding Gift

By Margaret Sorensen

Grandmother had been a young girl when she started to sew clothes for herself and her siblings. Her family encouraged her, and she became a very good seamstress.

Years later, she would sew for her two daughters and then her two granddaughters. Our clothes were often admired by friends and family.

I was ten years old before I realized that you could buy clothes in a store. The two stores in Delaware, Iowa sold no clothes and I always assumed that you made your clothes at home, and often from hand-me-downs from someone else.

Grandmother made all her own patterns from old newspaper. She sewed on an ancient contraption that required you to watch closely or the needle would go through your finger. This only happened once to me, but it left a lasting impression. In addition to watching your fingers, you also had a pedal which required both feet to move up and down. This propelled the machine to go forward or backwards. Throughout my childhood and even into young adulthood, my grandmother made my coats and hats, dresses and petticoats and also my pajamas and robes.

About a week before my wedding to Bill, my grandmother told us that our wedding gift was ready. She went to her closet and pulled out a large box, all wrapped and tied with wedding paper and large white bows. She gave us the box and we quickly opened it. Inside was a beautiful home-made quilt.

It was the prettiest quilt that I had ever seen. Grandmother had taken small pieces of cloth and sewed them into a pattern resembling a daisy. Each petal was made of a different piece of material. The center of the daisy was a solid piece of blue fabric.

I looked at the quilt for a long time, and then realized that each little piece of fabric that my grandmother had used for the quilt had been something I had seen before. She had saved a small piece of fabric from each of the many things she had made for me throughout my childhood, and had cut and sewed the pieces, and made them into a quilt.

`The quilt told the story of our life together and of all the important moments that we had shared. I recognized the fabric that grandmother had used to sew the dress I wore to my first day of school. Also, the ones from my confirmation and graduation, and everything in between.

My husband and I slept under the quilt for many years and it always reminded me of my grandmother, and the love we shared for each other.

Today, when I look at this quilt, I see a rare and wonderful piece of art, a one-of -a-kind treasure. Someday I may hang it on a wall in our home. In my eyes, it is more magnificent than a painting by Renoir.

Shirley Ullman

Shirley Ullman grew up in the Bronx, New York and after her disastrous employment as a bookkeeper found more suitable work with B'nai Brith as a secretary and receptionist, until she married. She and her husband went into the grocery store business. (before there were supermarkets) When her husband became a builder, the two worked together in that business for many years. After his death, she remarried and was again widowed.

Shirley has two children, two grandchildren and two great-grandchildren. Retired now, she enjoys every day of her life, which she says, is a "work in progress."

MMM

A Week in the Life of a Bookkeeper

By Shirley Ullman

There are times when looking back at my youth, I think that I'm looking through a kaleidoscope and so many different images of experiences come leaping out at me. One of them stands out like a beacon. I was sixteen, fresh out of high school in June 1935. Jobs were very scarce, lawyers, if they were lucky enough to have a job, were working for $5.00 a week. Macy's hired only college graduates or young women from England as salespersons and then there was me!

My parents were paying $25.00 a month for the apartment that we had moved into when I was a year old and the rent was long overdue. My father had no work, having lost what little he had in a grocery store and my mother worked as a baby nurse. She stayed away from home two to three weeks at a time earning $15.00 a week and this is what we lived on. During that time since I was an only child, it fell on me to clean the house, wash the windows, do all the laundry and cook for my Dad and myself. I became expert at it.

I was registered at every employment agency in the city. I worked as a shampoo girl in a beauty shop for $8.00 a week and on an assembly line packaging Christmas tinsel. In short, I tried my hand at whatever I could get. One day a cousin visited and said, "My friend Celia worked for such a wonderful man for 20 years and she just retired. He has a business making lace. I told her how badly you need a job so she told him all about you and *Voila* You have it! All you have to do is go to work at 9 a.m. on Monday. Here is the name and address."

I was dumbfounded! "What work would I have to do?" I asked. "Oh, you'll run the office, type, take some shorthand, answer the phone and do some bookkeeping." was her answer.

When I realized that I would not be going to college from high school, I knew that I would need some business acumen. I had switched from my academic course to a business course in my senior year. I became a whiz at steno and typing, but I knew nothing about bookkeeping. I really didn't know the difference between a credit and a debit.

When I said, "But Belle, I don't know a thing about bookkeeping, I have no idea at all," she said "Not to worry. Just call me as you go along and I will tell you everything you have to do."

The prospect of a salary of $22.00 a week was so overwhelming that I felt that I would walk on hot coals to do the job well. Monday morning I went to work scared to death and ready to face a tiger. I walked into a very large room with windows facing Broadway, in the middle of which was a space about 20' x 20' with a wooden railing 4' around it. In it there was a desk, a chair, a telephone, a typewriter and a filing cabinet. I was a fish in a fishbowl.

There was no way that I could make a call or hide a thing. There was a woman in the back who ironed lace all day long, a young boy who did errands and took packages to the post office and me.

My boss welcomed me and said that Celia had told him that he would love me, that I was accomplished and that he never had a girl like me. She was so right! The first thing he said to me was "Take down the journal and the ledger." I looked on top of the cabinet and there were four hard covered books there. I was nonplused and just stood looking.

He didn't say anything and put two books on the desk, opened them and said, "Post." There was no way in the world to call Belle so I said "Oh, I don't know if you post the way they did at my job for Clairol."

Well, that was the clincher. My ignorance was out, there was no way I could fool him after that.

My boss showed me how to post. Taking the figures from one book and transferring them to the other and putting a little check mark against every number. I was ready to choke when I realized that there couldn't possibly be more than one way to do that.

That poor man was a gem. When he was on the phone, he would call out to me. "Please give me Mr. Hakkis' folder." Now, how was I supposed to know that Hakkis began with a C? My boss and all his customers were Syrian and not one name was spelled the way it sounded. He might just as well have asked for Mr. Pneumonia and I would have looked under N!

Every day I came to work and prayed that the floor would open and swallow me. I could *never* quit, no matter what.

I had no problem with the steno and typing and as a matter of fact, my letters could have been framed

The worst part of this whole thing was the fact that I simply could not add. There was no adding machine and if there had been one, what would I have done with it?

It was the end of the month, and I was told to add all the columns on one side of the page and all the columns on the opposite side and that the answers should be the same.

There were about twenty lines of figures down the page in three columns on each side and every time I added a column I came up with a different sum. In self-defense I would add six numbers, put the figure down, add another six numbers and so on and then added all those sums together.

My boss came over to watch periodically and God only knows what he thought. My eraser received a great workout and I hate to tell you what the pages looked like. I would sit there with those numbers, look in the back room and think, now if I only had the job ironing lace, I would have no problem with that at all!

My mother asked me how I liked my job and I said, "To tell you the truth Mom, I don't think it will last;" never telling her anything about the difficulties I had there all that week.

The next day, praying for deliverance I went to work and was greeted by a slip of paper. On it there were numbers from 1 to 10. My boss said, "Please go home and practice how to write numbers."

Friday came and oh, blessed relief! My boss, very embarrassed and discomfited said, "Miss Fess, you are such a sweet young girl, your letters are beautiful. But you know that we don't do many of them and I really do need a bookkeeper. Please forgive me, but I won't need you any more."

I felt like throwing my arms around him and hugging him. He handed me my pay in cash. One week's salary and two weeks notice $66.00. WOW!

When I arrived home, I flew up the four flights of stairs, burst into the apartment and yelled "Mom, Mom, I was fired and we're rich!"

Susan Violante

I was born in 1963 in Maracaibo, Venezuela to Italian immigrants parents, where I did all my schooling, receiving a Bachelors Degree in Political Sciences and Business Administration. I moved to Caracas, where I got my first job as General Director of an Environmental Foundation.

After a year, I decided to open a Potter's studio in a little tourist town up in the Hills. It was there that I purchased an antique 1930s type writer and started writing outside of the notebook.

In 1989 my parents retired to Florida so I sold my studio and moved to Florida with them. Since I am a 100% fluent tri-lingual, (English-Spanish-Italian) an International Company sponsored my visa to work in the US as a Job Costing Accountant. A month later, I met my husband... and here I am, married with two girls.

My hobbies are painting, working clay, and restoring old furniture. I do not consider writing a hobby. Writing is a need I have to whisper to myself, to play with my dreams...to make them real on paper and to share them in publication.

MMM

I Remember...

By Susan Violante

I remember knowing it all, being tough, the leader of the gang. I was only twelve. I was in trouble in all my classes by the first quarter of 6th grade. I would cut classes and smoke cigarettes because I was cool.

Then one day I got caught, and sent to Detention, but I had done nothing wrong that day, according to me, so I detained myself at a friend's house, instead.

At about 5:00 pm I began to walk back to school, hoping my mother didn't go to pick me up early. I went through the back alley, so no one I knew would see me as I passed my grandmother's café, which was across the street from my school.

313

"Psst." I turned around. He must have been in his late twenties, with black curly hair, gray pants, and a white shirt.

"Where are you going beautiful?" I ignored him and started to walk a little faster.

Tum, tum, tum...I could hear his foot steps, or was it my heart beat. One more block, I thought...tum, tum, tum...He grabbed my arm from behind. I don't remember exactly what happened next. I can't see his face nor hear his voice anymore in my mind. I was scared.

I kicked him on his crotch. I remember him on the ground and me frozen next to him, laughing. To this day, I don't know why I was laughing. All I can remember is that I ran away as he started to get up.

I ran around the corner and stumbled onto my Grandmother who was coming out of my school looking for me. My mother had asked her to pick me up.

I made it back to school and got spanked for not being there, too. I never told anyone what happened. Why not? I don't know.

I do remember however, what I learned that day. I found out that I did not know everything and I was not the toughest kid after all. I remember learning about fear that day.

〰〰〰

The Hurt That Won't Go Away

By Susan Violante

I saw her rushing to the guest bathroom, and I knew. I interrupted my conversation and ran after her, grabbing the door before it shut and saw her sobbing.

"Why are you crying?" She was inconsolable. "What is it baby? Tell mommy what happened". Her silence began to worry me. I knew she was a sensitive nine-year-old, but this time I could feel the pain growing inside her.

"They all laughed at me mommy. Why are they so mean?"

My world came crushing down. My baby had discovered the hurt that won't go away. "Why can't they accept me?" I froze not knowing what to say. You see "they" are family.

"What happened?" I asked.

"Annie told me she is too cool to hang out with me. Why? mommy?"

"I don't know, honey. But didn't you tell her that because you're gifted you are too smart to try to be cooler than anyone?"

"I tried to tell her, but I couldn't. They were all laughing at me."

"Oh Baby, come here, give me a hug." My voice started to break. I was nine again. "This is part of life. Not everyone will like and accept you."

"Yes mommy, but no one defended me. I want to get back at them!"

"And be like them? Do you think you will enjoy making her cry the same way you are crying now?"

"No. But I want to get even."

"Nickie, remember Annie is family. You will keep seeing her over and over. Are you both going to try to be even each time?" She sighed, her little brain working...

"No" She answered. "I guess I'll have to teach her to be nice."

Again, she became my teacher. All my pain and fear when facing social groups, as I grew up, and as a grown up had a reason to be. I found that the pain that wouldn't go away had just left.

JoAnne von Born

Jo-Aynne von Born has written two feature length screenplays as well as two short plays which received stage productions in New York and in Los Angeles. Three of her poems are under contract with Blue Mountain Arts and she is currently working on a inspirational non-fiction book. She resides in South Florida and is the lucky mother of two teenagers who have taught her the value of patience and laughter.

MMM

Sal's Daughter

By JoAynne von Born

The withdrawn old woman in the rocking chair suddenly came alive at the sound of my introduction. She shot straight up on the front porch of her modest Long Island home as if she had shed 20 years and her voice screeched, "Oh my God! It's Sal's daughter! Where's my Sal? Where's my little Sal?"

I was fifteen years old and had just met my father's mother, my grandmother, for the first time in my life.

That same night I was whisked off to a christening held in a typical middle class, Italian New Jersey catering hall. When I entered the party room temporarily marked "Corrao" the florescent lights jarred my vision as a sea of thick, dark eyebrows descended upon me.

"Ow my Gawd! It's Sal's dawghter! The one from Flowrida. She looks just like Sal. No she looks like Valerie, Marie's dawghter. Oh my Gawd. Does she know where Sal is?"

I felt exposed and paraded around like a freak in a circus show. I was overwhelmed with these curious spectators called relatives who studied and dissected me and my relationship to a man I did not know.

I could not wait to get on the plane. All I wanted to do was go home to my sunny solitary life in Florida with my mother, and leave this mess behind.

Meeting my father's family for the first time and looking at a whole other half of where I came from, was too much for an insecure teenager already dealing with the pressures of boys and budding female identity.

Who were these people? How could I come from them? They were so different from who I thought I was. It shattered my mind to think I was one person yesterday and to realize that today I am someone else entirely.

I am Sal's daughter.

I do not even remember my father, except for the images burned in my mind from a few pictures of him that I have looked at over the years. It is the only frame of reference I have for the man who helped to conceive me.

For some mysterious reason, my mother awkwardly left New York and my father when I was two years old. Four years later it seemed my father totally vanished from this world. At least that is the last year his social security number had any reported earnings. It was also the last year his driver license was renewed and the year he vacated his last known address, a rented Brooklyn apartment.

"Mrs. Von Born," the kindly woman from the New York Bureau of Vital Statistics at the other end of my cell phone prepared me. "We have your father listed as deceased as of December 1967. However there is no death certificate and no known place or date of death. No one at the Bureau can figure out how or why your father is on the deceased list with no apparent information to back it up."

I cried all over my cell phone as I drove through my fancy Weston neighborhood in south Florida, where I imagined they all knew who their father was and had lots of warm memories of him. Suddenly my kids, strapped into their car seats in the back, started to shout loudly as they played a game and I had to fight to concentrate on my conversation.

"But that doesn't make sense," I garbled through my tears and tight throat. "His sister spoke to him on the phone a week before his January 22 birthday in 1968, a month after that. She invited him for dinner the following Sunday."

"Did he go?"

"He never showed up. He called that morning and said he had to help a friend move. That was the last she or anybody ever saw or heard of him again... hello? Hello?"

I was in a bad cell area and the call had disconnected but I did not care. It was useless. For almost thirty years I had survived without my father. He had nothing to do with my life. Why would I need to know about him now?

Then a memory flashed in my head.

I was in the kitchen and pregnant with my son. My two-year old dimpled daughter Kristina waited eagerly with her father at the kitchen table for the dinner I was preparing.

At that moment my mind was busy with what I was cooking, what I needed to do later that night and the next day to get everything in order for the soon to arrive baby. All the responsible things I needed to do to keep life together, to keep the sky from falling down, to keep myself from falling apart.

Behind me, I heard laughter. Kristina's laughter. I smiled at the sound of her reckless joy and felt happy that I had a home and a husband, a complete family, something much better than what I grew up with. I turned around to appreciate what I had.

What I saw rattled me in ways I could never imagine. My beautiful little girl sat bouncing on her father's knees, her messy blond pigtails dancing all around her head. She was smiling so large I thought her dimples would pop off. They were father and daughter in their own world of validation, love, security and connectedness.

Cruelly, I was slapped in the face with everything I had never had. For the first time it stood harshly before me like blinding spotlight over my childhood.

In the next instant, with no absolutely no control over it, I hated my daughter and I hated my husband. I hated them for what they shared and I hated myself for what I missed.

"Mommy, look at me and Daddy!" Kristina chirped as Steve continued to bounce her up and down.

I wanted to look. I wanted to be part of it but I could not. I could not handle the enormous amount of buried anger bursting through the scars of growing up without a father.

The Ending

By JoAynne von Born

The rain beats down on the pane of my kitchen window like the pounding of wild drums from an unfamiliar continent.

"Patta dum, patta dum, patta dum, dum, dum,"

I sit stiffly at my kitchen table and stare out into the gray, wet afternoon. My neck hurts. My shoulders are tight. I cannot get my short breath all the way down. Regardless, I am determined to focus my attention on the bowl of steaming hot beef stew I am about to eat in the frigid air-conditioned Florida condo I call home. Immediately, my mind wanders. This is the end of my life, as I know it.

Just weeks ago, I walked into my sunny office with a picture window overlooking a cascading fountain in the park. I was shaking on the inside. For three years I had enjoyed a lucrative position in advertising sales for a luxury yachting magazine. Yearly trips to the south of France for the glamorous Monaco Boat Show were a regular part of my job.

My plans this day were to make my usual calls to clients soliciting them for another 'biggest issue of the year,' the standard line, when I could not think of anything spectacular to say. Then five minutes before the day was over, I would drop my bomb, escape out the door and avoid the fallout.

By late morning I could not stand the tension building within me. Thankfully, it was broken when Karlene, the owner of the magazine called in her high pitched voice as she always did from her office next door.

"Jo, what's wrong with you today?"

Damn her! She always could read me like a book. Now, it was time to tell the truth, as ridiculous as she would think it was. Into her office I went, fearful of what I was about to do and what her reaction would be.

"Karlene, you know I love you," The tears came flooding out despite my intention to hold them back. Why am I such a wimp?

"I think the world of you but I'm just not happy. This is a great job that anyone would want but it's just not for me. I don't care about boats or billionaires. I care about people and the human condition. You know me. You've heard me talk. You know this life is not me. I mean I could do it. I can play the part but it's not what's in my heart." Oh God, I really am a wimp!

This beautiful model of a woman who should be on the catwalk instead of running a magazine, tenderly reached for my hand and said, "I knew you weren't happy. For over a year, I've known. Your work has not been so great lately but I didn't want to say anything."

I was squashed! Who the hell was she to say that? I worked my ass off bringing in new clients, more than tripled sales from the day I started while I efficiently covered for all her lies that backfired on clients. How does she have the nerve to say my work has not been so great? To think I was worried I would hurt her feelings by leaving! To think I even care about my performance at a job that was not 'me'!

Then there is Bob. The love of my life or so I thought. When my quest for a deeper spiritual life emerged within me, Bob was my handsome knight in shining armor who arrived on the scene complete with an intoxicating mix of intense sexuality and spirituality.

However, after numerous breakups that seemed to occur when I would intuitively sense his less than committed interest in me, he would suddenly declare, "You're too needy. Go find your own happiness."

And like a lightening flash, he was gone from my life only to appear a few months later with a smile on his face to see if I had fixed myself.

I did fix myself this one final last time. I went to a psychic who told me I would have several meetings with alien beings and that Bob was a floater in my life, present only to teach me about my anger.

I have never met the alien beings but as for the lesson of anger? I decided I had learned enough from Bob and spent a solid month meditating him out of my consciousness. Just to be sure I was cleansed of any residual negativity of my former Bob life, I quietly withdrew from all our common friends, who were really his friends to begin with, leaving me pretty much on my own.

The day I returned home from work and told my 15 year old daughter and 13 year old son that I had left the job that had afforded sleepaway camps, trips to Universal Studios, New York and Mexico, computers, bikes, toys and endless nights of eating out without looking at the bill, their mouths dropped opened.

"You did what?" my daughter Kristina demanded. "What are you going to do? How are we going to live? Are we still going to North Carolina for Christmas?"

I laughed out of nervousness. I had not even considered them in my decision.

"I can't believe you! What kind of 43 year old mother doesn't work?" she screamed as she slammed the refrigerator door shut and walked out of the kitchen. Furiously she dialed the phone to complain about what a loser I was to everyone she knew. Meanwhile my son Nikolaus lowered his head and let his hand drop the sandwich he was eating, on to the plate. He got up without a word and quietly walked past me.

"Nik, what's wrong?" I was familiar with his quiet display of disapproval. "It's going to be okay. I promise. I have to do this."

He did not respond and I did not know if it was really going to be okay.

Why do I have to be so different? Why is it that I cannot get into the flow with the rest of the world? Why is it that I cannot just get along with some happiness here and there instead of wanting it all?

This is where I am. Suddenly realizing I am alone in this journey called my life. How is that for a crisis?

Back to my lunch, a hearty beef stew that breaks all my rules of skinniness and health. Right now, all I want is comfort.

I have lovingly created this luscious stew for myself and I plan to eat it with complete attention just as I hope this break in my life will somehow teach me to live. Not to gobble up life like a feverish pig but to savor gently the magnificence and the power I have to create a life that is as satisfying as a home cooked meal.

This is the truth of beef stew. Today it is my prayer and meditation.

It is similar to the ones I learned in the zillions of workshops, retreats and houses of worship I frequented with Bob as we tried to find the definition of God that would ring most true from the multitudes offered. Only this time, there would be no mantras, no incense, no chants and no songs to get me in the mood. There would be no bibles, no books, no lectures and no fellowship. Not that there is not a time and place for that.

Just not now. No. Now it would be just me and whatever happens to be in front of me which at this moment happens to be my lunch.

What the hell am I saying? I have kids to support, a future to plan for. What about retirement? I am alone. I have no husband or family to rely on. Do I really think I can take this time to…..gross, I hate to say it, *find myself?*

Maybe I should just be quiet and eat the stew.

I lift the spoon to my mouth. I smell the aroma of garlic and onion. I taste the velvet like, buttery, tomato-beef flavors. I feel the sensations of a symphony playing its tune on my tongue. Even the ting of the spoon as it touches the bowl has a certain ring and the sight of the colorful stew set against the white bowl has an abstract impressionist feeling to it.

I think I feel happy.

Now that I look closer, I can see that the textures are soft, some fluid, others solid. The colors vary from warm hues of caramel brown to bright shades of carrot orange and summer squash yellow. Black pepper specs and fresh green peas dot the canvas of my bowl. Never have I noticed the intricacies of stew before, but today it is an amazing display of colors, shapes and free-floating designs.

This is an extremely focused moment for me. Wow, I feel really good.

My gaze falls upon one single blackish-brownish peppercorn that floats off to the side and hugs the rim of the bowl. It intrigues me. The dark, rugged roundness of it reminds me of a lost planet adrift in space waiting patiently for an explorer to come unlock its secrets. It also feels lonely to me. I am sad for it.

Okay, hold on. Am I cracking up here? Is this some sort of nervous breakdown? Since when can a peppercorn feel anything, let alone loneliness? My mind has wandered again. Get back to the stew.

Sorry. I want to know how this peppercorn got there. I want to know how it escaped the grinder. All the other peppercorns were neatly ground into specs just as they should be. But this one escaped. Why? Why did it have to be different?

The peppercorn silently stares at me without an answer. I stare back helplessly. Soon my eyes glaze over. My breathing slows. I do not hear the rain and I cannot feel my backside in this hard wooden chair.

Where am I going or where have I gone? I do not know.

I just give up and decide to give in to this mysterious peppercorn as it pulls me towards all the possibilities that a peppercorn could ever be.

Acceptance

By JoAynne von Born

Acceptance is not one of those qualities I have had an easy relationship with. Especially with my physicality.

Most people who meet me would never believe that both sides of my family came from the land of mozzarella and basil. To counteract my Italian heritage, I asked my mother for a nose job at sixteen and by twenty one I took to a bottle of golden blonde hair tint. At family reunions, I stand out like a marshmallow in a bowl of rocky road ice cream.

It's not that I don't love Italians. I do. They are warm, loving and full of life. I think what happened was, somewhere early on, between Twiggy and Cheryl Tiegs, I got the message that dusty blonde hair and a turned up nose were more acceptable than a greasy brunette with the ability to sniff the scent of olive oil and garlic a block away.

A few years ago, I went back to dark hair thinking that would help me to get more real with myself. Of course, I couldn't reverse my nose even if I wanted to. (it's ironic that all the fashion magazines now tout models with ethnic faces that glorify very prominent noses) But the funny thing was that the real me had become less "me" than the blonde persona I had fashioned, the one I had become accustomed to seeing in the mirror, the one I had learned to totally accept. I hastily went back to being the new real me.

Acceptance is what I am today. Not what I was back then or where I think I would like to be later on. Acceptance is this moment. It is who I am right now. And that is one sure thing I can have an easy relationship with.

Sharon Wasserman

I had never written anything, except for assignments and letters, until taking this class. .Also, I thought I was going to write about cancer, as s nurse who had cancer, and whose mother and husband were also afflicted with it.

I never did write about it, although it is still something that I have in mind to write about some day. But it doesn't speak to me. Yet. Perhaps that's a good sign.

I had been married and divorced when I was about 35, with three young children. I remarried a few years later and currently split the year living in Boca Raton and Highland Park, Illinois. Life can't get better than to be near my children and grandchildren, old friends and flowers and trees.

MMM

Work Memories

By Sharon Wasserman

As a young person, I knew in my heart that I would one day work with ill people when I grew up. My initial idea of being a physician was shot down by my family with, "girls can't do that."

I lowered my goal by presenting the possibility of becoming a nurse and was responded to with, "You shouldn't get your hands dirty." So, when I started classes at the University of Minnesota, I had no goals and majored in, what was an underlying theme at the time, achieving my "M.R.S."

Eventually I became aware of the school of radiology and received a positive response from my mother when I presented her with the idea of becoming a nurse. On my first day as a student I was matched with the certified tech in charge of the "G.I." rooms, the one rotation that everyone feared, due to some pretty wild stories that made the circuit of horrible happenings there.

I reassured myself that I would at least get this out of the way and not have to waste my time dreading it in the future. So there I was, the very first day in that department, on my hands and knees, cleaning up the huge mess that a patient had made when he couldn't hold the liquid barium that the radiologist had rectally inserted to x-ray his colon.

The patient had not cleaned himself out according to instructions, thus the explosion -- all over the doctor, the table and the floor. I had somehow managed to move out of the way, but it was my responsibility to clean it up and all I could think of while doing so was, "If my mom could see me now!"

I didn't tell her about this incident, as I was afraid she would cancel my enrollment. I guess she thought that chests and bones were what we mainly x-rayed!

I loved the environment of that bustling hospital, despite that jarring setback. Many cutting edge things were happening and our department was involved in it all.

Open heart surgery started there and I remember how we would all clamor to get a good seat in the viewing theater above the O.R., although we really couldn't see beyond the surgeon's head and hands. Sometimes we would be called into the O.R. to take an x-ray during this delicate surgery, and I remember those times as very dramatic with the surgeons exhibiting high anxiety and shouting to me to "hurry," and my cool response, "Please hold the patient the way I'm asking you to, so that I'll get it right the first time," I always did.

There were no jobs in the Twin Cities for me when I graduated, so I moved to Chicago where, with my good friend, Lynne, we obtained jobs quickly. She worked at what was then called "Wesley" hospital, and I at "Passavant," both of which are now connected under the auspices of Northwestern University..

We lived on Delaware and Rush streets in the hub of nightclubs, restaurants and folk music. It was safe to walk across the street at midnight to buy a pack of cigarettes as there were so many people out and about. The noise level at night was unrelenting, with cabbies honking and people shouting to each other.

The only time the noise bothered us was in the warm weather as we didn't have air-conditioning and the windows were open. The soot that spilled into our apartment and settled on the Venetian Blinds was unbelievable. Our building manager would send the "blind maid" to clean the blinds, which we thought was very funny.

The color scheme of our furnished rental was gray, not very creative, but we loved our independence and our new life style, which included one good free meal a day, uniform laundry, air-conditioning in the hot summer, and a burgeoning social life that stemmed from the presence of many other young people in our neighborhood looking to connect with each other.

After I married Tom, and moved to the suburbs, I no longer worked, due to a dearth of hospitals in the area. So I shelved my medical life until I heard of a local college starting a new nursing program where the students no longer had to sleep at the hospital or be on-call.

What a time I had! I met like-minded people, learned about illnesses I didn't know existed, and participated in healing and miracles.

I remember one Christmas Eve day, when the doctor handed the newly delivered baby girl to her mom, and said: "Merry Christmas, Audrey," and how those of us in attendance cried, as we didn't expect the baby to be alive.

I was drawn to working with cancer patients, probably as a result of my experience when my mom was terminally ill and in the hospital with round-the-clock nurses. I had observed some significant examples of human kindness.

I also had the privilege of meeting with Elisabeth Kubler-Ross when her first book on death and dying was published, and I was able too apply her expertise when I worked with critically ill people and their families. Some people grimaced when they learned of the population with whom I chose to work, but I always derived a great deal of satisfaction knowing I had done a good job. I think it's all about listening to the patient, just listening, and they'll eventually let you know their needs.

I was fortunate to work in the hospital when the nurse-patient ratio was low, and I felt safe for all of us. When the work environment started to change and become stressful, I chose to work in the field of home health and what an education I got there!

I learned my way around the county, saw neighborhoods I didn't know about, met people from every walk of life and from many different cultures. I loved the independence I had, and stayed in that arena until one day a little voice in my head said: "I don't want to do this any more."

I knew it was time to leave it, and I did, with no regrets and so many good memories.

Life Lessons

By Sharon Wasserman

The feeling of newly found freedom came with the zip of a shade! I listened with amazement to the silence...no words came from my mouth! It was then that I realized I had been greeting each day (for how long?) with: "f_ _ k the world!"

I knew this was an important time and needed to pay attention to what had just occurred, to understand my position in the moment. It was only yesterday that he had moved out of our house, he with his toxic ways, his irresponsible manner, his selfishness. And in his absence, a lovely sense of peace had floated in, a sense of hope for good days and lightness of spirit.

I wasn't sure when he had moved out of my life, mine and the children's, but out of the house was a wonderful beginning for the opportunity to live honestly, and perhaps to love again.

No more excuses to my lovely children as to why he didn't attend their school functions, or didn't come home to join them for dinner, or why he never made it to the emergency and hospital rooms.

And now, thirty-five years later, I still have one old fashioned shade that needs to be zipped up and is a reminder of one of the most promising and exhilarating days of my life.

Marsha D. Wilchfort

Marsha D. Wilchfort lives in Westhampton, New York. She is working on her memoir, three kidneys and a mini cooper. In her spare time, she is creating Tango for Klutzes.

MMM

A Sad Story

By Marsha Wilchfort

His body stiffened and his skin turned blue and his three kidneys stopped functioning -- the two kidneys he was born with and the one that was transplanted.

He looked upward toward the heavens and a god that he did not believe in, and died.

Two weeks later, I did the only thing I could. I bought a mini cooper and slept in his bed that night. The mini cooper smiled at me with its jaguarlike lights.

He had stopped smiling sometime after the stroke. He was really excited about the kidney transplant, thought he would be finished with dialysis and possibly living a somewhat normal life. He had waited five years for the kidney only to be told he also needed a new heart, that he wouldn't last five years.

If he was apprehensive about the surgeries he never showed it. He wanted to make it easier for me. He just went forward, never complained, never felt sorry for himself. He knew that self-pity would destroy him.

Yes, the mini cooper smiled at me with its jaguarlike lights. Did I say that the mini cooper was red? It had to be. It was my new traveling companion or should I say toy? I call her baby.

The mini cooper hugged my body. It was wide and short as he was long, lean and ill. It respects and accommodates my shortness. If I were a car I'd be a mini cooper. If I were a dog, I'd be a cat. If I could cry there would be no stopping.

"Cry me a river, I've cried a river over you," only it's not like that at all. If I let go, would my tear duct use its allotment of tears or do they regenerate or degenerate? It's not a crummy starfish. Is there such a thing as drowning in one's tears rendering them forever depleted so that you can never cry again? Do you lose your heart too or just the tear maker? How much does a tear weigh? Are they all the same size or do they not conform to anything? Could crying become a new weight loss program? It's not a snowflake, though it might as well be.

Is crying a physical activity? The loss of salt is tasty. I don't cry in tears. The future is forever becoming the past. The past lives deep in our space and time. I just want it all to slow down.

Ron didn't believe golf was a sport. He thought it was akin to gardening. When we went to affairs he would count how many people were in attendance. He would calculate how much gift money the bride and groom would have. He wasn't an accountant, he was an attorney. He would go from table to table at affairs having his picture taken.

After about six tables and three Bloody Marys, the photographer would say, "You--get out of this photo," Ron would put his arms around strangers smiling his vodka grin. This became some kind of tradition. When our friends would receive the photos they were either furious or hysterical, probably both. Ron would be systematically erased chemically, his sweet face left at the assigned table.

In the world of me minus Ronnie, I'm a widow, as was my grandmother before me at the same age. Her beloved David died and my middle name is Dayvi. My Aunt Edith, my mother's

Sister, lost her Alfred at the same age. My Aunt Beatrice, my father's sister, lost her Les at the same age as well.

Destiny, coincidence, chance.

Funeral Arrangements

By Marsha Wilchfort

My cousin arrived from Perry Point Maryland just in time to help make the arrangements. Ellen's good at that. She lost her younger sister, Judy at age 23 to uterine cancer, and we cousins are all unterusless. She does arrangements well.

The night nurse who was taking care of Ron at home said she would be leaving as Ron, too, was leaving us. The hospice nurse arrived, she took his pulse – that he did not have – checked his heart, then poured the morphine down the kitchen sink.

I wanted to know what it tasted like -- morphine, that is – why Ron grimaced so, when I gave it to him.What made it bitter, and why didn't I do something to make it sweet?

Please, god – don't let me become bitter. I wanted to taste what he tasted, I wanted to know what rolled and circled around his mouth that I kissed after he woke up from the coma, when I had another chance to get him back. We kissed fishy baby kisses. His eyes were like a new born and he was in some way, an innocent.

But I never want to know what it's like to have a stroke, a kidney transplant and a medical center that declares this abortion a success.

Ellen made some phone calls. Adam made arrangements to change the time of his tennis tournament. Life goes on. Ronny would have wanted that.

Before the man from the funeral home came and put Ron in a body bag, I thought I saw him move.

My father, Adam, and Ellen were going to the funeral home. I drove. Ellen sat in front with me. Adam was in the back seat with my father. I must say, I know of no one except for children who use rear seat belts, with the exception of my father who prays for just ten more years of life, and I know that he will outlive me. I find it curious that at 85, he is still greedy for life.

We arrived at the funeral home. I haven't a clue why it is called "home." – Fun –e-real—real fun home? Where is the morphine when I need it?

Well, Irving, as it turns out, can't get his lousy seat belt off. The car is five years old and no one has ever used that seat belt before. And my father is claustrophobic. His arms are flailing. He's sweating and screaming, "Get me the hell out of here!" He's scared.

I have an appointment with the funeral home man. Ellen is truly my sister by cousinhood and we can't stop laughing. I am very close to peeing in my pants. I will not be making a respectable appearance. Adam finds nothing funny about this, whatsoever.

Finally, I say, "Look, Dad, I'll leave the window open. I'll keep the motor on, and you just relax."

I am about to leave him when something unclamps it and he's free. I am laughing like it is any other day.

We walk inside. It smells of cover-up smells, oils, formaldehyde. And I smell like almost pee. Ellen and I cannot sit near each other because we are two very demented people who don't know how to behave ourselves.

Flunking Bereavement

By Marsha Wilchfort

Shit, I flunked bereavement! I was punctual, I attended every session except one—I went to a birthday celebration of Ron's parent's partners in business, in life, 87 years of life. I try to remember that some people live long lives. Celebrate other people's joys. Force yourself.

Pat, the facilitator of the group, liked me. She thought I was practical, I thought I was whimsical.

Ron's wallet and keys are in his night table drawer waiting for his return and so is his driver's license, the one where he looks like a Russian woman. (how he pulled that off only the goddess of Russian women knows).We used to imagine, if Ron were to be pulled over by a police officer, could he be charged for impersonating a (quite unattractive) female, or be charged with transgender dressing?.

I've been very economical these days. I've made my first major decision, to pick up the mail only once a week, only on Sunday in my pajamas.

I discard the discardable condolence cards, the meetings he needed to attend, the journals, the law bulletins, the legal supplement, the continuing education classes in cassette form. How much is a life worth in dollars in an accidental death?

I did receive a post card from T.J. Maxx. They miss me. No one else misses me. They are having a special sale for those who have been missing. Do they hire special staff to find who's been missing in this very tight economy? How frivolous! I only go where I'm invited. I'm going to T.J. Maxx, and that means I have to get dressed. I'll try. I could put my jeans over my pajamas. That could work.

I don't need anything. I have all the essentials, but T. J. Maxx misses me so I'll try to go. I'll shower the night before so I won't have any serious excuses, I hope. I'm on my way with my little post card of special discounts for the missed of heart.

I'm feeling pretty good in the store. I crave the home accessory department. I love sheets. My linen closet is becoming outrageously cluttered. I even have our first set of pillowcases that I purchased at E. J. Korvettes 32 years ago. They too no longer exist. Korvette's, not the pillowcases.

I can't fathom why I still have those cases. I'm not sentimental. I'm practical. They were so unattractive and cheap, a reminder of our humble beginnings, as well as our youth. I don't like to think about beginnings.

We had a king size bed. I was able to find a jungle print sheet set, two pillowcases, a flat sheet and a fitted one. I'm going to buy it. I don't need it. Most times I like to believe I am in the "less is more" Zen mode, or perhaps am I just an idiot phony who can't be trusted when I am in T. J. Maxx.

I also bought a basket made in Uganda with meticulous weaving and stitching with a tiny hook to hang on the wall.

When I return home, I realize the fitted sheet is all I need. I cautiously remove it and place it on my bed. It looks great and inviting. I carefully remove the price tag, pack it all back into the package minus the fitted sheet. Tomorrow I'm going to Marshall's to return it.

Marshall's took the set back, never realizing it was minus the fitted sheet. They didn't know it wasn't purchased there either. Not only did the return deception go smoothly but they priced it at $15 more than I paid at T. J. Maxx. I am rewarded for my deception. The customer service lady asked me if I would answer a few questions and they would give me a $10 gift certificate on their computer. I thought they had done that already. Hell, it's not a lie detector.

I think I have become a returnaholic. However what I did with the sheet was criminal. Shall I join a returnaholic support group sponsored by the kind, compassionate, dis-enfrachised ex-shoppers of T.J. Maxx of unemployed salespeople from Marshall's?

Perhaps the only ethical thing to do would be to turn myself in to the proper authorities, whoever that might be, to fill the empty hole inside of me that no baskets from Uganda or jungle print sheets can fill.

Elaina Zuker

A seasoned businesswoman, educator, author and consultant, Ms. Zuker has held executive positions in publishing, higher education and communications and a keynote speaker who has addressed meetings and conferences in industry, government and professional associations.

Her newest book, "The Seven Secrets of Influence" (McGraw-Hill), the recent Main Selection for the Business Week Book Club, has been translated into four languages. The author of "Mastering Assertiveness Skills", "The Assertive Manager", Career Success Series and the Day Timers Success Tapes, she has been featured on numerous radio and television talk shows and in many newspaper articles, "Creating Rapport" came out in June 2005. She is currently at work on "Success Secrets That Can Change Your Life".

Ms. Zuker has created custom publications on personal success for Time Magazine, Money Magazine, Hearst Publications, Hachette Publishing and Times Mirror Publishing. She has served on the faculties of Montclair State College (Division of Business), Mercy College, Pace University, and Marymount College.

Ms. Zuker's clients include: Avon Products, American Express, American Management Association, Chase Manhattan Bank, Chiron Corporation, Citibank, IBM, Lawrence Livermore National Laboratories, MCI, Ogilvy & Mather Worldwide, Sheraton Corporation, Syntex Pharmaceuticals and many other Fortune 500 Companies. Ms. Zuker conducts seminars in the U.S. and internationally on Influence, Assertiveness, Leadership, Creative Problem Solving, Goal Setting and Time Management.

Ms. Zuker holds a B.S. (Psychology) from Empire State College in NYC, and an M.S. in Organizational Behavior from Polytechnic Institute in Brooklyn

Princess of the Projects

By Elaina Zuker

April Fools' Day, 1999. I arrive at the lobby of the elegant Westmount building with two giant suitcases full of clothes. I feel like an immigrant, just like my ancestors who came to this bitter cold city from other cold cities like Minsk and Moscow.

In a sense I <u>am</u> an immigrant. I became an American citizen after living in New York for 25 years with a Green Card. I haven't lived in Canada as an adult since I was 22, in 1963. I don't think like a Canadian. Now I don't even speak the language.

Once, you could isolate yourself in one of the English speaking ghettos. Then, you only interacted with the "Pepsi's" (as some pejoratively called the French Canadians) if you employed them, or if they were the drivers of your taxi or bus, or the cleaning lady. The way they got that name, it was said, is that their breakfast fare was a Pepsi and a Mae West (a Canadian version of a Twinkie).

We never lived in one of those "uniculture" neighborhoods, though. My parents, poor as they were, considered themselves cosmopolites, citizens of the world. They liked living where there were families from all over. Our neighbors were Jamaicans, East Indians, Scandinavians. My mother, while she always said that we should learn to live with people from all cultures, and hated going to the Laurentians in the summer where only "those yentas" congregated, still sent us to a Jewish-only school, and had a fit when I wanted to date a "non-Jewish" boy, as they so quaintly put it in those days.

I left Montreal – in a five-piece pink linen suit with a matching picture hat -- headed for San Francisco on the Canadian Pacific Dome Car train across the Rockies to Vancouver and then on a Greyhound bus down the West Coast.. JFK had just been killed, girls my age were either getting married and having their first babies or reading *Sex and the Single Girl*. My friends and I were called "career gals."

We pretended to be very sophisticated (we didn't know the word "cool") going out with married men and meeting at the Little Hungary at 11 P.M. to sip cappuccino and listen to Leonard Cohen's plaintive songs and poetry. We worried about the Russians and the Cuban missile crisis.

I left town because <u>my</u> married man, Howard, had been killed in a plane crash, exactly one week after that awful Nov. 22 Friday. It was the Air Canada flight to Toronto. I had made the booking, since I was his secretary and it crashed in the woods north of Montreal four minutes after takeoff.

So now here I was back home, having lived four lifetimes away. This was only temporary, though, until I could afford the crazy prices of Northern California real estate. When I left the townhouse in Sausalito, I put everything in storage. All my consulting clients were on the East Coast - most of them in New York, and the Canadian currency was at an all time low. My friend Gisele suggested, "Why don't you spend the summer in Montreal, enjoy all the Arts Festivals, rent an inexpensive flat and give yourself a break from the pressure of hunting for decent housing in the crazy Bay Area market?"

My sister cried with happiness when I told her I was coming back. We have never lived in the same city as grownups, although I am 10 years older, we grow closer every year. All the time I lived in California, we spoke on the phone at least once a day.

I speak to the kids a few times a week, too, although now that they're 16 and 21 they have no time for their Auntie, even though they still think I'm the "coolest".

This building facing Westmount Park is very genteel. Bob, the doorman is hovering, asking if I need anything else, telling me the "mail is in." (the highlight of the day here, I suspect). Nothing like the indifferent doormen in New York whose "wadddya want?" attitude I had grown accustomed to.

Westmount! I've come a long way, baby. This is the most chic neighborhood in town. Once it was an "Anglo only" place. Now the affluent "francophones" as they are called, form almost half of the population.

"Not bad, ay, Momma?" I say to my dead beautiful mother, who answers in my head, "You couldn't have moved back here while I was alive? So you could finally give your mother some pleasure, some naches? And after all these years, you couldn't afford one of those really big houses in <u>Upper</u> Westmount, on the mountain instead of just an apartment down in the flats? What did you do with all your money? Alright, so you had 'adventures.' You lived in New York, you traveled the world, you became a 'success.' But you should have married a rich man, so you wouldn't have had to struggle and worry like I did."

"It's still worlds away from the projects, Momma," I say aloud, as if the fantasy were real.

I've regressed to mid February in 1954. I'm in the seventh grade. My alarm has already gone off half an hour ago, but I'm still lying curled up like a snail under the heavy quilt in my white and blue haven. I have a real bedroom set, even though it's made from some dubious form of plywood. It's white with gold trim. It has a full headboard with nooks for my Nancy Drew books, my diary and my own powder blue Princess phone.

I hear Mother's high heels clicking along the long dark uncarpeted corridor to my room. I've always had my own room, since I had to be quarantined when I had Scarlet Fever at six.. Then Dick and Karen came along, but I wouldn't share a room with anyone, even though sisters usually did. So I commandeered the back room in our cold water flat, and growled at all who tried to approach.

Mom gently pushes the door open. She is already dressed in a beautiful silk blouse and wool suit for her job downtown as a legal secretary. "I go to business," as she put it. Her black hair was done once a week, permed once a month. Even though she typed all day, her nails were always manicured. Her make up was already complete with brown-penciled brows and she smelled of *Midnight in Paris* (at 6 a.m.!)

Soon, she'll put on her black Borgana fake fur coat, wool hat and warm boots over her nylons, to wait for the 161 bus, from which she will transfer twice to get to work at nine. She'll carry her high heels along with her lunch to the office.

She wakes us all up, tosses us out of the beds so she can make them, fixes all our school lunches and marinates something for dinner while she and Dad talk about the news, laugh about the movie or the Sid Caesar show.

I am going to be picked up by the school bus, to take me to The Peretz Shule, which is in the real Jewish Ghetto district. After the bus drops us kids off, it will turn into a "limo" for my grandfather.

Zaide, or "Chaver Tzooker" as he was called by his comrades and cronies, was one of the founders of this school. He and several of his pals, young Labor Zionists/Socialists had come to Canada from the Polish area near Minsk at the turn of the Century, and immediately plunged into furthering the "movement" in the new country.

The school was private, and taught Yiddish language and culture, not religion. They were always short of funds, so Zaide would jump on the school bus and be driven around to all the wealthy Jews who were business owners and captains of industry, like the Bronfman and Steinberg families, and hit on them for money for the "shule," for the "Farband," for the "library," for the "kinderveldt." (kids' summer camp).

My mother's beautiful contralto voice, restrained at this time of morning, is still humming one of those dreadfully perky "good morning" commercials. She feels around the blue quilt to see where my head is. Everything is blue in that room. No greens are allowed there, or any other color for that matter. Mom says that since I have her periwinkle eyes I have to wear only blue to bring them out. Besides, only homely people and gentiles wear green.

She makes her way over to my bed across the little room, and like she did every day, hands me my underwear and towels, all warm and toasty, which she had heated up for me on the one space heater in the front hall.

Jolted out of my reverie by Bob, who takes my bags, I leave the frigid back room cold water flat in the projects, elevated to this elegant proof of success. Yet somewhere, tugging at my gut, there is the feeling that no Westmount kid ever felt so loved, and so pampered. as I, when I was the Princess of the Projects.

Back from Ground Zero

By Elaina Zuker

After being glued to CNN and the other networks for 2 months, reading every word in the NY Times, crying while reading and saving the daily "Portraits of Grief" section, and several aborted trips (couldn't get the business meetings lined up, places to stay, etc) I finally went to New York last week for a few days.

The business meetings didn't all materialize, but I couldn't wait any more. I had been feeling "stranded," out of town and away from my city which had been so mortally struck, my city where I had lived for almost 30 years. I felt guilty that I wasn't there in the early days, when I might have been able to help - donate blood, go down "there", serve food, comfort people, whatever.

I had been scheduled to fly on Sept. 11th, and when I heard the news (in French) at the nail salon here in Montreal, I came screeching home to watch it all unfold on TV. Watching and taping all the memorial and fund-raising concerts. Listening to every word from Dan and Peter and Wolf (where was Bernard Shaw when we needed him?) Paying close attention to the pundits, "terrorism experts," and ex-generals weighing in, hearing the numbers of "missing" with horror. Walter Cronkite, a guest with the newly sobered and dignified David Letterman said it best, "We must never round out those numbers. Each one, each life, is important."

The first few days, I was as dumbstruck as everyone else, plus worried about my brother who was in Yemen on a World Bank project. He left in a hurry in an Air Yemeni flight ("not El Al", as he put it) to Paris and the safety of friends in the Canadian Consulate.

The first thing that was strange was riding in from Newark airport. There's that curving stretch on high ground around Weehawken after you have suffered all the ugliness of Elizabeth and the rest of that wasteland, and you know when you turn the next bend towards the Lincoln Tunnel, you'll be rewarded with the most stupendous view of the skyline. There it was, all perfect, all those familiar skyscrapers, except, except.....

But it goes by so fast, you hardly have time to take in the amputated scene. In the city, heading up 8th Avenue, everything *looks* pretty normal, except for the zillions of flags everywhere - in front of delis, porn shops, restaurants, flying from taxis, trucks, buses.

During the few days I spent there, I did familiar things with familiar old friends: Capuccino with the "girls" (Dorothy, Karen and Lori) at Caffe Bianco in my old upper E. Side 'hood, tea with Nancy at the Algonquin, bean and barley soup with Albert at the Polish Tea Room in the Edison, the Met *(that* is indestructible and forever, right?) with Sonya, to see the Indian jewelry show (reminded me of my time in India, where I bought a burqua because it was a pretty color, then threw it in the trash when I realized its meaning) tea with Carole at home, same old spinach and turkey salad with Joan at old O'Casey's on 41st St. near the Library; dinner with old business partner Joan on the Upper West side, old style Italian food with Paul and Jack, the Comfort Diner (!) on East 86th St. for cheeseburgers (warm food and drink with warm friends) Nothing new and trendy for me this trip.

I went to some business meetings -- business is awful. Everyone says it will get better. Nobody knows when. At a roundtable meeting of luxury marketers, executives pondered how to get people back into the stores to buy Gucci and Prada bags, high-end jewelry and apparel. Tough road, when even the knockoffs on Canal Street remain unsold in stall after stall. My friend Carole, the quintessential shopper, confesses she was right in front of a Loehmann's and had no desire even to go in and look around.

I asked everybody where they were on that day, did they know anyone, had they been "there?" What was it like?

Finally, I could put it off no longer. I noticed how queasy and anxious I was as soon as I got into the subway, and on a simple trip (for me) of taking the R from the Carnegie Hall stop to Lexington and then transfer to the 6, I managed to screw up and found myself on the sidewalk of 3rd Avenue and 60th St. Could it be that I, who pride myself on keeping my eyes on the same paragraph of the newspaper and still getting out at the right stop, couldn't figure out the subway anymore?

I finally rode down to Fulton Street. The first thing that hits you is the smell. If you've been there you know what I'm talking about. If you haven't, I can't even describe it -- like burning rubber, electrical wires, burning....we all think it, can't even say it. Makes you long for the good old days of smelling regular New York pollution.

Along lower Broadway, there are crime scene barriers all along the site, so you can't even see the rubble, except for the giraffe-like cranes and equipment sticking up from the ground. You can see the ruins of about 6 or 8 stories of the WTC, just like we've seen on TV, except in reality, it is many shades of brown and black, the window frames all jagged, once ordinary offices.

In front of St. Paul's church, miraculously undamaged, there's a sign that says, "We are open for volunteers and rescue workers only." There are huge walls/fences on every block, every square inch filled with poems, photos, messages, flowers, flags, and candles. Most of it is looking pretty frayed by now, but there are *fresh* flowers in some places. Tourists climbing up the barriers to get photos of the wreckage are shooed away by weary cops. Hawkers are (quietly) selling neckties, pins, hats and other stuff with Americana motifs.

There's stillness down there. It's a glorious sunny fall day, just like *that* day. I walked a few blocks south slowly, still couldn't absorb the reality. That's the weird thing. Everything is so slow down here. Slow is not the way *any* street in New York is supposed to be.

For some reason, I turned west on Liberty Street, and that's when it hit me. I guess each of us has the "moment", when it finally sinks in. That corner is where, if you were going to an appointment at WTC, you would

340

turn towards the entrance. The street would be in shadow, even at high noon, because of the heft of the buildings. And today it was bright with unobstructed sunshine from the West. *No* buildings there.

I gasped, actually couldn't breathe.

I wanted to get the hell away from there, then I wanted to stay .I was in kind of a tailspin - couldn't leave, couldn't stay. The thought of my original plan, to head for SoHo and browse in galleries and shops, made me feel like retching. Browsing through sterile, brightly lit galleries - after this, as just the next thing on today's agenda? I don't think so.

You still feel like you haven't done a proper homage. What should one do?

There's nothing more to do. Just keep the images forever.

I got back on the 6. People were jostling, talking, pushing.

On the Crosstown bus, two women got into a squabble. "Oh right, just push to the front as though you're the only one on the bus," one said. "I wouldn't *have* to push, if you weren't blocking the whole entrance," said the other.

I couldn't help myself. "It's nice to see things are getting back to normal" I said out loud. The whole bus erupted with laughter.

Maybe that's a teeny thing to be thankful for.

MMM

Women Entrepeneurs of the East Side

By Elaina Zuker

It's 6 a.m. and I'm coming down East 78th Street, half asleep, to pick up my New York Times at Alters and read it as I eat the dollar and a quarter two-egg special at the Greek luncheonette. First Avenue looks like a battle zone, the streets still slick from last night's rain, and sawhorses cordoning off Con Edison's recently dug trenches.

As the robotic rhythmic traffic light turns green, I see two figures crossing, approaching me. One is Mrs. Lee, carrying an overstuffed shopping bag. Twenty paces behind her is the Venerable One, carrying two shopping bags. They are the Management of the Mun Lee Laundry Co. of East 78th Street.

Mrs. Lee's peppered hair is rolled in a neat pageboy, like a 1950's home perm. Her cherubic Oriental face disguises for a moment the tired lines around her eyes. She gives me half a smile and mutters "good morning." The Venerable One is now passing me, her pale watery slanted eyes stare through me unseeingly.

In what Chinatown tenement, sleeping on floor mats, did they start *their* day, I wonder. Do the shopping bags contain laundry work they take to do at home?

The Mun Lee Laundry will open at 7 AM. in time to service its customers. The Eastsiders whose lives are full of careers, tennis, evening classes, dates, dinner parties, backgammon, therapy, rap sessions, health clubs, meditation groups, Club Med, Fire Island and Stowe are much too busy to do their own laundry. Even at 60 cents a pillowcase, they're glad to give it to Mun Lee.

At 7:15 the place is already packed. There's a line of scrubbed, business-suited men and women, standing impatiently with their bundles. Some actually do the jobs their costumes portray, like the young man with the Burt Reynolds mustache, who works as an account executive for an ad agency. Others do not, like the tall blonde woman in the chocolate brown pin-striped suit and tan stilettos. She will get off the subway at Canal Street, walk up four flights in an old factory building to the office of the plastics jobber she works for. She'll carefully drape her suit jacket over the back of her chair, then look through the pile of papers on her desk to decide what to type first.

Later that morning, I take a break from the work on my desk and go to pick up my sheets. On the grimy storefront window, peeling painted letters spell "Mun Lee - Hand Laundry." Inside, the Puerto Rican presser, a sloppy woman wearing a loose jersey and fuchsia nylon slacks, stands over a crumpled heap of sheets, her old fashioned iron sputtering and spewing water and steam. Without missing a beat or glancing up, she announces "customer" in a raspy, jaded voice. Sizzling sounds and the smell of onions frying, signal lunch cooking in the back room.

Mrs. Lee comes out. She wears jacquard patterned polyester knit slacks, a pale green pajama-like blouse, and embroidered canvas Mary Janes. She would probably be surprised to learn that it is the latest look from Bloomie's China promotion.

The Venerable One, white hair pulled back in a pigtail from her parchment skin, sits by an emptied bag of unwashed shirts, needle and thread in her hands, staring vacantly. Did this shuffling rag doll with the yellow elephantine skin ever dance? Hard to imagine, but at one time those ovaries gushed monthly blood.

Mrs. Lee takes my yellow ticket and slowly pokes with her pole among the precariously stacked piles. How will she ever find my expensive new Country French sheets in this mess? And why doesn't she step on it? Does she think I have all day? I'm not one of these spoiled, pampered, husband-supported Vuiton'd matrons from East End Avenue. I'm a working woman, just like you, I want to shout at her. And so far, I haven't done anything this morning that I'm likely to get paid for. You've probably made more money so far than I have today.

Once, when I asked for restitution from Mrs. Lee for bleaching the color of my favorite Indian tie-dyed shirt, I realized how well she had learned to self advocate. In her broken English, she firmly asserted my carelessness in having purchased such an item from a country where it is well known that dyes are never "fast." As befit her position on the organizational chain, she referred me to her 15 year old daughter who, in impeccable English corroborated her mother's position, adding that it was not in their policy to guarantee color fastness.--- a good lesson for me in entrepreneurial buck-stopping.

In my work as a management consultant, I counsel women on careers. I stress the virtues of planning, devising a market strategy, targeting one's product or service carefully, pricing competitively.

In seminars, the women do role plays and learn about "risk taking," entrepreneurship, collaborative decision making, delegation and division of labor. They're asked to think of a role model, someone they see as successful, a woman they admire. They often come up with Diane Von Furstenberg, Barbara Walters, Katherine Graham, Jane Evans, Martha Stewart. Women Tycoons.

Not all East Side career women wear suits and carry briefcases.They don't all wake to a Sony clock radio in a high rise or brownstone apartment, where they live alone or with a husband, lover, roommate or pet. They don't all jog along the East River or the Park in their Adidas, and then shower and blow dry their layered hair. Not all primp with the latest Monteil burgundy eye shadow and don their "Investment Dressing" tailored tweed suit, with the standard "feminine" silk blouse and coordinated scarf. And they don't all read the Wall Street Journal while waiting for the Water Street Express bus or for the downtown Lexington Avenue IRT.

The women of Mun Lee may not fit into that mold, but they are *my* secret role models In fact, I reflect, they're more entrepreneurial than I am. They ventured into a strange neighborhood, negotiated a lease, decided what services they would offer and at what prices, and then figured out who would do what.

As for me, I invest in no capital equipment, work in my brownstone apartment, employ no full time workers, and take few risks.

It's 11.45 p.m. I'm returning from a dinner party in the neighborhood. As I approach my apartment building, I see two women walking wearily towards me. First, the Venerable One, clutching her shopping bag. Now, Mrs. Lee and I are face to face. "Good night," I say. "See you tomorrow." She smiles.

AFTERWORD

And so hopefully, you've read many of the stories, wondered why I chose some, and if you were in any of my classes, wondered why yours were not chosen.

My choices were based on a few criteria. Some of the stories in here met them all. Some met enough for me to believe that they were viable for the book. I was looking for a good or unusual "story," a compelling description of some specific time, tradition, custom, or general life condition which, though specific to the writer, had an appealing universality. I also included some personal musings on life and the lessons we take away from mere observations or personal struggles. And I deliberately included some very simplistic writings that in some way were touching and human and warm.

Some people wanted merely to record stories without caring much about the writing process. Other wanted to learn how to improve their writing skills as their memories were recorded. In the end, I believe everyone became more conscious of words and how to use them more effectively.

Perhaps you can identify the writers with exceptional talent. They do exist within these pages.

And since so much of life is random and for many logistical reasons, these were the stories in my computer pool. Many others, equally representative, were not accessible to me, and many other talented writers who were in my classes will continue to write their stories with an eye to "Showing" – rather than "Telling." Several books, by the way, have emerged from class attendees, and others are still in the works.

Bottom Line: We Do Have Fun.

ABOUT THE EDITOR

ERosen424@aol.com

Although Emily Rosen's "work" life seems disparate and unconnected, she insists that the threads are there and form a well focused pattern. After earning three Master's degrees, appearances might indicate that she deviated from her academic training in the late '70s and early '80s for about 8 years when she became the co-owner of a very successful singing telegram company, *Witty Ditty*. "But," she says, "I did in-depth interviewing about the recipients and customized all the lyrics," definitely a precursor to her future involvement in memoir writing. After selling that business she has continued writing personal poetry for her new business, *Pryme Rhymes*. "We write 'em. You recite 'em"

She began her career as a copywriter, switched to teaching which led to counseling, while simultaneously freelancing as a feature writer for local and national media.. Her column, *Everything's Coming Up Rosen* appears in the *Deerfield Beach Observer.*

In Florida, as a retiree, she has devoted many volunteer hours to leading therapy and support groups for *The Center For Group Counseling* in Boca Raton. Instructing the writing workshops feeds into her writer/teacher/therapist self.

There is also the travel-adventurous part that began with a trek through the Himalayas in Nepal and has lead her through a variety of other off-the-beaten track outdoor travel experiences..

And lest she leave out the cog around which all her wheel-parts revolve, she lives in Boca Raton with her retired dentist husband. She has two sons, and two pre-teen age grandchildren, the latter of whom live a frustrating 1500 miles away outside of Philadelphia.

And – just to keep her wheels turning, she rides her bicycle daily.